Sexuality in
eighteenth-century Britain

Sexuality in eighteenth-century Britain

PAUL-GABRIEL BOUCÉ
editor

MANCHESTER
UNIVERSITY PRESS

BARNES & NOBLE BOOKS
TOTOWA, NEW JERSEY

Published by Manchester University Press
Oxford Road, Manchester M13 9PL

British Library cataloguing in publication data

Sexuality in eighteenth-century Britain.
1. Sex (Psychology)—Addresses, essays, lectures
I. Boucé, Paul-Gabriel
155.3 BF692

ISBN 0-7190-0865-4

First published in the USA 1982 by
Barnes & Noble Books
81 Adams Drive
Totowa, New Jersey, 07512

ISBN 0-389-20313-0

Printed in Great Britain by
Butler & Tanner Ltd, Frome and London

Contents

The Contributors

ROY PORTER
Lecturer in Social History of Medicine, Wellcome Institute for the History of Medicine, London

PAUL-GABRIEL BOUCÉ
Professor of English Literature at the Sorbonne Nouvelle, Paris

NORAH SMITH
Lecturer at Napier College of Commerce and Technology, Edinburgh

ROBERT A. ERICKSON
Associate Professor of English, University of California, Santa Barbara

G. S. ROUSSEAU
Professor of Eighteenth-century Studies, University of California, Los Angeles

PETER WAGNER
Lecturer, Sprach- und Literaturwissenschaftliche Fakultät, Universität Eichstätt

RUTH PERRY
Associate Professor of Literature, Humanities Department, MIT

JOHN VALDIMIR PRICE
Senior Lecturer in English Literature, University of Edinburgh

DOUGLAS BROOKS-DAVIES
Senior Lecturer in English, University of Manchester

ARTHUR H. CASH
Professor of English, New Paltz College, State University of New York

ROBERT ADAMS DAY
Professor of English and Comparative Literature, Queens College and the Graduate Center, City University of New York

PAT ROGERS
Professor of English Literature, University of Bristol

Preface

Now that sexuality has become a respectable, if somewhat overexploited, topic even in Academe, the jaded reader may well ask: 'Yet *another* book on sexuality? And on the eighteenth century at that? Don't we know all about that notoriously libertine age of free and easy sexual antics in the boudoirs and the haystacks?' Such a 'sagacious reader', as Henry Fielding would no doubt have dubbed him, is of course entitled to wonder, like James Thurber in 1929: 'Is Sex Necessary?' He may also side with that other humorist, George Mikes, who in his most memorable and shortest chapter in *How to be an Alien* (1946) wrote: 'Continental people have sex-life; the English have hot-water bottles.' Mikes has had to qualify his peremptory judgement, rather grudgingly and ungenerously, by admitting in *How to be Decadent* (1977) that things have 'progressed here because the English now have electric blankets. It is a pity that electricity so often fails in this country.'

Fortunately for those who lived and loved in the eighteenth century, candle power was less apt to fail suddenly. Not that the eighteenth century in Great Britain, or on the Continent, was in actual fact a sort of erotic paradise teeming—according to the facile but still widespread literary, iconographic and filmic clichés—with 'buxom wenches', usually with generously *décolleté* neck lines, 'lusty swains' and 'amorous beaux'. The works of Michel Foucault, Lawrence Stone, Jean H. Hagstrum, to name but a few scholars in the field, should be enough to lay such a sexy ghost for ever. But its autopsy should one day be performed by an interdisciplinary team of specialists in eighteenth-century literature, history and art. I have always suspected that John Cleland and Sade on the one hand, and popular reproductions, on the other hand, of Watteau, Boucher and Fragonard, have much to answer for. On the contrary, the prints of Hogarth, and especially Rowlandson, afford a much less frivolously ethereal vision, to say the least, of sexuality in eighteenth-century Britain.

Yet, in spite of the present interest in the study of sexual mores and *mentalités*, much remains to be done. No book dealing with sexuality at a given period may claim to be exhaustive, because of the symplectic ramifications of a subject at the core of everyday life. The aim of this volume is simple enough: to present an interdisciplinary approach to a Protean and inescapable phenomenon. About half of the book deals with the socio-cultural context of sexuality, with particular, but not exclusive, emphasis on the medical and/or para-medical background (Roy Porter, P.-G. Boucé, R. A. Erickson, G. S. Rousseau). To this section also belong Norah Smith's study of sexual mores in Enlightenment Scotland, and Peter Wagner's analysis of a much publicised epiphenomenon, namely pornography and its already frequent brushes with the law. It is on purpose that this book has kept well away from the adjacent fields of erotica and pornography, although incidental references are made to such sub-literature. The field has already been well covered, and more studies of that rather special realm are under way. At first sight erotica and pornography appear to offer a rich lode of information, yet too often they prove to yield but a disappointing handful of fool's gold. What I personally call 'invariable geometry' in eighteenth-century erotic or pornographic writings turns out to be strikingly and tediously similar to the recently reprinted excerpts from the naughty Victorian magazine *The Pearl*, or Anaïs Nin's wearisomely repetitive *Delta of Venus*. 'La petite mort'—as orgasm was referred to in eighteenth-century French—can also be deadly: 'O cruel Nymph! a living Death I bear', as Dapperwit exclaims in canto V of *The Rape of the Lock*. Without denying at all that erotica and pornography can be viewed as meaningful socio-cultural data, one may well wonder how much light they actually shed on the sexual *mentalité* of most individuals. Pity, rather than scholarly envy, should be felt at the thought of the poor bemused sociologists, historians or critics in a couple of hundred years' time who will have to wade through the nauseous spate of written and visual pornography which has been flooding sex-shops in Soho, Pigalle or any other purlieus notorious for sexploitation throughout the world over the last two decades.

Regrettably few critics bear in mind that in the eighteenth century the borderline between 'science' and literature was not as sharply defined as now. Science, especially medicine in its early days, was still accessible to most educated readers. On a more popular level the immense success of such para-medical publications as *Aristotle's Masterpiece* and *Onania* throughout the eighteenth century, and well into the nineteenth century, contributed to the dissemination and crystallisation of sexual beliefs and myths, some of which can still be traced today both in Britain and on the Continent. Therefore, the general axiology of this book is based on the notion that no artificial separation should be effected between acknowledged 'great literature' and its contemporaneous subsoil of pseudo-/para-/meta-/literature. For instance, the much-studied concepts of love in Richardson's, Fielding's or Smollett's novels should be related to the then current knowledge, beliefs, values and myths pertaining to sexuality. Virginity, its medical and mythical lore, provide an apt illustration to the point. The desperate struggles of Richardson's Pamela, Fielding's Sophia or Smollett's Emilia (in *Peregrine Pickle*) in order to remain *virgines intactae* before marriage will appear much less artificial and contrived in our *blasé* late-twentieth-century eyes if we are aware of the medical and socio-cultural beliefs then prevalent about the loss of the precious hymen. Which does not mean, of course, that all literature should be explained away in reductive terms of mere sociological context. But at a time when structuralism and post-structuralism are making their fashionable, and at times objectionable, inroads into Anglo-American literary criticism, the importance of such basic contextual data has to be firmly reasserted.

The transition from the socio-cultural background to the more specifically literary topics can be made smoothly enough with Ruth Perry's analysis of Mary Astell's feminism and Arthur Cash's study of Sterne's fictional treatment of Dr Burton as Slop in *Tristram Shandy*. John V. Price and Robert A. Day deal with sexual patterns in the novels of Defoe, Fielding, Richardson and Smollett. Douglas Brooks-Davies analyses the mythology and the iconography of love in Pope, Fielding, Cleland and Sterne. Pat Rogers explores the titillating sexual ambiguities of the popular 'breeches parts' on the Restoration and eighteenth-century stage, with particular attention to Peg Woffington and Charlotte Charke. If this volume has managed to throw a bridge over the sadly widening gap between literary criticism and social history, then all the contributors will feel that their endeavours have not been totally in vain.

A pleasant task remains for the editor: first, to thank the international team of contributors who have borne with my coaxing and nagging while the volume was in preparation. An editor assumes the thankless duties of a sheepdog vigilantly watching over his wayward flock, and occasionally snapping at some unfortunate laggard who has fallen behind. I also wish to thank the staffs of the North Library, and especially of the Cambridge University Rare Books Room, for their unfailing and generous help. My own research was materially facilitated by a British Council grant in aid during the 1980 summer in Cambridge, for which I am deeply grateful. Once again, I wish to express my gratitude to Wolfson College, Cambridge, for its continued hospitality in the summer, and its much appreciated friendliness. There, thanks to Professor Mary Hesse's kind help, I was able to meet Dr Roy Porter. Last but not least, a special niche in all the contributors' gratitude, and first and foremost in mine, should be reserved for John Banks, our editor at Manchester University Press, for his most courteous patience.

Sorbonne Nouvelle PAUL-GABRIEL BOUCÉ
(Université de Paris III)
September 1981

ROY PORTER

Mixed feelings: the Enlightenment and sexuality in eighteenth-century Britain

I

The social and cultural historian of England may expect to find that Enlightenment attitudes had some impact upon sexual practices and the values which underlay them. After all, the aim of the *Aufklärer* was not just theoretical, but about changing what people did; and England was by common consent amongst the most Enlightened nations in Europe.[1] But we must not be looking for the wrong things in the wrong places. It would be surprising to find eighteenth-century English people writing systematic and philosophical treatises on the subject of sex. Because the Enlightenment was 'established' in England, 'progressive' thinkers did not need to produce basic treatises argued from first principles on subjects of fundamental importance. Enlightenment ideas filtered down through more pragmatic, allusive and 'applied' channels: essays, fiction, coffee-house conversation, daily practice in the family or the doctor's consultation. Also we should not expect to find all sectors of society equally affected. The Enlightenment began as a self-consciously élitist movement within polite and predominantly male society. At the same time, because literacy was high and culture was becoming more commercialised, England had a growing general public eager to read about, see and share in the tastes of their betters.[2] How far Enlightenment ideas (on sexuality or anything else) percolated down society is a fundamental question. Neither can we presume that Enlightenment attitudes to sexuality must automatically have been secular and radical. Precisely because England was a nation in which the main battles of the Enlightenment—against feudalism, absolutism and ecclesiastical obscurantism—had already been won, the views of most liberal and rational writers were primarily practical and accommodating, operating within a broad Latitudinarian Christian framework. Above all, we must not presume that Enlightenment views on sexuality necessarily anticipated those of latter-day liberals. Attitudes towards eroticism are complex; sex is not something that whole groups and movements are simply 'for' or 'against'.

Lastly, we obviously need to be cautious before attributing changing patterns of sexual behaviour to intellectual 'causes' or 'influences' such as the Enlightenment. For instance, demographic rise and the growing incidence of bastardy, especially in the second half of the century, quite likely bear witness to increased sexual activity amongst large sections of the population. But it is probably premature to attribute this (without internal evidence) to a revolution in sexual attitudes amongst working people (as Shorter does) and amongst women in particular (as does Branca).[3] They have seen these groups affirming a new commitment to positive sexual enjoyment. More probably, however, population rise was a response to a world in which impediments to copulation and marriage (such as servants living in) were diminishing, and economic incentives to larger families were strong.

In this brief essay, I shall explore the main issues about the place of the Enlightenment in changing English attitudes towards sex.

II

In their quest for modes of life which were rational, liberal, polite and happy, men of the Enlightenment habitually contrasted themselves to the common people (whom they regarded as leading lives dominated by custom and superstition, little better than animals), and the courtly aristocracy (whose lives were artificial, dissipated and useless). At the dawn of the Enlightenment those two strata were leading very distinct sexual lives, both of which were unacceptable to Enlightenment opinion. On the one hand, the sexual lives of the mass of the population were dramatically circumscribed. First, they were limited by suspicious and guilt-ridden attitudes towards the body. Within popular religion, and seventeenth-century Puritanism in particular, sensuality was associated with the Fall and with sin. Folk wisdom and proverbs predicted that those who wallowed in the lusts of the flesh paid for their pleasures: venereal diseases and bastards were the wages of sin.

Popular bawdy embodied subconscious male fears of cuckoldry, castration, impotence and the insatiability of women.[4]

Second, they were circumscribed by a family, domestic and village economy in which prudence sternly dictated the regulation of family size, and the production of offspring only under favourable circumstances. Pre-marital sexuality was repressed, and particularly in the seventeenth century marriage for both men and women was postponed into the late twenties. Within marriage, abstinence and *coitus interruptus* helped to trim family size to economic openings; affect was geared to income. Family disgrace, community shame and the Church courts punished those who stepped out of line.[5]

Third, popular eroticism was probably inhibited by the limiting conditions under which sexual activity took place. Dirt, disease, modesty, physical inhibitions and lack of privacy created conditions in which for many people sex was neither the incarnation of love nor an *ars erotica*, but rather infrequent, functional, perfunctory and repetitive.

At the other end of society there was the Restoration court. Sexual libertinism was of course rife in royal circles.[6] But much Restoration eroticism was obscenity. The desire to arouse was matched by a self-conscious desire to shock (and solid gentry and burgher opinion were indeed revolted by court morals). The rejection of Calvinist values was undertaken by men such as Rochester who were still themselves Puritans at heart. Sexuality was still naughty and pleasures were guilty. Restoration pornography was chiefly aggressive, aimed to disgust; its drama cynical about love and marriage, encouraging defensive laughter at old goats, cuckolds and the impotent. As Roger Thompson has written,

> Plainly many late seventeenth-century Englishmen shared an obsessive yet apprehensive view of sexuality. For all their libertine philosophising and summonses to merriment, they seem profoundly inhibited and uncomfortable about the subject. They cannot treat it in a matter-of-fact, balanced way; they cannot laugh about it without sniggering, or describe it straightforwardly, joyously, even innocently. Their reaction is disproportionate, discordant, distorted and disassociated. Pepys cannot appreciate the pleasure and the fun in *L'Escholle des Filles*; he is tantalised, drunkenly horrified; he ejaculates, he destroys. Shame is the spur.[7]

Enlightenment thought rejected traditional plebeian modes of behaviour, but also traditional courtly and aristocratic forms as well.

Enlightenment writers attempted to set conduct upon a sounder footing, a psychology grounded upon a proper science of human nature. Rejecting Calvinist notions of original sin and the corruption of the flesh, they argued that Nature was good, and that proper behaviour should seek to realise human nature, rather than to deny, fight and conquer it. Man's nature lay in his senses, and resolved into a capacity to be happy. It was not only those who called themselves Utilitarians who believed that ultimately happiness and virtue were heads and tails of the same coin.

For some thinkers, such as Shaftesbury, man had been programmed with faculties or senses (such as benevolence) which produced pleasure. For others, from Locke to the Utilitarians, man's character was a *tabula rasa*, yet he had a basic drive to pursue pleasure and avoid pain, upon which basis all subsequent action was learnt by experience and engraved by association. In both cases, the pursuit of pleasure, leading to happiness, became seen in Enlightenment writers, from Locke and Addison to Chesterfield and Bentham, as the behaviour dictated by Nature to man. 'Pleasure is now, and ought to be, your business', Chesterfield told his son.[8] The tendency to produce happiness was the only ultimate yardstick of right and wrong, good and evil.

If Nature was good, then desire, far from being sinful, became desirable. And the sexual instincts were undoubtedly natural desires. Giving pleasure, such passions were thus desirable and to be approved. 'The Venereal Act . . . when it is performed in obedience to nature' is 'highly delightful', argued Robert Wallace.[9] Or, in Boswell's words, there is no 'higher felicity on Earth enjoyed by man than the participation of genuine reciprocal amorous affection with an amiable woman'.[10] For Erasmus Darwin, 'animal attraction' was 'the purest source of human felicity; the cordial drop in the otherwise vapid cup of life'.[11] Sex was also useful. David Hume argued that erotic attraction was the 'first and original principle of human society'. Because it was habitually associated with beauty and benevolence, it was a constructive rather than an anarchic passion.[12]

These naturalistic and hedonistic assumptions—that Nature had made men to follow pleasure, that sex was pleasurable, and that it was natural to follow one's sexual urges—underpinned much Enlightenment thought about sexuality.[13] Thus Jeremy Bentham argued that the ascetic Pauline condemnation of fornication outside marriage was counter-utilitarian: 'when viewed in an unprejudiced point of view, and by the standard of utility, sexual gratification in those modes, against which popular antipathy is apt to rage with greatest fury, will be seen not to belong to the department of morality'.[14] They constitute the psychological morality which informs John Cleland's aptly titled fiction of Fanny Hill, *Memoirs of a Woman of Pleasure* (London, 1749). Throughout this work, the 'principle of pleasure'[15] was presumed to be the *primum mobile* of human action. Mrs Cole, the bawd, 'considered pleasure of one sort or another as the universal port of destination, and every wind that blew thither was a good one, provided that it blew nobody any harm'.[16] Of the pleasures, sex was reckoned to be supreme and natural. Fanny was 'guided by nature only'.[17] Fanny wrote, 'I began to enter into the true unalloy'd relish of that pleasure of pleasures, when the warm gush darts through all the ravish'd inwards; what floods of bliss... too mighty for nature to sustain';[18] her sexual encounters with Charles were 'the most delicious hours of my life'.[19]

Furthermore the sexual urges were often portrayed as instinct within the mechanical constitutional of mankind: 'I had it now,' wrote Fanny Hill, 'I felt it now, and beginning to drive, he soon gave nature such a powerful summons down to her favourite quarters, that she could no longer refuse repairing thither; all my animal spirits then rush'd mechanically to that centre of attraction.'[20] At the same time, spreading sexual joy was equated with the maximising of public happiness. When Fanny ceased to be a kept woman and became a public prostitute, she saw herself 'passing thus from a private devotee to pleasure into a public one, to become a more general good, with all the advantages to put my person out to use either for interest or pleasure or both'.[21] Thus in Enlightenment fabrics of thought, the felicific calculus of happiness came to be closely linked to sexual gratification. When Boswell wanted to ask Louisa when she would allow him to have sex with her, his question was 'How then can I be happy? What time?'[22]

This hedonistic liberation of the libido was all the more acceptable because it fitted easily within wider contexts of Enlightenment outlooks. The naturalistic drive of Enlightenment philosophy encouraged materialism and monism. The body became the seat of sensation, of consciousness; within the Condillacian tradition, touch became the prime sense.[23] In the mechanistic associationism of Hartley, Priestley and others, reductionism was collapsing the psychological into the physiological. Thus for Erasmus Darwin, ideas of beauty arose as a result of infants' associations of the shape of the 'female bosom' with generosity and fertility.[24] The penis could be seen as 'a wonderful machine'.[25] Sexual stimulus and response thus became part of the cause and effect inevitability of the mechanical universe.

Not least Enlightenment hydraulic physiology, linked to traditional medicine, could see regular sexual discharges as requisite for health. 'I was afraid I was going to have an attack of gout the other day,' wrote Lord Carlisle, 'I believe I live too chaste. 'Tis not a common fault with me.' Erasmus Darwin, sire of fourteen children himself, recommended marriage (i.e. sexual outlet) as a cure for psychosomatic disorders.[26]

The Enlightenment was interested in the 'natural philosophy' of sex, its 'art and science', which as Fanny Hill said, 'resided in the favourite centre of sense'.[27] It even toyed with a kind of sexual religion. James Graham, the sex therapist, set up a Temple of Health, which housed his celestial bed in a chamber called 'the holy of holies'. Erasmus Darwin's *Temple of Nature* was a paean of praise to the 'Deities of Sexual Love', for it was they who created evolutionary progress, through the superfecundity of the generative powers. Life rose from asexual to sexual reproduction, which was 'the chef d'œuvre, the master piece of nature',[28] not only improving and diversifying the stock, but being more fun as well. The poem's apparatus of the Eleusinian mysteries celebrated the marriage of Cupid and Psyche: 'All forms of Life shall this fond pair, delight / And sex to sex the willing world unite'.[29]

Thus in Enlightenment thought, sexuality pervaded the universe. Cosmic poetry celebrated the recent confirmation of plant sexuality. Erasmus Darwin in his *The Loves of the Plants* (which used a sexual classification) depicted in a mock-heroic way the sexual activities of the plant world. Thus, for instance, the gang-bangs of Maedia: 'MAEDIA's soft chains *five* suppliant beaux confess / And hand in hand the laughing belle address'.[30] Darwin's evolutionary concept of the development of life saw sexuality as the animating cause. Sexual selection was an important element in improvement of stock. The strength of sexual desires was always threatening to overstock the environment; the survival of the fittest weeded out the surplus.[31]

Seen now less as a sin or vice, and more as part of the economy of

Nature, sexuality figured largely in eighteenth-century intellectual discussion, an object for natural science. Travellers' reports and the emergence of anthropology familiarised the English with the polygamous societies of the South Seas. For many this image of a society without sexual possessiveness, guilt or jealousy was attractive: as also, doubtless, for men the prospect of legitimately enjoying several wives (Boswell called it being 'patriarchal'). 'Free love' was much discussed (there was a Whitby collier of that name in the 1760s). Boswell believed that even as a married man he should be free to follow his sexual instincts. Predictably, he would not allow the same freedom to women.[32] Jeremy Bentham for his part advocated legalised divorce, partly to free women from the tyranny of sexual slavery: 'to be constrained to receive [an unwanted husband's] embraces, is a misery too great to be tolerated even in slavery itself'.[33]

Another aspect of this intellectualisation of sex was the growing discourse about sexuality as a facet of personal relations. The desirability of open sexual discussion was often stressed:

> It would be proper to familiarise the sexes to an unreserved discussion of those topics which are generally avoided in conversation from a principle of false delicacy; and that it would be right to speak of the organs of generation as freely as we mention our eyes or our hands,

suggested Mary Wollstonecraft.[34] Manuals appeared, discussing sexual techniques, compatibility, venereal diseases, fertility, birth limitation and reproduction.[35] Above all, sex therapy burst upon the scene. The most famous exponent was James Graham, who set up his headquarters first at the 'Temple of Hymen' at the Adelphi in the Strand, and then later at St James's. Graham lectured to fashionable crowds about the invigorating properties of happy sexuality, and gave instructions as to how it could be made more successful and enjoyable. Amongst other techniques for stimulating eroticism, Graham advocated the use of pornography. People should have 'their passions aroused and excited, by the sight of rich warm or what are called lascivious prints, statues and paintings'. Similarly, when wives had failed to get pregnant 'in the ordinary course of things' he recommended 'celebrating the rites of Venus in a variety of ways'.[36] He also hired out his 'celestial bed' to barren couples at £50 a night. Its properties (exploiting, claimed Graham, electro-magnetic energies which flowed through the universe and which the bed tapped) would restore potency and fertility.

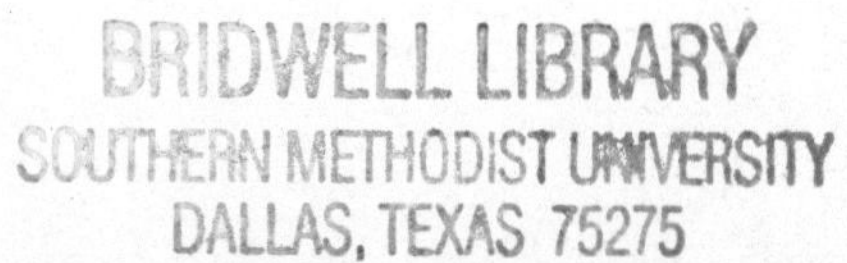

III

Enlightenment England—I have been arguing—reconceptualised sexuality as being an essential part of Nature. As integral to human nature, it was an important component of happiness. As part of the universe, it was to be studied. But did this evaluation have any impact upon sexual practice? Perhaps the most marked feature about Georgian sexuality was its public nature, its openness and visibility. There were so many manifestations that in this brief paper there is room to do no more than mention some of them.[37]

First, sex was a prominent part of the written and printed culture. There was both high-class and popular pornography.[38] Pornographical journals began appearing from the 1770s, starting with *The Covent Garden Magazine or Amorous Repository*, which contained sexy stories and advertisements for prostitutes and brothels (including prices). Sexually and scatologically explicit prints were commonplace, engraved by leading artists such as Gillray, Rowlandson and Morland. Obscene and scatological sexual references to royalty and politicians were the staple of newspaper reporting (Pitt the Younger appeared as 'The Bottomless Pitt', 'stiff to everyone but a lady'). Newspapers advertised sexual services of all kinds, from gigolos to aphrodisiacs, V.D. cures and abortifacients such as Farrer's Catholic Pills, and Velnos's Vegetable Syrup. Adultery and 'innocence destroyed' were the staple themes of titillating novels such as *The Innocent Adultress* (1777) and *Fatal Follies* (1788), read—as the age deplored—by young ladies. Take for example this synopsis in the *Monthly Review* of *The Ramble; or History of Miss Evelyn*,

> A young lady in love with her supposed uncle. An old dotard in love with this same young lady, his supposed grand-daughter.
>
> These amours made honest by the help of a gypsey, whose child the loved and loving fair one is said to be. Her virgin chastity attempted by the ancient lover, and rescued by the younger. Her virgin chastity again attempted by the friend of her beloved *Adonis*, and again rescued by a mad adventurer. The rescued fair conducted by her new inamorato to the mouth of a dismal cave, (in which he threatens to end his life before her eyes, unless she consents to repay his services with those charms which he had preserved) and there terrified into a promise of marriage. A *third ravishment*, and a murder, introduced for the sake of *variety* and *entertainment*, into the husband's story of himself. The wife, unmindful of her holy vow, on a sudden suffering her first passion to rekindle. Her husband in a fit of jealousy, encountering his innocent rival. The hapless fair rushing between their swords. Wounded. Expiring. Lamented.[39]

The Gothic novel multiplied these sado-masochistic thrills. Helpless women were humiliated in *The Monk*; the tyrannical father in *The Castle of Otranto* plotted to marry his son's bride. There was an extensive literature about prostitutes from *Moll Flanders* to *Fanny Hill*, warmer, more erotic and less disgusting than its Restoration predecessors. The voguish novels of Laurence Sterne took much of their success from their ingrained sexual *doubles entendres* in words, psychology and situation.[40] Erotic literature evidently sold well: *Memoirs of a Woman of Pleasure* is reputed to have made its publisher Ralph Griffiths £10,000.

Secondly, sexuality was very visible in the public arena. Throughout the century women's garb was conspicuous by its extremely low *décolletage*. Prostitution swarmed on to the streets. In London, prostitutes numbered probably over ten thousand, at all levels from the kept woman to the street walker, the amateur to the professional, the sixpenny whore to the high-class and well-bred courtesan who—Casanova thought—might cost six guineas for a night at a bagnio. Prostitutes plied their trade on the streets with almost no interference. They advertised in directories such as Jack Harris's *The Whoremonger's Guide to London*.

Many other sexual entertainments were available. Bagnios and serails catered for specialised tastes such as flagellation. Men of pleasure had their own private clubs, most notably that of the 'Medmenham Monks'. There were shows which featured naked dancing and copulation, as for example that run by Mrs Hayes where—she advertised—'at 7 o'clock precisely 12 beautiful nymphs, spotless virgins, will carry out the famous Feast of Venus, as it is celebrated in Tahiti, under the instruction and leadership of Queen Oberea (which rôle will be taken by Mrs. Hayes herself)'. Sex in public was quite acceptable. Prostitutes and their clients copulated in St James's Park (where William Hickey's first experience took place). James Boswell christened the recently opened Westminster Bridge one May evening in 1763:

> At the bottom of the Haymarket I picked up a strong, jolly young damsel, and taking her under the arm I conducted her to Westminster Bridge, and then in armour complete did I engage her upon this noble edifice. The whim of doing it there with the Thames rolling below us amused me very much.[41]

Third, there was a good deal of casual, easy-going, promiscuous behaviour, some of it vicarious, which few thought to question. It seems to have been taken for granted that maid-servants were fair game for men's advances: the men were not the worse thought of so long as they made arrangements for any bastards that resulted. Although women were clearly victims of unwanted attentions, many seem to have been compliant or active. Young William Hickey was first seduced at the age of ten by a maid, Nanny Harris. One of his early memories was of awaking one morning to find himself between Nanny's legs: 'with one of my hands upon the seat of Love where I have no doubt she had placed it'.[42]

Men such as Hickey and Boswell found no difficulty in getting sexual partners amongst women who were not prostitutes. Actresses and dancers were assumed to be sexually easy. Many females obviously felt better off as the kept women of gentlemen than as servants or as wives. Some high-class demi-mondaines and courtesans, such as Kitty Fisher and Fanny Murray, won fame and respect (and became much-prized models for leading painters). Women of easy virtue were not automatically outcasts. In the 1780s Francis Place had as his master a London leather-breeches-maker, Mr France, who had three daughters by a first wife. 'His eldest daughter was and had been for several years a common prostitute. His youngest daughter, who was about seventeen years of age, had genteel lodgings where she was visited by gentlemen; and the second daughter ... was kept by a captain of an East India ship, in whose absence she used to amuse herself as such women generally do.'[43] Evidently neither Place, nor France, nor the women were embarrassed by this situation. It was commonplace for respectable men to keep mistresses and to walk out in public with them, as for instance did the Duke of Grafton with Nancy Parsons. Wives were often complaisant in their husbands keeping mistresses (they might be glad of the chance of avoiding getting pregnant). Well-to-do young men in London were expected to be *honnêtes hommes*. 'Where', asked John Wesley,

> is male chastity to be found? Among the nobility, among the gentry, among the tradesmen, or among the common people of England? How few can lay any claim to it at all? How few desire so much as the reputation of it! How numerous are they now even among such as are accounted men of honour and probity who are as fed horses, every one neighing after his neighbour's wife.[44]

At least in high society, adultery, *ménages à trois* and shifting sexual liaisons seem to have been early assimilated; certainly they were matters of intense gossip and amusement, but not necessarily the cause of matrimonial breakdown, duels or psychic disaster. Wives were often prepared to put up with their husbands' affairs. Boswell's friend, the Honourable Mrs Stuart, wife of James Archibald Stuart, told Boswell

That from what she had seen of life in this great town she would not be uneasy at an occasional infidelity in her husband, as she did not think it at all connected with affection. That if he kept a particular woman, it would be a sure sign that he had no affection for his wife; or if his infidelities were very frequent, it would also be a sign. But that a transient fancy for a girl, or being led by one's companions after drinking to an improper place, was not to be considered as inconsistent with true affection.[45]

Few men were ashamed of owning their bastards. Erasmus Darwin had two illegitimate daughters, whom he brought up openly on intimate terms with his second wife and her children. He founded a school at which they became the governesses. He had no thought that this might damage his reputation as a Midlands physician. Similarly, the tenth Earl of Pembroke fathered children on two mistresses. His illegitimate son was close friends with his father's heir and with the Countess (who, however, insisted that the bastards should not take the family name of Herbert). Bastards might even marry well. The illegitimate daughter of Sir Edward Walpole married Lord Waldegrave, and on his death, George III's brother, the Duke of Gloucester.

I want to emphasise several aspects of this public visibility and tolerance of sexuality. Firstly, it encompassed a large section of society, certainly much more extensive than the libertine élite of the Restoration court. Admittedly, other wedges of society were engrainedly straitlaced, not least the Dissenting community. And of course the flaunting of sexuality was much more evident in large towns, above all London. Yet this does not diminish the extraordinary openness of sexuality, in contrast to other ages. *A View of London and Westminster, Or the Town Spy* reckoned in 1725 that there were 107 brothels within the Hundred of Drury alone. In mid-century John Shebbeare noted that 'every print-shop has its windows stuck full with indecent prints to inflame desire through the eye, and singers in the streets charm your ears with lascivious songs to waken you to the same employment'. Francis Place confirmed that in the 1780s quite respectable shops sold pornography. Mrs Roach, the owner of one, 'used to open a portfolio to any boy or to any maidservant ... the portfolio contained a multitude of obscene prints ... she encouraged them to look at them. ... This was common to other shops. ...'[46] The omnipresence of prostitutes, bawdy prints and titillating novels all indicate that sexual indulgence and tolerance were not just confined to a tiny libertine rakish fringe.

Furthermore, sexual indulgence seems—by the standards of other ages—to have been remarkably open, easy and unrepressed. Sexual adventures were described by diarists such as William Hickey without the slightest sense of guilt or furtiveness. Seeking to enjoy himself on a sunny afternoon, Hickey would often call in at a brothel, pick up some girls, and take them into the country or up the Thames. In a letter to David Hume, Lord Denbigh quite routinely mentioned how he, in company with Lord Sandwich, Lord Mulgrave and Mr Banks, had taken 'two or three ladies of pleasure' up to the inn at Spine Hill near Newbury for the better part of a week, noting that they intended 'to pass all this week and the next'.[47]

Sexual indulgence was less likely to ruin a reputation, even that of a lady. 'No one is shocked', wrote Lady Mary Wortley Montagu, 'to hear that Miss So-and-So Maid of Honour, has got nicely over her confinement.'[48] Looking back from the more straitlaced nineteenth century Francis Place observed,

> want of chastity in girls [of the tradesmen's class] was common, but it was not by any means considered so disreputable in master tradesmens families as it is now in journeymen mechanics families. A tradesman's daughter who should now misconduct herself in the way mentioned would be abandoned by her companions, and probably by her parents.[49]

There was even great freedom of expression. The *Monthly Review* believed that *Memoirs of a Woman of Pleasure* was a book not 'offensive to decency'. Robert Bage's novel *Mount Henneth* (1781) includes an episode in which the women characters discuss sexual intercourse after they have seen a stallion copulating with a mare. David Hume could discuss incest without awkwardness or a sense of taboo. And certain forms of hypocrisy were conspicuous by their absence. For example, it was commonly admitted that the widespread practice of beating (e.g. in schools) was sexual in nature—an association repressed and buried in Victorian times.[50]

In fact sexual liberty and libertinism were often boasted about. Philandering was construed as free and liberal behaviour. It was manly. Men such as John Wilkes and Charles James Fox gained as much in public acclaim from their sexual exploits as Pitt lost for lack of them. In 1784, when Fox was charged in a case of assault, he gave as his alibi that he had been in bed at the time with Mrs Armistead (she was willing to swear to it). He was much admired for his frankness. Sometimes sexual activity was represented as part of the Englishman's birthright. At the mock election at Garret in Surrey, a man qualified for the franchise by having 'enjoyed a woman in the open air in the vicinity'. Fanny Hill conceived of herself as some sort of national utility: of her employment at the brothel she says there was an 'open public enjoyment' of her[51] (and yet there was freedom too. She was 'at [her] liberty to refuse the party').[52]

This exultation in sexual freedom was often contrasted—in ways utterly characteristic of the Enlightenment—to its opposites: the sick scourging of the flesh and the abomination of institutional chastity in Catholic monasteries and nunneries, and the denial of the body by canting killjoy Puritans (who, in the Enlightenment stereotype, almost always turn out to be Tartuffian hypocrites). Charles Surface and Tom Jones might be promiscuous, but they had good hearts. Men such as Joseph Surface who paraded their virtue turned out to be concupiscent repressed lechers. In life and art, the Georgians did not demand that the sexually exuberant came to a sticky ending. Not all harlots' progresses were downhill all the way. Mrs Hayes, the society brothel keeper, retired reputedly worth £20,000. Fanny Hill made £800 clear profit out of two years as a whore. Both *Fanny Hill* and *Moll Flanders* had happy endings (Fanny's career was described in typical Enlightenment terms as 'a rare alliance of pleasure with interest').[53]

What is very conspicuous is that both influential public opinion and the authorities throughout Enlightenment England made so little attempt to curb this sexual Eden. There was little continual and overriding public fear, for most of the century, that God's wrath was about to descend upon His priapic people (though there were occasional and temporary panics, as after the London earthquakes of 1750). Though many worried that sexual indulgence was leading to national corruption and anarchy, little was done about it. The general preference for liberty and decentralisation over central police action applied equally to sexual matters. The Church courts, which had been the chief enforcers of sexual morals in previous centuries, were allowed to wither (though not quite to disappear). Parliament took no national, concerted action against prostitution, pornography or obscenity (though *ad hominem* prosecutions were occasionally brought, especially when libel was involved, when there were personal axes to grind, as in the prosecution of John Wilkes's *Essay on Woman*).[54]

There was more public willingness to exonerate sexual misdeeds. Henry Fielding, analysing the causes of crime, specifically exempted girl prostitutes from blame for their offences: they were 'whores through necessity'.[55] Similarly the Magdalen Hospital for Penitent Prostitutes was founded not to punish or correct the whores, but out of 'pity', as a 'retreat', and to reform them.[56] The age also saw the setting up of Foundling Hospitals, and of Lock Hospitals for treating venereal diseases, despite the views of some fundamentalists that sexual crimes were thereby being condoned.

Certainly, there were groups in Georgian England who were horrified that rampant sexuality was undermining the moral fibre and godliness of the nation. Early in the century Societies for the Reformation of Manners were set up to bring prosecutions against prostitutes, pornographers and homosexuals, as well as against other lewd people such as sabbath breakers and swearers.[57] In 1787 the Proclamation Society was founded for the same purposes, developing into Wilberforce's Vice Society of 1802. But two points need to be made.

First, these societies won only limited amounts of popular and official support. The Societies for the Reformation of Manners were resented and ridiculed. Their vigilante smuthounds were sometimes beaten up. They had declined by the 1740s.

Second, the moving forces behind these anti-sex movements were deeply hostile to all facets of the Enlightenment. The Reformation Societies early in the century were reincarnations of Stuart Puritanism. Attacks on the immorality of the stage came above all from the High Churchman Jeremy Collier. The Hutchinsonians, who attacked lax sexual morals and decadence in high places, were implacably opposed to Locke, Newton and Rational Christianity. John Wesley, a passionate anti-Latitudinarian, attacked sexual indulgence. His *Arminian Magazine* talked of 'the deluge of depravity which has been pouring upon us'.[58] Wesley was a Bowdleriser *avant la lettre*. And not least of course the late-eighteenth-century Evangelicals who formed the core of the Vice Society were entrenched against liberal politics (especially the French Revolution), rationalism and natural religion. Typical

Enlightenment figures such as Sydney Smith and Byron were the sworn foes of such societies.

In other words, there was a close alignment between sexual permissiveness and endorsement of other Enlightenment outlooks. It would be hard to prove that adherence to or rejection of Enlightenment beliefs *caused* individual courses of sexual behaviour; yet the correlations are close enough to be persuasive.

IV

I have not been arguing that Enlightenment opinion thought that sex was 'a good thing' *tout court*. It was much more complicated than that. In sexuality, as in matters of child-rearing, personal freedom and government, Enlightenment belief in liberty and indulgence had well-defined limits, its own pressures and intolerances, contours and chiaroscuro.

Firstly, the much-bandied freedoms were to apply principally to males. Male Enlightenment attitudes were highly ambiguous with regard to women.[59] On the one hand, there were deeply ingrained misogynistic beliefs which saw women as men's playthings, or attributed overwhelming and grotesque sexuality to women (and early eighteenth-century female writers such as Mrs Centlivre and Mrs Manley were happy to admit to female sexuality). Certainly Enlightenment men did not seek to deny female sexuality. There was no Georgian Dr Acton who thought that to attribute erotic passion to women was 'a vile aspersion'. Boswell thought 'I have my own private notions as to modesty, of which I would only value the appearance; for unless a woman has amorous heat, she is a dull companion'.[60]

Furthermore, eighteenth-century English women were allowed a real measure of freedom, which shocked some foreign visitors. Le Blanc noted that Englishwomen have 'no false modesty'. 'If a girl fancies a man and can't get to know him, she will send him a message with her proposal, or advertise.'[61] Many currents of Enlightenment thought insisted that women were intelligent and rational creatures, and there is much evidence from middle- and upper-class households of women being treated in a more egalitarian way (e.g., having greater say in choice of their own marriage partner).

Yet one strategy women followed (and some men complied) to enhance their status as rational, sensitive and refined creatures was to deflect attention from, or deny, their sexuality. The English bluestockings, such as Hannah More, highlighted the intellectual and moral abilities of women by repudiating traditional emphasis on beauty and charm.[62] In her early years as a radical intellectual, Mary Wollstonecraft carried into practice her principles of the rights of women, but only through personal chastity and denial of common ideas of marriage. In any case, liberal and Enlightened men no less than crusty reactionaries were unwilling to accord to women the full freedoms they sought for themselves. The sexual fidelity of wives seemed essential to prevent bastards who would bring confusion to family property and inheritance. The more Enlightenment sentimentality enhanced woman's special role as mother, the less her sexual independence would be.

The Enlightenment mentality was also frightened of plebeian sexuality. Just as one didn't talk atheism in front of the servants, so eroticism wasn't for them either. The title of one of the more widely circulating pornographic magazines makes this point very clearly: *The Covent Garden Magazine, or Amorous Repository, Calculated Solely for the Entertainment of the Polite World* (1774). In part the fear was that sexual licence would slide into general disorder and anarchy. But the far greater fear was that the masses were fast-breeders; they would outrun their ability to look after their own offspring, and also the national economy's capacity to absorb them. Economists and political arithmeticians were all too well aware of the swelling ranks of paupers and the vast increase in the poor rates. That late Enlightenment figure, Thomas Malthus, put the picture most scientistically when he axiomatically deemed that population growth had a tendency to outrun food supply. Failing voluntary moral checks amongst the poor (abstinence from sex by, for example, late marriage), positive checks, such as famine or war, would supervene. Enlightenment men such as Bentham devoted great effort to persuading the poor that it lay in their interests to curb their own sexuality in the cause of minimising poverty. Lower down the social scale rationalist radicals such as Francis Place could see the wisdom of family limitation. But also, as good Enlightenment figures, they accepted the joy of sex. The answer: the legitimising of contraception. What needed to be suppressed was fertility and poverty, not sexuality.

The Enlightenment's toleration of sexuality was drawn to exclude two other groups. Firstly, the young. From early in the century there was a growing torrent of medical and moral opposition to masturbation, directed primarily against young people.[63] Characteristic were the warnings of James Graham. The young who masturbated, he pronounced, would suffer

> debility of body and of mind,—infecundity,—epilepsy,—loss of memory,—sight, and hearing,—distortions of the eyes, mouth and face,—feeble, harsh and squeaking voice,—pale, sallow and blueish black complexion,—wasting and tottering of the limbs,—idiotism,—horrors,—innumerable complaints—extreme wretchedness—and even death itself. . . . Every act of self-pollution and even every repetition of natural venery with even the loveliest of the sex to which appalled or exhausted nature is whipped and spurred by lust, habit, or fiery unnatural provocations;—but especially every act of self-pollution!—is an earthquake—a blast—a deadly paralytic stroke.—to all the faculties of both soul and body! . . . Thrice happy! supremely blessed! in my opinion, are those young men and women, who live, till they are at least *twenty* years of age without ever once having had even one seminal emission in their whole life, asleep or awake, voluntarily or involuntarily![64]

Such opposition came in part from those groups generally hostile to sexual liberalism, but it also came from medical men and educators otherwise enlightened in their outlooks. It arose partly at least because it was feared that masturbation would jeopardise other cherished ideals of the Enlightenment. Warm and mutual relationships within the affectionate, companionate family was increasingly valued. The denial of original sin made childhood seem a time of innocence.[65] Under these circumstances teenage sexuality became less acceptable. Furthermore, as Enlightenment thought put more stress upon individual responsibility and success, anything that threatened these needed to be rooted out. Masturbation became a convenient explanation of why some people remained feeble in mind and body, plagued by lassitude and melancholy.

Secondly, Enlightenment sexual tolerance extended only as far as heterosexuals.[66] The German traveller Von Archenholz noted that 'unnatural pleasures are held in great abhorrence with the men. In no country are such infamous pleasures spoken of with greater detestation.'[67] In London at least there were of course clubs for upper-class homosexuals, whose practices, if discreet, were tolerated. But the law on buggery remained capital, and was sometimes executed with full savagery against members of the lower classes. Some of the more notorious homosexual men of Georgian England, such as William Beckford, found it prudent to live abroad or in seclusion. Enlightenment writers showed no sympathy towards homosexuality. The kinds of masculine culture which produce undercover homosexuality, such as superfine courtliness or Spartan ruggedness, were out of fashion. Enlightenment writers endorsed the time-honoured depiction of buggery as 'a crime against nature': the strongest term of condemnation they knew.

Practically all Enlightenment figures recommended the pleasures of the flesh. This is not of course to say they neglected or despised the pleasures of the mind. As Cleland has Fanny Hill say, the two are mutually enhancing. It was only slightly eccentric thinkers such as William Godwin who from Enlightenment stances downgraded the body. Godwin believed that as men grew more rational, superior intellectual joys would increase and taste for inferior bodily pleasures would atrophy. This would not threaten the regeneration of the species, since life would be ever more and more prolonged.[68]

Yet Enlightenment values strongly opposed the blind and merely animal indulgence of sexual cravings. For sexuality to be enjoyable, it had to be refined, decent, polite. The Enlightenment legitimated sexuality at the cost of making it decorous.

This civilised pursuit of pleasure took several forms. Often the emphasis was upon the *rational* quest for sexual joy. Fanny Hill described one of her older men as a 'rational pleasurist';[69] 'He loved me with dignity in a manner equally remov'd from the sourness, the forwardness, by which age is unpleasantly characteriz'd', while being 'much too wise to be asham'd of the pleasures of humanity'.[70] Sometimes the emphasis fell chiefly upon polish and gentility. Fanny Hill recounted how she and others had found the secret of having the most 'libertine pleasures' yet of reconciling 'even all the refinements of taste and delicacy with the most gross and determinate gratifications of sensuality'.[71] Sex should be neither savage nor sinful, but civilised: there was, she wrote, 'no stiffness, no reserve, no airs of pique, or little jealousies, but all was unaffectedly gay, cheerful, and easy'.[72]

A sexual etiquette needed to be negotiated which would guarantee pleasure without embarrassment. Polite society sought to have its liberties without offending. For example, at Devonshire House in the 1790s the Duke and Duchess shared a *ménage* with the Duchess's closest friend, Lady Elizabeth Foster. The Duke's legitimate children were brought up alongside his children by Lady Elizabeth. Yet propriety was strictly observed. Lady Elizabeth's illegitimate children were all born in secrecy abroad (as was a bastard of the Duchess by Lord Grey). The paternity of Lady Elizabeth's children was concealed from the children themselves. Similarly, for his part, James Graham the sex therapist emphasised the decorum of his lectures: 'Ladies of rank and character are assured, that nothing will be said or seen, which çan give even the smallest offence to the chastest and most delicate female eye or ear, and that every thing will be conducted with the most perfect decency and decorum'.[73] Above all, perhaps, the late Enlightenment cult of sensibility came to inform notions of decent sexuality.[74] Enlightenment thought saw emotional refinement as enhancing sexuality. As Francis Hutcheson put it,

> The inclination to procreate is excited, or at least generally regulated in its choice of partner, by many delicate sentiments, and finer passions of the heart of the sweetest kind ... The esteem of virtue and wisdom, the desire and love of innocence of manners, complacence, confidence, and the tenderest good-will, are the most natural incitements and concomitants of the amorous desire, and almost obscure the brutal impulse towards the sensual gratification, which might be had with persons of any character.[75]

Sexual attraction came to be expressed in an aesthetic, elevated rococo language, brimful of feeling. Tenderness was underlined by the growing delicacy of the language employed. *The Memoirs of a Woman of Pleasure* notably contains no four-letter words. Sexual feelings were increasingly filtered through sensibilities of tenderness, ardour and pre-Romantic passion. It was sentimental sex that gave *Tristram Shandy* and *A Sentimental Journey* their power. Fanny Hill wrote of her own 'sensitive soul':[76] 'Love, that made me timid, taught me to be tender too.'[77] For her the male member was a 'sensitive plant'.[78] In Mrs Cole's brothel, 'good manners and politeness were inviolably observ'd; here was no gross ribaldry, no offensive or rude behaviour or ungenerous reproaches to the girls for their compliance with the humours and desires of the men'.[79]

Within this sentimental framework, Fanny fell in love with the man to whom she gave her virginity, and eventually settled down with him.

Refined sexuality had its advantages. It was presumably more erotic. It was also less dangerous to health. Lord Chesterfield urged his son to get his sexual experience with a refined Parisian lady rather than with a streetwalker because it was more educative and the chances of catching the pox were so much slimmer:

Un arrangement, which is, in plain English, a gallantry, is at Paris as necessary a part of a woman of fashion's establishment as her house.... A young fellow must therefore be a very awkward one to be reduced to, or of a very singular taste to prefer, drabs and danger to a commerce (in the course of the world not disgraceful) with a woman of health, education and rank.[80]

Above all, sex with sensibility seemed to solve that constant problem of the English Enlightenment: how individuals could indulge their own selfish passions without danger to the social order.

V

Within limits, English Enlightenment attitudes sought to permit free play of individual sexuality (in much the same way as it encouraged freedom of thought and expression, religious toleration, and the free disposal of capital and property). These attitudes carried over into action. Although these values were élitist, there was probably a wider range of public sexual indulgence than in the preceding or succeeding centuries. Seventeenth-century religious anxieties about the flesh were being soothed away. Certainly what is often thought of as the 'Victorian' obsessional repression of sexuality—seen as fatal both to individual psychic equilibrium and to family and social order—was long pre-Victorian in origins. But it sprang more from the rejection of Enlightenment beliefs than from their culmination.

The rejection of Enlightenment sexuality crystallised in two movements. On the one hand Romanticism repudiated Enlightenment sensuality as gross and materialistic. The idealisation of love, and particularly of woman, was central to the Romantic quest. Blake wanted to liberate the body from prohibitions and inhibitions. But he also wanted to liberate it from Enlightenment conventions of politeness and from merely natural desires. As Price has written, 'When Blake calls for the improvement of sensual enjoyment, it is as a means of freeing the individual from the merely vegetative and natural. The intensity of consummation becomes an annihilation of selfhood and an entry into the realm that transcends the temporal, the Eternal.'[81] Blake was an advocate of the lineaments of gratified desire, but he thought desire would be gratified only within the religious–mystical framework of prelapsarian Adam reborn. Even the division of the sexes was for Blake a continuing indictment of man's fallen nature. Shelley longed for a unique, passionate and all-consuming ideal love (as in *Epipsychidion*), while also remaining an adherent of a Godwinian/Wollstonecraftian 'free love'. The mundane sexuality of the Enlightenment *homme moyen sensuel* was rejected by Romantics; they wanted a more transcendental kind of love.

Contemporary with Romanticism was the movement, led by the Evangelicals, to banish hedonism in general, and sexuality in particular, from the respectable consciousness and from public life.[82] In this transition, as Byron put it, 'from cunt to cant', the pursuit of pleasure fell under deep suspicion. 'Let us give ourselves a little respite [on Sundays] from the fatigue of pleasure', recommended Bishop Porteus.[83] One needed to be on guard against pleasure's darts: 'Novels generally speaking are instruments of abomination and ruin. A fond attachment to them is an irrefragable evidence of a mind contaminated, and totally unfitted for the serious pursuits of study, or the delightful exercises and enjoyments of religion.'[84] In his *Essay on the Stage* the Methodist John Styles argued that 'in the choice of a wife, a gentleman should peremptorily reject every female who has been five times at a Theatre in the course of the last two years of her life'.[85] Of the many manifestations of pleasure, sexuality was the most sinister and sinful. Bowdlerism, Grundyism, prudery, repression, anxiety and shame were summoned up to put sexuality back in its rightful place. Sensuality came to be practically the antonym of respectability.

My point is that those who at the end of the eighteenth century rejected Enlightenment attitudes towards sexuality were those who were comprehensively rejecting all aspects of the Enlightenment beliefs and the prevalent mores of Georgian culture. By that emphatic and self-conscious denial, they bring into focus the reality of distinctive Enlightenment attitudes towards sexuality.

NOTES

1 For a more fully developed account of the view of the Enlightenment in England advanced here, see Roy Porter, *English Society in the Eighteenth Century* (Harmondsworth, 1982); *idem*, 'The Enlightenment in England', in Roy Porter and Mikuláš Teich (eds.), *The Enlightenment in National Context* (Cambridge, 1981); *idem*, 'Science, Provincial Culture and Public Opinion in Enlightenment England', *British Journal of Eighteenth Century Studies* III (1980), 20–46; and *idem*, 'Medicine and the Enlightenment in Eighteenth Century England', *Bulletin of the Society for the Social History of Medicine*, XXV (1979), 27–40.

2 See J. H. Plumb, *The Commercialization of Leisure in Eighteenth Century England* (Reading, 1973); *idem*, *Georgian Delights* (London, 1980).
3 Edward Shorter, *The Making of the Modern Family* (London, 1976); P. Branca, *Women in Europe since 1750* (London, 1978). For a criticism see C. Fairchilds, 'Female Sexual Attitudes and the Rise of Illegitimacy: a Case Study', *Journal of Interdisciplinary History*, VIII (1978), 627–67.
4 For recent discussions, see L. Stone, *Family, Sex and Marriage in England, 1500–1800* (London, 1976), ch. XII, and Roger Thompson, *Unfit for Modest Ears* (London, 1980), p. 214. See also F. Bottomley, *Attitudes to the Body in Western Christendom* (London, 1979).
5 Community control of individual sexual behaviour has been stressed by Peter Laslett, most notably in *The World We Have Lost* (London, 1965), and recently in the work edited by Laslett, Karla Oosterveen and Richard M. Smith, *Bastardy and its Comparative History* (London, 1980). See also Keith Wrightson and David Levine, *Poverty and Piety in an English Village: Terling 1525–1700* (London, 1979). Of course, controls were much laxer in big towns such as London. There Francis Place thought that in the late eighteenth century 'want of chastity in girls was common', M. Thale (ed.), *The Autobiography of Francis Place* (Cambridge, 1972), p. 57. In villages there were always some women who were sexually easy-going: G. R. Quaife, *Wanton Wenches and Wayward Wives* (London, 1979). Such groups of men as soldiers notoriously sowed wild oats, and prostitution abounded.
6 I. Bloch, *A History of English Sexual Morals*, trans by W. H. Fostern (London, 1958), ch. VIII; Stone, *Family, Sex and Marriage*, p. 530f.
7 Thompson, *Unfit for Modest Ears*, p. 210.
8 C. Strachey (ed.), *The Letters of the Earl of Chesterfield to his Son*, 2 vols. (London, 1932), II, p. 133. For brief introductions to this trend of moral thought, see L. A. Selby-Bigge, *British Moralists*, 2 vols. (Oxford, 1897); D. D. Raphael, *British Moralists 1650–1800*, 2 vols. (Oxford, 1969); J. Passmore, *The Perfectibility of Man* (London, 1970), esp. chs. VII–X; and E. Halévy, *The Growth of Philosophic Radicalism*, trans. by M. Morris (London, 1928). In *Memoirs of a Woman of Pleasure* (London, 1749; edit. quoted, Mayflower Books, London, 1977) John Cleland has the prostitute heroine Fanny Hill say that though she knew that as a whore she was engaging in vice, yet 'to say the plain truth, the dissipation and diversion I began to find in this new acquaintance' cured her of anxieties (p. 83).
9 Quoted in N. Smith, 'Sexual Mores in the Eighteenth Century: Robert Wallace's "Of Venery"', *Journal of the History of Ideas*, XXXIX (1978), 419–33, p. 426.
10 F. Pottle (ed.), *Boswell's London Journal 1762–1763* (London, 1950), p. 84.
11 Erasmus Darwin, *Zoonomia*, 2 vols. (London, 1794–6), I, p. 147.
12 L. A. Selby-Bigge (ed.), David Hume: *A Treatise of Human Nature* (Oxford, 1978), p. 486. I owe this point to Sylvana Tomaselli.

13 For the rise of egoistical, individualist, sensationalist hedonism in the context of the wider European Enlightenment see L. Crocker, *An Age of Crisis: Man and World in Eighteenth Century French Thought* (Baltimore, Md., 1959); R. Mauzi, *L'Idée du Bonheur dans la Littérature et la Pensée Françaises au XVIII*[e] Siècle (Paris, 1960); F. E. and F. P. Manuel, *Utopian Thought in the Western World* (Cambridge, Mass., 1979), ch. XXII, 'New Faces of Love'. Crocker controversially sees the movement culminating in de Sade.

14 Quoted in M. Williford, 'Bentham on the Rights of Women', *Journal of the History of Ideas*, XXXVI (1975), 167–76, p. 172. Bentham claimed that sex was a legitimate pleasure in its own right, and denounced those moralists who argued 'a man is to convert the highest enjoyment that kind nature has bestow'd upon him into a mechanical operation to make children' (Bentham Papers, University College, London, Box 74, fol. 8). I owe this point to David Liebermann.

15 Cleland, *Memoirs*, p. 10. For discussion of Cleland's overt debts to the *philosophes*, see Leo Braudy, '*Fanny Hill* and Materialism', *Eighteenth Century Studies*, IV (1970–1), 21–40, and also W. H. Epstein, *John Cleland, Images of a Life* (New York, 1974), ch. VI. Of course, what actual, as distinct from fictional, women of pleasure thought is a separate issue.

16 Cleland, *Memoirs*, p. 33.

17 *Ibid.*, p. 36. Cf. p. 51: 'I did what I did because I could not help it.'

18 *Ibid.*, p. 57.

19 *Ibid.*, p. 68.

20 *Ibid.*, p. 81. Cf. p. 121: 'O how powerful are the instincts of nature! How little is there wanting to set them in motion!'

21 *Ibid.*, p. 114.

22 Pottle, *Boswell's London Journal*, p. 116.

23 S. Moravia, 'The Enlightenment and the Sciences of Man', *History of Science*, XVIII (1980), 247–68; A. Vartanian, *La Mettrie's L'Homme Machine* (Princeton, N.J., 1960).

24 Darwin, *Zoonomia*, I, p. 146. Fanny Hill by contrast refers to the male genitals as the 'originals of beauty', objects 'above all the imitation of art'. Cleland, *Memoirs*, p. 59.

25 Cleland, *Memoirs*, p.36. See also Braudy, '*Fanny Hill* and Materialism'.

26 See D. King-Hele, *Doctor of Revolution* (London, 1977), p. 255; *idem*, *The Essential Writings of Erasmus Darwin* (London, 1968), p. 81.

27 Cleland, *Memoirs*, p. 33.

28 Erasmus Darwin, *Phytologia* (London, 1800), p. 103.

29 Erasmus Darwin, *The Temple of Nature* (London, 1803), canto II, lines 245–6.

30 Erasmus Darwin, *The Botanic Garden* (London, 1791), canto I, lines 61–2. In his *Essay on Woman* (London, 1763) John Wilkes expressed this cosmic philosophy of sex in summary form: 'Life can little else supply / But a few good fucks and then we die.'

31 King-Hele, *Doctor of Revolution*, p. 242f.

32 Boswell expounded to Belle de Zuylen how, within marriage, he would expect to be free to pursue his sexual appetites where they took him. When she replied she would expect the same freedom, he termed her a 'frantic libertine'. F. Pottle (ed.), *Boswell in Holland 1763–1764* (London, 1952), p. 279. Boswell remained deeply troubled as to how to square his desire for sexual freedom with his Christianity: see C. Ryscamp and F. A. Pottle (eds.), *Boswell: the Ominous Years 1774–1776* (New York, 1963), p. 74.

33 Williford, 'Bentham', p. 171.

34 Quoted in G. Rattray Taylor, *The Angel Makers* (London, 1958), p. 7.

35 A. McLaren *Birth Control in Nineteenth Century England* (London, 1978), ch. I; J. Blackman, 'Popular Theories of Generation: the Evolution of *Aristotle's Works*. The Study of an Anachronism', in J. Woodward and D. Richards (eds.), *Health Care and Popular Medicine in Nineteenth Century England* (London, 1977), pp. 56–88. Francis Place reported reading *Aristotle's Masterpiece* while still at school. More generally on the development of intellectual discourse about sex see M. Foucault, *The History of Sexuality*, vol. I, *An Introduction*, trans by R. Hurley (London, 1978).

36 For discussion of Graham see E. Jameson, *The Natural History of Quackery* (London, 1961), ch. VI. For a French parallel, see R. Darnton, *Mesmerism and the End of the Enlightenment in France* (Cambridge, Mass., 1968).

37 Plentiful evidence can be found in books such as Bloch, *History of English Sexual Morals* (London, 1958); M. M. Hunt, *The Natural History of Love* (London, 1960); N. C. Epton, *Love and the English* (London, 1960); G. Rattray Taylor, *Sex in History* (London, 1959).

38 D. Foxon, *Libertine Literature in England 1660–1745* (New York, 1965).

39 *Monthly Review*, LII (February 1775), p. 186.

40 R. Alter, '*Tristram Shandy* and the Game of Love', *American Scholar*, XXXVII (1968), 316–23. F. Brady, '*Tristram Shandy*, Sexuality, Morality, and Sensibility', *Eighteenth Century Studies*, IV (1970–1), 41–56, where on p. 49 Brady writes of Sterne's 'hedonistic delight in the joys of the senses'.

41 Pottle (ed.), *Boswell's London Journal*, p. 255. 'Armour' is of course a condom.

42 A. Spencer (ed.), *Memoirs of William Hickey*, 4 vols. (London, 1923), I, p. 12.

43 Quoted in A. Parreaux, *Daily Life in England in the Reign of George III*, trans. by C. Congreve (London, 1969), p. 127.

44 Thale (ed.), *Autobiography of Francis Place*, p. 71.

45 W. K. Wimsatt and F. A. Pottle (eds.), *Boswell for the Defence* (New York, 1959), p. 76. Of course, there were limits to tolerance, In 1792 Mrs Siddons took it very badly when her husband gave her the pox.

46 Quoted in Stone, *Family, Sex and Marriage*, p. 621.

47 J. Greig (ed.), *The Letters of David Hume*, 2 vols. (Oxford, 1932), II, p. 319.

48 Quoted in Taylor, *The Angel Makers*, p. 191.

49 Thale (ed.), *Autobiography of Francis Place*, p. 81.

50 This point is well made by T. Gibson, *The English Vice: Beating, Sex and Shame in Victorian England and After* (London, 1978), p. 12. See for example this verse on a child's sampler of 1842 (in the Doll's Museum, Warwick):

> How gracious and how wise
> Is our chastising God
> And Oh how much the blessings are
> Which blossom from his rod.
>
> He lifts it up on high
> With pity in His heart
> And every stroke his children feel
> May grace and peace impart.

51 Cleland, *Memoirs*, p. 138.

52 *Ibid.*, p. 141.

53 *Ibid.*, p. 115.

54 It is notable how little groups seeking to clean up public life (such as the Evangelicals) looked to parliamentary legislation to serve their purposes. Public opinion remained heartily opposed to literary censorship. Early attempts at Bowdlerisation (usually called 'castration') were staunchly resisted by figures such as Dr Johnson. See N. Perrin, *Dr Bowdler's Legacy: a History of Expurgated Books in England and America* (New York, 1969). Chaucer was first expurgated in 1795 (p. 53). Expurgation got up steam in the 1790s.

55 Henry Fielding, *An Enquiry into the Causes of the Late Increase in Robberies* (London, 1751), p. 47.

56 H. F. B. Comston, *The Magdalen Hospital* (London, 1917), pp. 42–3. Of course, humanitarianism had its limits. In 1783 the Hospital refused to admit a black woman (p. 200).

57 E. J. Bristow, *Vice and Vigilance* (Dublin, 1977); see also J. Redwood, *Reason, Ridicule and Religion* (London, 1976), pp. 182f.

58 *Arminian Magazine*, XII (1789), p. 496.

59 For basic inequalities see K. Thomas, 'The Double Standard', *Journal of the History of Ideas*, XX (1959), 195–216; P. M. Spacks, '"Ev'ry Woman is at Heart a Rake"', *Eighteenth Century Studies*, VIII (1974–5), 27–46. For Enlightenment upgrading of women see E. Jacobs, W. H. Barber, J. H. Bloch, F. W. Leakey and E. Le Breton (eds.), *Woman and Society in Eighteenth Century France* (London, 1980); M. Williford, 'Bentham'; M. LeGates 'The Cult of Womanhood in Eighteenth Century Thought', *Eighteenth Century Studies*, X (1976), 21–40; K. B. Clinton, 'Femme et Philosophe: Enlightenment Origins of Feminism',

Eighteenth Century Studies, VIII (1975), 283–300. For Mary Wollstonecraft, see C. Tomalin, *The Life and Death of Mary Wollstonecraft* (London, 1974).

60 C. Ryscamp and F. A. Pottle (eds.), *Boswell in Extremis* (New York, 1970), p. 180.

61 Taylor, *The Angel Makers*, p. 4.

62 For this retreat into primness see A. Wallas, *Before the Bluestockings* (London, 1929); M. A. Hopkins, *Hannah More and her Circle* (New York, 1947).

63 A. Comfort, *The Anxiety Makers* (New York, 1969); E. H. Hare, 'Masturbatory Insanity: the History of an Idea', *Journal of Mental Science*, CVIII (1962), 1–25; R. H. MacDonald, 'The Frightful Consequences of Onanism', *Journal of the History of Ideas*, XXVIII (1967), 423–31.

64 J. Graham, *Lecture on the Generation, Increase and Improvement of the Human Species!* (London, n.d.), p. 20.

65 L. DeMause, 'The Evolution of Childhood', in L. DeMause (ed.), *The History of Childhood* (New York, 1974), pp. 1–73; P. Coveney, *Poor Monkey: the Child in Literature* (London, 1957).

66 H. Montgomery Hyde, *The Other Love* (London, 1970); A. L. Rowse *Homosexuals in History* (London, 1977), where on p. 111 Rowse writes 'Regency society was flagrantly shameless in its sex life, provided it was heterosexual'. A. D. Harvey, 'Prosecution for Sodomy in England at the Beginning of the Nineteenth Century', *Historical Journal*, XXI (1978), 939–48; A. N. Gilbert, 'Sexual Deviance and Disaster during the Napoleonic Wars', *Albion*, IX (1977), 98–113. Lesbianism seems to have been regarded by men with tolerant condescension.

67 Quoted in Taylor, *The Angel Makers*, p. 274.

68 W. Godwin, *Enquiry Concerning Political Justice*, ed. by I. Kramnick (Harmondsworth, 1978), p. 756. From Enlightenment individualistic and libertarian principles Godwin pronounced marriage the 'worst of monopolies' (p. 762), and demanded emotional and sexual freedom.

69 Cleland, *Memoirs*, p. 207.

70 *Ibid.*, p. 135.

71 *Ibid.*, p. 117.

72 *Ibid.*, p. 117.

73 Advertisement taken from *A Collection of Cuttings ... referring to Graham* in the Library of the Wellcome Institute for the History of Medicine, London, Acc. No. 73143.

74 For the medico-physiological background see G. S. Rousseau, 'Nerves, Spirits and Fibres: Towards Defining the Origins of Sensibility; with a Postscript, 1976', *The Blue Guitar*, II (1976), 125–53; *idem*, 'Science and the Discovery of the Imagination in Enlightened England', *Eighteenth Century Studies*, III (1969), 109–35; *idem*, 'Psychology', in G. S. Rousseau and Roy Porter (eds.), *The Ferment of Knowledge* (Cambridge, 1980), 143–210; S. Moravia, 'From *Homme Machine* to *Homme Sens-*

ible: Changing Eighteenth Century Models of Man's Image', *Journal of the History of Ideas*, XXXIX (1978), 45–60.

75 Francis Hutcheson, *A System of Moral Philosophy*, 2 vols. (Glasgow, 1755), II, pp. 151–2.

76 Cleland, *Memoirs*, p. 150.

77 *Ibid.*, p. 48.

78 *Ibid.*, p. 192.

79 *Ibid.*, p. 146.

80 Strachey (ed.), *Letters of Chesterfield*, II, p. 59.

81 M. Price, *To the Palace of Wisdom* (New York, 1964), p. 444; for the complexities of Blake's attitudes to the body see T. R. Frosch, *The Awakening of Albion: the Renovation of the Body in the Poetry of William Blake* (Ithaca, N.Y., 1974), and more broadly, J. Benthall, *The Body Electric* (London, 1976).

82 See Taylor, *The Angel Makers;* Ford K. Brown, *Fathers of the Victorians* (Cambridge, 1961); M. Quinlan, *Victorian Prelude* (New York, 1941); M. Jaeger, *Before Victoria* (London, 1956); P. Fryer, *Mrs Grundy: Studies in English Prudery* (London, 1963); E. Trudgill, *Madonnas and Magdalens* (London, 1966). Nineteenth-century sexual repression of course often took the form of physical mutilation of manuscripts, to expunge sexual passages, as happened to Francis Place's collections. David Vincent has recently pointed out how working-class autobiographers in the nineteenth century found it impossible to discuss their sex lives: 'Love and Death and the Nineteenth Century Working Class', *Social History*, V (1980), 223–48.

83 Beilby Porteus, *Works*, 6 vols. (London, 1811), II, p. 217.

84 *Evangelical Magazine*, I (1793), p. 79.

85 John Styles, *Essay on the Stage* (London, 1806), p. 37.

PAUL-GABRIEL BOUCÉ

Some sexual beliefs and myths in eighteenth-century Britain

Although in recent years scholarly works dealing with sexuality in eighteenth-century France or Britain[1] have begun to dispel some of the more tantalising obscurities shrouding our forebears' intimate lives, much remains to be done in order to gain a deeper knowledge of the then current sexual beliefs and myths which, more or less consciously, influenced and shaped their attitudes to the anatomy and the physiology of sex. Valuable information may certainly be culled from such works as Dr Robert James's *Medicinal Dictionary* (London, 1743–5), a mammoth compilation of six million words in three folio volumes, which may be taken as fairly representative of the state of mid-eighteenth-century medical knowledge. But at the forbidding price of £4.00 in eighty one-shilling fortnightly instalments,[2] it was impossible for lower-class or even middle-class readers to have easy access to such a work of reference. On the other hand, such books as John Wesley's *Primitive Physic* (London 1747), sold for one shilling, proved immensely and durably popular, being reprinted well into the nineteenth century: unfortunately, the book has little or nothing to say about sexual matters. The case is quite different with such anonymous publications as *Aristotle's Compleat Masterpiece In Three Parts; Displaying the Secrets of Nature in the Generation of Man: ... to which is added*, A Treasure of Health; *or*, The Family Physician (London, 23rd ed., 1749), or the three following companion volumes, no less spuriously attributed to the Greek philosopher, *Aristotle's Book of Problems ... Touching the State of Man's Body* (London, 25th ed., 1710?), *Aristotle's Compleat and Experienc'd Midwife* (London, 10th ed., 1750?) and finally *Aristotle's Last Legacy Unfolding the Mysteries of Nature in the Generation of Man* (London,

1749). It would be a fascinating and most informative piece of bibliographical research—well beyond the scope of this essay—to trace the intricate and instructive printing history of these little books still published in the 1930s, and possibly still nowadays. Their first editions date from the late seventeenth century, 1684, for *Aristotle's Masterpiece*, but their sources go back to Greek and Latin Antiquity, the Middle Ages and the Renaissance: the most direct ancestor of *Aristotle's Masterpiece* was a folio published in Venice in 1503.[3] Such durable popular success was often sadly misunderstood and soundly condemned, even by the distinguished medical historian, Sir d'Arcy Power, who could see nothing in *Aristotle's Masterpiece* but a 'hoary old debauchee acknowledged by no one', and who, somewhat uncharitably, conjectures the existence of a 'large class of persons in England possessed of prurient minds and so uneducated that the pseudoscience of the middle ages still appeals to them'.[4] Sir d'Arcy Power, who was writing half a century ago, wilfully ignores that basic urge for sexual knowledge analysed by Michel Foucault in his *La Volonté de savoir* (1976): 'Depuis le dix-huitième siècle le sexe n'a pas cessé de provoquer une sorte d'éréthisme discursif généralisé' (p. 45). One may well disagree with Foucault's strident over-emphasis of the political and socio-economic factors in what he aptly calls 'le grand prêche sexuel' (*ibid.*, p. 15), but it remains largely true that ethico-sexual attitudes in the eighteenth century were obsessively haunted by the often asserted need for a booming demography capable of providing the nation with a cheap and readily available labour force, not to mention cannon fodder in times of (frequent and murderous) European conflicts. But both Sir d'Arcy Power and Foucault ignore the individual's basic and instinctive curiosity concerning his own sexuality, and especially the physiological processes of procreation. Such works as *Aristotle's Masterpiece* were the humble, often misleading, forerunners of our scientifically better informed sex manuals. They follow, more or less closely, the actual progress of science which they assimilated and vulgarised in their countless English and American successive reprints, and thus assumed, in spite of their numerous errors, a pervasive didactic role rendered all the more necessary by the chaste and chastening silence enforced by families, schools and universities, not to mention that arch-silencer for centuries, the Church. To the same deep and normally healthy curiosity for sexual matters may be attributed the immense and lasting success of Dr

Nicolas Venette's *De la Génération de l'homme, ou tableau de l'amour conjugal* (Amsterdam, 1687), reprinted well into the twentieth century, and translated into most European languages. The English version, *The Mysteries of Conjugal Love Reveal'd*, first appeared in London in 1703. Just as in the case of *Aristotle's Masterpiece*, such prolonged success stirred up the moralistic wrath of the usual self-appointed 'censores morum',[5] especially in the nineteenth century.

Not only do such books contain obvious scientific errors, especially about spermatogenesis and the psychology of pregnancy, but they carry in their mixed streams beliefs and myths dating back to Hippocrates and Galen. Such beliefs and myths originated in ancient and medieval medicine, but often their sources are so diffuse that it becomes wellnigh impossible to separate them from traditional medicine, folklore, legends and superstitions which weave their elusive way into medical or para-medical discourse on eighteenth-century sexuality. Such beliefs and myths are characterised by their chronological instability: they may well be indignantly rejected by a late seventeenth-century author, but they reappear in full mythical force half a century later. Sexual beliefs and myths appear as a loose constellation of pseudo-scientific lore so firmly anchored in people's minds that some of them still continue to obtain in our supposedly better informed and more enlightened times. They are reflected in popular handbooks, and far from being grounded in a rational approach of the scientific type, they presuppose a deliberate suspension of the critical faculties. They are not only illogical—hence their sporadic recurrence—but stem from a pre-logical, or possibly a-logical, *mentalité*, which makes light of contemporaneous scientific advances, while paying lip-service to pseudo-experimentation or clinical observation. Thus, sexual beliefs and myths are also characterised by their insidious and obstinate remanence, as they fail to develop in a linear or chronological way. The dividing line between 'beliefs' and 'myths' is often blurred by constant symplectic interpenetration. Myths obviously thrive on beliefs, but they also connote something larger and more diffuse, viz. the often violent collusion (and also collision) of the most secret impulses of the individual psyche with the imperative pressures of our social existence.[6] The social function of sexual myths should never be lost sight of: doubtless, in a period of great physical insecurity, where the quasi-omnipresence of disease and death was constantly to be felt, much more sharply so than in our highly medicalised modern world, myths contributed to spread a diffuse but reassuring sense of community. Such pseudo-scientific beliefs assumed a mythical dimension of inevitability and universality.

Among the more tenacious anatomical myths, which can still be traced nowadays in our subculture, those concerning the size of the male and female sexual organs take pride of place in popular medical handbooks. They certainly reflect, especially for men, a latent anxiety—a sort of pre-Freudian 'Angst'—which would tend to prove that the male psyche is deeply marked by a constant over-valorisation of the phallus. In *Aristotle's Masterpiece* is to be found the origin (for the eighteenth century) of this most extraordinary anatomical myth, which establishes a size-relationship between the nose and the penis. The bawdy allusions or references to the myth are countless in eighteenth-century literature, as may be readily gathered from Sterne's chapters in books III and IV of *Tristram Shandy* on a seemingly inexhaustible source of puns, jokes, innuendoes and spicy *doubles entendres*. In popular sexual semiotics, the size of the nose was a physiognomic indication of penile size, as is made plain from a section of *Aristotle's Masterpiece* entitled: 'Of Judgments drawn from the Nose': 'He who hath a long and great Nose is an admirer of the Fair Sex, and well accomplished for the Wars of Venus'.[7] The nostrils also enabled a knowledgeable observer to guess at the putative size of another man's sexual organs: 'When the Nostrils are close and thin, they denote a Man to have but little Testicles, and to be very desirous of the Enjoyment of Women, but modest in his Conversation. But he whose Nostrils are great and wide, is usually well hung and lustful.'[8] The myth is confirmed by the erudite Dr Venette, who launches into considerations liable to surprise modern specialists of Roman history:

> Admitting it true what Physiognomists say, *viz.* That Men with big Noses have also stout Members, as also that they are more robust and couragious than others, we have no reason to wonder at *Heliogabalus's* (whom Nature had favour'd with swinging Parts, as *Lampridius* reports) making choice of big nosed Soldiers, that he might be able to undertake great Expeditions with small Numbers, and oppose his Enemy with greater vigour. But at the same time he did not take notice, that well hung Men are the greatest Blockheads, and the most stupid of Mankind.[9]

This does not mean that Venette either rejects or accepts all phallic myths in the lucid light of medical experience or scientific knowledge: he often wavers between uncritical credulity and justified rational doubt. For instance, he does not seem to favour the then current practice of midwives who immediately after delivery would see to it that 'the Navel-string is cut as long as possible, if a Boy, and short, if a Girl. All this is done by the order of the Matron, who fancies that the Member of a Boy will be bigger for it, and the Girl will be more streight',[10] the narrowness of the vagina being currently regarded as a sign of virginity.

As far as this myth of penile size is concerned, it is virtually impossible to separate the anatomical elements from the physiological and socio-cultural ones. Modern feminists would rightly accuse the surgeon John Marten of rampant phallocratic chauvinism in his very serious *Gonosologium Novum* (London, 1709), when he asserts blandly that the penis 'is a Part in great Esteem among the Women; for if by any accident they see it, so as not to be seen or known they see it, it instantly inflames their Hearts with a Passion not presently assuag'd' (p. 10), an all too lightly proferred accusation of scoptophilic lechery. But this phallic voyeurism finds its confirmation in numerous erotic or pornographic scenes in eighteenth-century literature (or sub-literature) and graphic arts: Fanny Hill's amorous ardours are fanned by much peeping through convenient chinks in walls and partitions. Marten also indulged in functional considerations on the various penis sizes (p. 10):

> and as the *Stones* differ in several people as to magnitude, so doth the *Yard* both as to thickness and length; in those that are not much given to Venery, it is bigger and longer, say some, others the quite contrary; and in short Men is generally observ'd to be longer than in tall Men. In half-witted People it is generally pretty large, the length of the largest being commonly, when erected, nine Inches long, and four Inches in circumference.

No doubt modern sexologists would reject all of these pseudo-observations, but the myth is still current, especially in rural districts, that mental deficients are often endowed with abnormally large sexual organs. In a pamphlet—'By a Physician'—also published in London in 1709 in spirited defence of the *Gonosologium Novum*, all these myths are neatly summed up in the following lines: 'Men's Tools according to their Noses grow; / Large as their Mouths, are Women too below.' Traces of such popular sexual semiotics still exist nowadays: what budding, or experienced, Don Juan fails to notice the thickness or the thinness of the lips of a girl or woman he plans to seduce?

A marked difference between our present time and the eighteenth century lies in our much greater permissiveness and tolerance about female unchastity, especially the anatomical absence of the hymen, the guaranteed label of chastity for the 'virgo intacta' until her wedding night. In a pre-capitalist society where property was transmitted according to the right of male primogeniture, it was indispensable, if the first born was a male, that the father should have material proof of his wife's absolute chastity before marriage. As Stone remarks, 'Pre-marital chastity is a bargaining chip in the marriage game, to be set off against male property and status rights.'[11] Hence the mythical aura surrounding female virginity, the anatomical signs and physiological symptoms thanks to which its presence or absence could be detected, and hence also, the lengthy developments of medical authors on the subject. *Aristotle's Masterpiece* and Venette's *Mysteries of Conjugal Love* devote whole chapters to it. After a careful scrutiny of these chapters, the twentieth-century reader is left with a rather confused welter of often contradictory statements. The only point which is relatively clear is that the medical pundits then were not even agreed about the anatomical existence of the fragile and elusive membrane, which assumes an even more mythical dimension. In both works, a moderate, commonsensical opinion prevails. If the bridegroom on the wedding night, when deflowering his bride, sets a few drops of precious virginal blood flowing, then, yes, the hymen did exist. But if no such thing happened, then this non-occurrence was *not* to be interpreted as proof of the bride's sexual misbehaviour before marriage, as the hymen 'may be broken so many other ways, and yet the Women [be] both Chaste and Virtuous'.[12] What mishaps or accidents could destroy the precious membrane, still colloquially known in French as 'le petit capital', a palpable linguistic proof of socio-economic realism? *Aristotle's Masterpiece* obligingly lists quite a few possible causes, such as its accidental destruction at birth by clumsy midwives; stoppage of urine; corrosion by acrimonious humours during the menses; fits of coughing; violent straining; sudden sneezing, not to forget the girl's erratic fingers when she scratches her itching vulva. Venette is quite as cautious in the matter, and in his section 'Of Signs of a Maidenhead being present', after rejecting the mythical signs listed by the ancients, he concludes rather wisely that 'fries'd and curl'd Hair in the amourous Parts, a moist and open Chink, absence of the membrane Hymen, shaggy and discolour'd *Nymphae*, the interior

Orifice of the Womb widened, and the Voice chang'd is no sufficient Evidence of a Woman's being a Prostitute.' (p. 61). The same sagacious moderation marks the next section—or 'article', as it was then called: 'Of Signs of an absent Maidenhead' (pp. 63–9), but, significantly enough, Venette devotes great care to examining the anatomical problem of the hymen's presence or absence. This is doubtless an indication that the more or less diffuse myths about anatomical virginity were still very much alive and tenacious. A proof is furnished 'a contrario' by the next chapter in which Venette—like so many of his colleagues both in France and in Britain—seeks to clarify whether there are medicines capable of restoring a lost maidenhead (pp. 70–6). Venette's answer does not lack a certain logical cogency: 'As there are no signs that can clearly discover it, so there are no Medicines that can restore it when once lost. It may be in our power to mimick Nature, and to produce a counterfeited one; but all our force will not reach so far as to Re-establish the Natural, which is the most precious, and most valuable' (p. 70). But the cunning Dr Venette all the same goes on—not without some seemly deontological hesitations—to give his readers a list of styptic and astringent remedies in order to help out the unfortunate maids whose sexual parts are naturally too loose, which defect might excite the unwarranted and jealous wrath of suspicious husbands: 'The Vapour of Vinegar, wherein a piece of red hot Iron, or a well baked hot Brick is quenched: The astringent Decoction of *Acorns*, *Sloes*, *Myrrh*, *Provence Roses* and *Cypress Nuts*, distilled Waters of *Myrrh*, astringent Oyntment of *Fernelius*; are Remedies that streighten the genital Parts of Women when too wide' (p. 72). The socio-cultural myth of anatomical virginity must have been so potent—as is made plain by many scenes in eighteenth-century fiction, where prostitutes like Smollett's Miss Williams in *Roderick Random* (1748), or Cleland's Fanny Hill in *Memoirs of a Woman of Pleasure* (1749), sell several times their deftly patched up virginities for a high price—that Venette does not hesitate to recommend among his medical remedies what amounts to a genuine cheat, 'for the Preservation of Peace in her Family, to take all the pains imaginable to be thought a discreet Woman by her Husband' (p. 73). Let the bride insert two or three little pellets of dried lamb's blood into her vagina just before going to her nuptial couch, and the trick (used in *Fanny Hill*) will be played! John Marten in his already quoted *Gonosologium Novum* (1709) even goes so far as to recommend that the wedding should take place neither immediately before nor after the menses, because at such times, 'the *Hymen* and wrinkled Membrane of the Sheath are so relaxed ... that the Bridegroom's *Virile Member* may enter without any manner of Obstruction, whereby he may suspect tho' without Cause, that he had not married a Maid. These things have in some been the cause of very unhappy Lives' (p. 74). Marten is also perfectly aware of the astringent ways of producing artificial maidenheads, down to placing 'a little Fish-bladder of Blood so, as to be broke in the Encounter' (p. 75). Such harlots' tricks he denounces with a puritanical wrath far removed from Dr Venette's much more urbane and tolerant attitude.

It would be both unfair and clumsy to rail too quickly at these anatomical myths, about which it has several times been remarked that they are far from having totally disappeared today. Such is also the feeling of G. L. Simons in *Sex and Superstition* (London, 1973), who in his chapter VI, 'Modern superstition', asserts that 'One myth with enduring currency is that a girl with a large mouth has a large vagina, and that a large male nose suggests a large penis. It is still believed that a man who drinks vast quantities of milk will ejaculate a greater volume of semen, and that a woman with a dry vagina during intercourse has been unfaithful' (p. 166). The perseverance of sexual myths is therefore no myth, even in our so-called liberated and 'permissive' society, in spite—or because?—of the 'great sexual preaching' analysed by Foucault, which may well convey as much media-processed rubbish as the pseudo-scientific discourse of eighteenth-century medical handbooks.

Physiological beliefs and myths are even more numerous than anatomical ones. This can be partly explained by the fairly slow progress of actual scientific knowledge in the seventeenth and eighteenth centuries. For instance, William Harvey's discovery of blood circulation in the early seventeenth century (1616), and Leeuwenhoek's of spermatozoa about 1676, were not easily accepted. The fecundation process of the ovum by the spermatozoon gave rise to a virulent and intricate controversy between ovists and animalculists: it ended only two centuries later when the German biologist Oscar Hertwig (1849–1922) demonstrated that fecundation actually resulted from the fusion of the nuclei of both spermatozoon and ovum. Owing to the usual gap between the latest and most advanced scientific research and its vulgarised version in popular medical handbooks, physiological myths were bound to proliferate. Only a few will be briefly examined: those concerning the menses; conception and the signs of conception; and lastly, the devouring female.

Biblical influence has permeated so deeply and lastingly into the British psyche that it is hardly surprising to see to what extent the sexual interdicts of Leviticus and Deuteronomy have helped the proliferation of myths concerning female sexuality, especially that physiological phenomenon, menstruation, which for so long has retained its mysterious, malefic and anxiety-making aura,[13] as is made painfully clear by its popular synonym, 'the curse'. *Aristotle's Book of Problems*—which has little or nothing to do with Aristotle[14]—reads like a kind of physiological catechism, which examines man and woman literally from head to foot. It is a rich lode of startling beliefs and myths, always carefully grounded in humoral pseudo-demonstrations, which convey to the 'explanations' a deceptive gloss of science and logic deliberately made accessible to a popular public. The author—or rather, the authors—of the *Problems* are convinced that a pregnant woman no longer has any menses because the humoral surplus is transformed into intra-uterine nourishment during pregnancy, and into milk afterwards.[15] The reader learns that the catamenial flow is not of the same nature as the substance on which the foetus feeds, or which is transformed into maternal milk, 'because the first [the menses] are unclean, and unfit for that purpose, but the other very pure and clean, therefore fittest for generation' (p. 63). When Molière was making devastating fun of the 'virtus dormativa' type of Galenic argument in *Le Malade imaginaire* (1673), he could hardly imagine that the same pseudo-logical form of hoaxing logic would still be widely used in medicine a century later. Since the physiological mechanisms of fecundation were not known precisely, it was still accepted that women could conceive during their menstrual periods, the subject being handled with various degrees of distaste and tolerance. But in such cases of intercourse during the menses, women were likely to give birth to puny, sickly, red-haired babies, such a colour being due to a sort of mythical catamenial mimesis. It would be wrong to believe that *all* authors accepted such myths, which were rejected with great strength and indignation. But the very fact that such forceful language was necessary to combat them bears witness to their tenacious implantation and stubborn resistance. John Marten, for instance, in his *Treatise of all the Degrees and Symptoms of the Venereal Disease in both Sexes* (London, 6th ed., 1708?) indignantly denounces the apparently widespread belief that intercourse during the menses could excoriate the man's glans and prepuce, and even infect him with venereal disease. The following quotation (p. 71) sums up fairly well most of the menstrual myths as they are denounced by Marten in his *Gonosologium Novum:*

> They [the authors he is attacking] say further, that the Breath of a *Menstruous Woman*, or one that has her *Courses* upon her, will give a lasting Stain to Ivory, or a Looking-glass; and that a little of the Blood drop'd upon a Vine, or Corn, or any other Vegetable, will blast or cause the same to die: That if a Woman with Child be so defiled with the *Menses* of another Woman, it will cause her to miscarry: That if a Dog tasts [*sic*] the Courses of a Woman, he will then run mad: That if a Man tastes them, it will render him Epileptick; which, with almost innumerable other ridiculous and foolish Fancies, tho, related by grave and great Authors, are yet justly to be rejected as having no Foundation of Truth, or Reason to support them.

Marten displays optimistic faith here in man's rational powers when all such beliefs and myths stem from a pre-scientific apprehension of physiological phenomena, a mode of thinking certainly still current today in view of the superstitions attached to menstruation.[16]

The mystery shrouding the physiological mechanisms of conception in the eighteenth century could but give birth to a rich pullulation of mythical lore on procreation and the signs of pregnancy. The problem—'Is it going to be a boy or a girl?'—has not changed, and popular magazines today still exploit the gullibility of expecting mothers: the slightly anguished curiosity is the same, although our modern answers are probably closer to scientific reality. The great aim of eighteenth-century medical handbooks is to help procreation as much as possible: the century of Malthus was also a period when depopulation (especially of rural areas) and a supposedly flagging demography haunted the national conscience. Before Malthus's *Essay on the Principle of Population* (1798), most writers, even of fiction—such as Smollett in *Humphry Clinker* (1771)—seem to have been obsessed with a putative decrease of the British population, which would have laid the country open to a French invasion. All these medical handbooks contain chapters on male or female sterility, and its possible remedies. On the physiological plane, it is possible to trace a recurrent principle which may be called 'mimetic osmosis'. In order to cure frigidity (and hence sterility), men or women in such a plight must be given 'hot foods', made up of genital organs of creatures well known for their amorous propensities:

Such therefore ought to feed upon Cock-stones and Lamb-stones, Sparrows, Partridges, Quails and Pheasant Eggs; for 'tis an infalliable aphorism in Physick, that whatsoever any Creature is extreamly addicted to, they operate to the same End by their mumial [*sic*] Virtue in the Man that eats them. Therefore Partridges, Quails, Sparrows, etc. being extreamly addicted to Venery, they work the same Effect on those who eat them: And this likewise is worthy to be noted, That what Part of the Body the Faculty that you would strengthen lies, take the same Part of another Creature, in whom that Faculty is strong, as a Medicine.[17]

Such a quotation affords the key to the composition of all the potions, confects, elixirs, boluses, pills, meant to cure barrenness. Mothers and fathers to be were also advised to pay heed to the cycle of the seasons. Dr Robert James in his *Medicinal Dictionary* (1743–5) does little but repeat, in more formal language and with a few impressive authorities thrown in for good measure, the seasonal advice given in the *Problems*. It is in summer that women feel most amorous, while for man the 'hottest' season is winter, because of their opposite humoral natures, woman being cold and moist, man hot and dry. Man loses some of his strength in summer, whereas the contrary obtains for woman. Therefore, as Dr James advises in his articles 'Venus' and 'Ver', couples should make love in spring, less definitely in winter, certainly not in summer, 'but the most dangerous of all the four, by many Degrees, is the Autumn' (*s.v.* 'Ver'). No 'mellow fruitfulness' then in autumn. Pregnant women should watch their diet, and make a point of avoiding, among other things, fogs and damps, but also going out when either the north or the south wind blows, the former causing rheums, colds and catarrhs which may provoke abortions, exactly as the latter, but for unspecified reasons.[18] Likewise she should avoid 'all extraordinary Sounds and Noises ... especially the ringing of Bells, and the Discharging of great Guns: neither ought she give Way to either immoderate Laughing or Weeping, or to Anger, or any other Passion, for that may be prejudicial to her',[19] such advice not being devoid of a modicum of common sense, but sounding rather alarmist all the same. To this already well-filled list of potentially abortifacient factors, Dr John Maubray adds a few causes in his *Female Physician* (London, 1724), such as violent exercise, bad weather, stenches, and the astrological influence of Saturn on the eighth month of pregnancy, an influence which is so nefarious that if a child is born in the eighth month, he will remain sickly and puny, often half-witted, and probably will not live very long. However, those born in the seventh, ninth or even tenth months will prove all right, being placed under the life-giving influence of the Sun and Moon (p. 140).

The great 'medical' sollicitude lavished on conception and pregnancy finds its natural complement in the elaboration of a mythical semiology of pregnancy. By what signs can a woman's pregnancy be known? First of all, orgasmic pleasure, as it seems to open the way through the vagina and the uterus for the semen, is reckoned as a most favourable sexual omen. This the anonymous 'Physician' explains—rather mechanistically—in his *Rational Account of the Natural Weaknesses of Women* (London, 2nd ed., 1716): 'the falling of one of the little Eggs from its Cell in the Ovaria, through one of the Womb Trumpets, into the Womb, often occasions an uncommon Sensation and gentle shivering of the Body after the Conjugal Act, which is therefore a Sign of Conception' (pp. 60–1). Such a notion of female orgasm is, to say the least, rather pragmatic. Apart from the clinical signs, observed with more or less accuracy,[20] popular medical handbooks describe—and prescribe—rather bizarre fertility-tests, such as the 'flower pot' test. Take two handfuls of barley or corn and soak them separately in the husband's and the wife's urine, then plant each separately in a flower-pot, and water with the husband's and wife's urine respectively: whichever grows the more quickly is the more fertile, and if the grain does not grow at all, then both husband and wife are barren.[21] 'Pregnancy tests' also existed, for instance the following ones, taken from among many others, and irately denounced by John Marten in his *Gonosologium Novum* (1709): 'There are many fabulous Stories concerning whether a Woman be with Child or not; such as by putting the Woman's Urine in a Glass, and stopping it close for three days, and then straining it through a fine Linen Cloth, wherein, if she be with Child, you will find many small living Creatures; and that by putting a green Nettle into the Woman's Urine, and covering it close, letting it remain therein a whole Night, if she be with Child, you will find the Nettle the next Morning to be full of red Spots; and if not with Child, with black Spots' (p. 137).

But the acme of mythical lore is to be found in the great 'Boy or Girl?' guessing game—still going on with more or less scientific official sanction. Even more thrilling, and of infinitely deeper socio-cultural significance, were the 'recipes' openly purporting to give the *power of choosing* the sex of the baby at will. It is well to bear in mind here again the socio-economic context of such an immensely popular myth: the transmission of property to male heirs. Here is certainly one of the most widespread sexual myths in the eighteenth century, but also one of the most violently attacked as early as the seventeenth century. The myth of 'right and left' probably goes as far back as the Greek philosopher Anaxagoras born in 500 B.C. The genesis of this physiological myth affords an admirable example of naive but triumphal phallocratism. The right side is the stronger (in most people) and hence the nobler one: 'dextra est validior manuum'. Therefore, it can but be reserved to the nobler species *par excellence*, viz. Man. Consequently, only the *right* testicle is capable of elaborating the male-producing seed, and only the right side of a woman's womb can bear a male foetus. Therefore, should you wish to have male offspring, you must bind up your left testicle, so that only the right one will function in copulation. Just to be on the safe side, ask your wife to lie on her right side so that the precious seed will fall into the adequate part of the womb, i.e. the *right* one, whereas the left can only bring forth inferior, female, creatures. Such is the mythical opinion to be found in *Aristotle's Book of Problems* (pp. 39–41), quoting Hippocrates as its revered authority, and in the all too credulous Dr John Maubray's *Female Physician* (pp. 55–6). Maubray also quotes Lactantius, to the effect that if a male is conceived of seed fallen on the left side of the womb, he will be half womanish, and conversely, a female conceived in the wrong side of the womb will show marks of virility in her stature, limbs, hairy face, and voice. Likewise, if a pregnant woman feels her child on the right side; if her right breast is more swollen than the left; if the right nipple is redder; if she sets down her right foot first when she gets up in the morning, she is expecting a male. Such mythical beliefs still triumphed in the 1776 London edition of *Aristotle's Last Legacy*, but it is noteworthy that they had been rejected nearly a century before by Dr Venette in *The Mysteries of Conjugal Love* (p. 7):

> For all *Hippocrates*, there is no reason to believe his position, *viz*. That the right Testicle is hotter than the left; and also that it engenders Males, whereas the other produces only Females. Experience and reason oblige me to be of a different Sentiment from that Physician, for we know that the Seed mixing

together, when 'tis sallying out, the effect we perceive, can't be attributed more to one Testicle than another, but rather to the Complexion of the Man's and the Woman's Body . . .

Further on (p. 380). Dr Venette makes fun of farmers who tie the left testicle of stallions or bulls in order to have male animals, or *vice versa* in order to obtain females. The anonymous author of the *Ladies Dispensatory, or, Every Woman her Own Physician* (London, 2nd ed., 1740) even notes that men possessed of only one testicle have begotten both male *and* female children (p. 182).

But in spite of all the righteous expositions of the myth, it is likely that it has had a long and happy life. This may result partly from the ambiguous contradictions of a pre-scientific mode of thought. Dr Venette is an apt illustration of such (more or less conscious?) 'double-think'. After having rejected—as already seen—the 'right and left' myth in the opening pages of his manual, and again in what is the second volume of the original edition, he nevertheless devotes a whole chapter to the question 'Whether there is an Art in getting Boys or Girls',[22] and he even goes so far, in his own tortuously cautious way, as to give 'some Rules for engendering of such Matters and Spirits as may contribute to the difference of Sexes' (p. 381). The age of the prospective parents, proper humoral attention to their diet (game, for example, being a 'hot' food, as opposed to milk which is a 'cold' food); sexual moderation or excess—'Impatient Gardiners never gather the Seeds in season' (p. 382), in less metaphorical parlance, too much sexual ardour is apt to debilitate the spirits of the semen, which then can but produce females!—the times of intercourse either before or after the menses; the climate—Venette notes that there are six times as many females as males in the south of France, because heat there again dissipates the strength of the semen, whereas in the north the cold wind constricts our pores and thus prevents our natural heat from evaporating, which helps the procreation of male children—such are the 'rules' listed by the pawky La Rochelle doctor. His conclusion is couched in engagingly personal but wary forms: 'I am very well satisfied, by the experience I have of it, that they will sooner get a Boy than a Girl' (p. 386), if, of course, the parents have been wise enough to abide by Dr Venette's rules.

All these anatomical and physiological beliefs and myths tend to merge into an archetypal conception of woman as a sexually insatiable creature when her desire is aroused. This is one of the major sexual myths traceable in many medical handbooks, and certainly underlying much eighteenth-century fiction. Because of their aphrodisiac recipes rather lightly camouflaged as remedies to cure male impotence or sterility, eighteenth-century medical handbooks, especially the more popular ones, can hardly mask a more or less unconscious 'Angst' in front of the female sexual organ, the notorious and obnoxious 'vagina dentata' of psychoanalysis. Roger Thompson makes a similar point when in the conclusion of his recently-published book *Unfit for Modest Ears* (London, 1979) he states that 'Impotence stalks the pages of Restoration erotica, leaving a debris of unsatisfied women' (p. 212). Could Venette be considered as the distant forerunner of Freud? Not quite, but some of his descriptions of woman as she is recovering from the pangs and fatigue of childbirth read curiously like an anguished portrait of the dark devouring female, 'her genital parts growing more and more ardent, and more amorous, more unquiet, more inconstant and susceptible of Lasciviousness. They are a Creature in another Creature, that often causes so many Disorders in the Bodies of Women, as to oblige them to find out means to sooth and appease it, to prevent it being hurtful' (p. 99). A consequence of the flame that devours them is that women have a shorter life-span than men, who would no doubt be surprised to discover exactly the contrary in our century of statistical studies: 'Besides, they are much more amorous than Men; and as Sparrows do not live long, because they are too hot, and too susceptible of Love, so Women last less time; because they have a devouring heat, that consumes them by degrees' (p. 83). The good phallocratic Dr Venette was consciously ignoring the extremely high death rate of women in pregnancy and after childbirth due to rudimentary gynaecological and obstetrical care, and the murderous incidence of infectious diseases, not to mention the physiological wear and tear of repeated pregnancies. There is little doubt too that the biblical background—even more acutely pervasive in a Protestant country than in Venette's Roman Catholic France—contributed to the development of such a myth in men's self-righteous, moralistic minds, as can be seen from the following quotation: 'The Womb of a Woman is in the Number of the insatiable things mentioned in the Scriptures [Proverbs xxx: 15?]; and I cannot tell whether there is anything in the World, its greediness may be compared unto; neither Hell fire nor the Earth being so devouring, as the Privy Parts of a Lascivious Woman' (p. 123).

But it is only fair to note that, like most beliefs and myths briefly studied here, the 'Devouring Woman' myth was also attacked violently and rejected with heartening commonsense, as for instance in the *Ladies Physical Directory* (London, 8th ed., 1742) the author—'a Physician'—condemns this 'antient vulgar Error, which even to this Day much obtains amongst Men of inferior Rank in point of Knowledge, greatly to the Disadvantage of the *Fair Sex*, namely, That in celebrating the Rites of Love, a Woman is too many for a Man, and capable of tiring him quite down: This silly Notion seems to infer, that Women are warmer in their Nature, or more desirous than Men, which is absolutely false in Fact' (p. 70). This staunch defender of the female sex goes on to explain that woman, being the weaker and finer vessel, but of a much colder complexion than man, is in fact unable to experience sexual pleasure half so often as man, another eighteenth-century misconception at variance with the current, if at times strident, feminist emphasis on multiple orgasm. More constructively, the author, in very modern fashion, condemns brutal sexual intercourse without any foreplay. The anonymous author's prose is decidedly more formal than in Dr Alex Comfort's *Joy of Sex*, but the message (p. 70) rings strangely similar:

> But this idle and most erroneous Notion takes its Rise from this, that for the most Part, Men heated by immoderate Desire, rush into the Embraces of Women at once, without prior Endearments, and proper Dalliance to raise their Inclination also; and by that Means immediately consummate, or finish their own Bliss, when they have but even just rous'd up an Inclination or Desire, in their Paramours. By thus hastily rushing into a Woman's Arms, a Man may enjoy a great many Times, without her having, properly speaking, enjoyed him once.

This is a fine analysis of the physical causes of sexual frustration in females, but the percipient author can hardly escape the devious socio-cultural pressures of his own male-centred, if not phallocratic, times, so that he somewhat smugly concluded that, after all, this is a most fortunate state of things that women do not experience sexual pleasure as often as men, since 'it would soon reduce them to a most miserable weak Condition, and quickly deprive them of Life' (p. 71). 'Mourir de plaisir' was hardly, at least for women, the order of the day.

In order to be impartial, this essay should also make some mention of another myth to counterbalance the 'Devouring Woman': it could be called the 'Precious Sperm'. That vital liquor in most eighteenth-century medical handbooks appears, literally, as an elixir of life, distilled from the choicest blood, and able to cure a variety of female disorders in a wellnigh magic way. Chlorosis—the 'green sickness' of love-lorn maids—or cachexy, melancholy and hypochondria vanish when sperm comes to the rescue. Our grandmothers believed that sperm, internally applied, was a miracle cure for juvenile acne, a belief still probably shared by some of their 'liberated' great grand-daughters. Dr Robert James in his *Medicinal Dictionary* (*s.v.* 'Venus'), after denouncing excessive venery and its debilitating sequels, goes on to assert:

> It is, also, certain, from Experience, that Venery both alleviates and removes various Disorders incident to Women: for the male Semen, consisting of a fine elastic Lymph, rarefies and expands not only the Egg, but, also, the Blood and Juices in the Vessels of the Uterus, the Fibres of which it likewise strengthens. Hence the Reason is obvious, why Venery, or Coition, cures Women, rendered cachectic by a Suppression of the Menses, and generally restores that salutary evacuation.

No doubt in the eighteenth century as in ours a potential healer slumbered in the soul of every man.

At the close of this rapid and fragmentary survey of an immense topic[23] it is impossible not to stress the extraordinary resistance of sexual myths concerning virginity, the penis, menstruation or pregnancy, to name but a few. Sexual beliefs and myths of the eighteenth century are not only interesting *per se*, but also because a synthetic approach to them enables a twentieth-century reader to gain access to the very core of a system of symbolical representations inherent in any society which is born, grows and dies, without ever disappearing completely.

NOTES

1 See for instance: Michel Foucault, *La Volonté de savoir* (Paris, 1976); Pierre Darmon, *Le Mythe de la procréation à l'âge baroque* (Paris, 1977); Paul Hoffmann, *La Femme dans la pensée des lumières* (Paris, 1977); Peter Laslett, *Family Life and Illicit Love in Earlier Generations* (Cambridge, 1977); Lawrence Stone, *The Family, Sex and Marriage in England 1500–1800* (London, 1977); Pierre Darmon, *Le Tribunal de l'impuissance: virilité et défaillances conjugales dans l'Ancienne France* (Paris, 1979); *Dix-Huitième Siècle*, No. 12, 1980 (a special issue of 604 pages devoted to the representations of sexuality). The list is by no means exhaustive.

2 See Robert James, *Proposals for Printing a Medicinal Dictionary* (London, 1741). Samuel Johnson helped his Lichfield schoolfellow to write them.

3 On these extremely popular medical handbooks, see Otho T. Beall, '*Aristotle's Masterpiece* in America: a Landmark in the Folklore of Medicine', *The William and Mary Quarterly*, 20 (1963), 207–22—in which the author traces at least thirty-two American editions between 1766 and 1831; Janet Blackman, 'Popular Theories of Generation: the Evolution of *Aristotle's Works*, the Study of an Anachronism', in John Woodward and David Richards (eds.), *Health Care and Popular Medicine in Nineteenth Century England* (London, 1977), pp. 56–88; also Roger Thompson, *Unfit for Modest Ears* (London, 1979), pp. 162–8.

4 Sir d'Arcy Power, *The Foundations of Medical History* (Baltimore, Md., 1931), p. 147: the whole essay, 'Aristotle's Masterpiece', pp. 147–78, is still well worth reading; see also Joseph Needham, *A History of Embryology*, 2nd ed. (Cambridge, 1959), pp. 91–2, where the author stresses the link between *Aristotle's Masterpiece* and the *De Secretis Mulierum* of Albertus Magnus (1206–80).

5 See, for instance, *s.v.* 'Venette' (1632–98), Michaud's *Biographie Universelle*, 2nd ed., tome 43 (Paris, 1854–63), and Charles Nisard, *Histoire des livres populaires ou de la littérature de colportage* (Paris, 1854), I, p. 271.

6 See Roger Caillois, *Le Mythe et l'homme* (Paris, 1972), p. 11, and *passim*; see also Roland Barthes, *Mythologies* (Paris, 1970), *passim*.

7 *Aristotle's Compleat Masterpiece*, 32nd ed. (London, 1788), p. 105; all further references to this edition.

8 *Ibid.*, p. 106.

9 Nicholas de Venette [*sic*], *The Mysteries of Conjugal Love Reveal'd*, 2nd ed. (London, 1707), p. 27; all further references to this edition.

10 *Ibid.*, p. 91.

11 Stone, *op. cit.*, p. 636.

12 *Aristotle's Masterpiece*, p. 34.

13 On this topic, see Penelope Shuttle and Peter Redgrove, *The Wise Wound* (London, 1978), reprinted in Penguin Books 1980.

14 See Sir d'Arcy Power, *op. cit.*, pp. 149–65; and also the introduction to the Loeb edition of the *Problems*, by W. S. Hett, vol. I (London, 1961), p. vii.

15 *Aristotle's Book of Problems*, 29th ed. (London, 1775), p. 62; all further references to this edition. Sir d'Arcy Power, *op. cit.*, p. 178, mentions a Latin edition of the *Problemata* (London, 1583).

16 On the topic see G. L. Simons, *Sex and Superstition* (London, 1973), p. 167, and also *The Wise Wound*, *passim*.

17 *Aristotle's Masterpiece*, p. 51.

18 *Ibid.*, p. 58.

19 *Ibid.*, p. 59.

20 See *Aristotle's Last Legacy* (London, 1776), pp. 42–3.

21 *Aristotle's Masterpiece*, pp. 52–3.
22 Chapter VI, pp. 375–86.
23 See my essay 'Aspects of Sexual Tolerance and Intolerance in Eighteenth-Century England', *British Journal for Eighteenth-Century Studies* III (autumn 1980), 173–89, dealing with masturbation, and sexual intercourse in marriage; also, my 'The Secret Nexus: Sex and Literature in Eighteenth-Century Britain', to be published in Alan Bold (ed.), *The Sexual Dimension in Literature* (Vision Press).

NORAH SMITH

Sexual mores and attitudes in Enlightenment Scotland

> The *English*, she said, often take Liberties after they are married, and seldom before; whereas the *Scots* Women, when they make a Trip, it is while they are single, and very rarely afterwards.... Now as she had condescended to own that the *Scotish* Females are frail as well as ours, though in different Circumstances of Life... I could not... persuade myself to mention another Difference, which is, that the *English* Women are not so well watched.[1]

With what enviable confidence these generalisations are made; it would be gratifying if distinctions between the two countries could in fact be so clearly drawn, and indeed, if distinctions between attitudes and behaviour in the social classes and regions of Scotland itself were within the scope of an essay of this length.

The Union of Parliaments in 1707 made certain Scots acutely aware of the importance of adopting English culture and language in order to make Scotland's presence felt in Europe. Deprived of a Parliament and united with a wealthier and more powerful nation, other Scots felt the need to retain and cultivate their national heritage. It is not surprising, therefore, that even within Edinburgh itself very diverse attitudes to sex, and what it is possible to say about it in print, are to be found. Lord Kames reflects a rather different picture of the 'Progress of the Female Sex' in his *Sketches of the History of Man* from Allan Ramsay's in, say, 'Lucky Spence's Last Advice'.

The national institutions remaining to Scotland after the Union were her Church and the Law. Both played a significant part in shaping sexual mores and attitudes. In England, Lord Hardwicke's Marriage Act of 1753 replaced Canon Law, transferring the right to set up conditions for valid marriage from Church to State and for the first time making marriage a public and certain contract.[2] The Act was designed to prevent clandestine marriages and the ceremony now had to be performed in a parish church after proclamation of banns. In Scotland, however, the Act did not apply and even in the mid nineteenth century English parents of property were reputedly reluctant to send their eldest sons to Edinburgh University 'from the justifiable apprehension that they might succumb before the facilities of the law and the charms of the women of Scotland'.[3]

To an outsider procedure in Scotland was baffling. According to Edward Topham, 'even an Englishman looks upon the solemnization of [marriage] as a serious thing; but here, it is a matter of merriment, and no ceremony at all is necessary. A man, indeed, in Scotland, can scarce be said to know whether he is married or not, as his own consent is no part of the business.'[4]

The laws relating to marriage in Scotland were confusing to the Scots as well, and even legal minds did not always agree. Both 'regular' and 'irregular' marriages had legal validity, although irregular marriage was subject to statutory penalties, for the celebrator and witnesses, as well as the couple themselves.[5] Regular marriage was always preceded by banns read publicly in church and celebrated by an authorised minister, which in the eighteenth century meant a minister of the Church of Scotland, Episcopal, or Roman Catholic Church, but not a Presbyterian dissenter.[6] Proclamation of banns was designed to prevent bigamy and incestuous marriage; the alternative of publishing a notice of intention to marry in the Registry of Births, Marriages and Deaths was not introduced until 1878.[7]

Clandestine marriages were usually celebrated by ministers.[8] Though legal, such marriages constituted a breach of Church order, and it was known for deposed ministers who tried to scrape a living by officiating to be imprisoned or banished.[9] As in England prior to Hardwicke's Act of 1753, a marriage was clandestine either if banns were not proclaimed or if it was not celebrated by an authorised minister.

The most notorious form of irregular, but legal marriage, was by declaration:

> A marriage may be constituted, according to the law of Scotland, by declarations made by the man and the woman that they presently do take each other for husband and wife. No sacerdotal benediction is required to make this a valid marriage. The declarations may be emitted on any day, at any time, and without the presence of witnesses. Such a marriage is as effectual,

to all intents and purposes, as a public marriage solemnized *in facie ecclesiae*. The children of it would be legitimate; and the parties to it would have all the rights in the property of each other, given by the law of Scotland to husband and wife.[10]

A distinction was made between marriage by declaration and a promise to marry, followed by intercourse, however. The latter constituted not marriage, but pre-contract and required proper solemnisation or a decree of the Consistorial Court ordaining that the marriage should be solemnised.[11] Consent or promise to marry in the absence of a clergyman, followed by intercourse, had been described not as 'clandestine marriage' but as 'filthie huirdom and sclanderous fornicatioun'[12] and cohabitation where a couple were presumed married provided only evidence from which marriage might be inferred: cohabitation and repute did not in themselves *make* marriage.[13]

Confusion as to what did or did not constitute marriage gave rise to several legal cases,[14] but as Fraser makes clear, only regular (public), clandestine or declared marriages were legal, along with marriage by promises *cum copula* with decree or declarator. Couples sometimes went before a magistrate, confessing themselves clandestinely wed and the magistrate's decreet was thereafter taken as evidence of marriage.[15]

Edgar calls for the laws on marriage to be more explicit and illustrates the problems of marriage by declaration by citing the case of a man who was proclaimed with one woman and claimed by another. The claimant alleged ' "that in the end of harvest, four years, one night he and she met in a glen . . . and repeated the words of the marriage oath to one another; and that, as there were no witnesses present, the said Robert took heaven and earth to witness, also the moon and stars, wishing they might never shine upon him, and that he might never see the face of God in mercy, if he did not observe his marriage engadgment" '.[16] The Kirk-Session was advised by the Presbytery to investigate the man's denials further and if necessary to put him on oath. He ultimately took the oath and proclamation of banns proceeded. As Edgar points out, there were two implications: one, that in the eyes of the Presbytery what happened in the glen, if acknowledged, would have constituted a marriage; and also, that in the absence of corroboration, an oath by either party would be sufficient to terminate a marriage that was in fact legal.

While divorce by Private Act only was obtainable in England until the Matrimonial Causes Act of 1857 (passed largely on the recommendation of a commission of 1853 which pointed out that divorce costing £20 to £30 in Scotland cost at least £700 to £800 in England),[17] the Common Law of Scotland had granted divorce for adultery since 1560. At the Reformation the Protestant Church rejected the view that marriage was a sacrament 'and professed to be guided in all matters relating to it by the canon of Scripture. Whether the alteration of the law was made on this ground, or from broad and general views of worldly expediency,' says Fraser, 'it is now impossible to ascertain.'[18]

The special Act of Parliament required prior to 1858 in England was 'entirely discretionary in the legislature to grant or withhold the remedy' and despite a number of attempts, no Act of Parliament was ever passed granting divorce on grounds of the husband's adultery.[19] From 1858 a husband could divorce his wife for adultery, but she could divorce him only if adultery were combined with incest, bigamy, gross cruelty or 'other aggravated circumstances', or with desertion for two years without reasonable cause (20 and 21 Vict. cap. 85, sec. 27).[20]

In Scotland, divorce for adultery committed by *either* partner could be obtained from 1560 and a statute of 1573 (cap. 55) recognised malicious desertion if continued for four years as another ground for divorce.[21]

In the case of a woman whose proclamation of banns was sisted because she was reputed to have previously married a sailor, the Kirk-Session, in the face of conflicting evidence, ruled that she should produce a written statement from her alleged husband '"signifying that he had no claim to her as his wife"'.[22] This would have been sufficient to grant her freedom, but while the case illustrates a somewhat relaxed attitude to the marriage bond, it also reveals the uncompromising side of Church discipline: the sailor had set off for an unknown destination and the woman remained under scandal for four years, unable to contract a marriage, until the Session conceded to her request to be freed from scandal, in view of '"the distance of time when this was alleged, and the depositions of two witnesses"'.

The General Assembly soon after the Revolution Settlement of 1690 became very active in matters of Church discipline.[23] It had not met for forty years and the Covenanting troubles had taken precedence over all else. *The Form of Process* of 1707 standardised discipline: chapter 4 deals with 'the sin of Fornication, Adultery and scandalous

Carriage tending thereto', which though lacking the same biblical opprobrium as, say, pride or greed, tended to have more tangible consequences—one reason, perhaps, why of all sins, the sexual dominated Kirk records. Until the consequences materialised, however, Kirk-Sessions were advised to proceed with care:

> In delations about the sin of uncleanness, it falls frequently out, that when the matter is put to the strictest trial, all that can be proven is presumptions of guilt or scandalous behaviour, and not the act of uncleanness, the same being a work of darkness; and therefore this should oblige the kirk session to be very cautious how to admit the public entering a process without good warrant, where there is not a child in the case, unless the scandal be very flagrant.[24]

It has been argued that Kirk discipline protected the unwed woman by punishing the father of her child as well so that she did not face disgrace alone, and often by promoting marriage.[25] The English traveller Edward Burt offered an opposing viewpoint: 'when any thing is whispered, though by few, to the Disadvantage of a Woman's Reputation, and the Matter be never so doubtful; the Ministers are officiously busy to find out the Truth, and, by that Means, make a Kind of Publication of what, perhaps, was only a malicious Surmise'. Should the woman be guilty, the procedure had the benefit, he pointed out, of serving 'for a Direction where to find a loving Girl upon Occasion'.[26]

It also gave opportunity to 'Sets of Fellows, Enemies to Love, and Lovers of Profit', who spied on strolling couples and at the first sign of intimacy ('or perhaps none at all') 'demand the *Bulling-siller* (alluding to the Money usually given for the Use of a Bull;) and if they have not something given them (which to do would be a tacit Confession) they, very likely, go and inform the *Kirk Treasurer* of what perhaps they never saw, who certainly makes the Man a Visit the next Morning'.[27]

But in theory, at least, discipline, by being made public, reminded the sinner that he was part of a Christian community, so that 'both he and the community might by this outward act learn the Christian way of life'.[28] Even Burt admitted that it had an influence on national morals, when he quoted the case of a woman seduced and made pregnant on the eve of her wedding by her betrothed, who then delayed the ceremony, bringing about her disgrace and sudden death. The young gentlemen of the town immediately announced to all keepers of local taverns and coffee-houses 'that if ever they entertained that Fellow, they would never after enter their Doors' and the man was ostracised and ultimately obliged to leave the country. 'I am afraid', Burt confessed, 'your smart ones in *London*, would have call'd this Act of Barbarity, only a Piece of Gallantry; and the Betrayer would have been as well received among them as ever before.'[29]

Nor was discipline entirely punitive: the Session Book of Wigtown recorded in the entry for 20 March 1701 that a couple had lived separately for some time, for no known cause. By 3 April the couple had met with the minister and the Provost several times 'and after much dealing' with the husband 'they prevailed with him to take home his wife'.[30]

On another occasion, a pregnant girl 'was examined upon the nature of faith and repentance and found very ignorant. Pains were taken to instruct her, and the Session thought not fitt as yet to admitt her to publick compearance but appoynts her to continue to converse with the minister and elders privatly.' Only after instruction was she allowed to do penance.[31]

An Act concerning the Method and Form of procedure of Judicatories of the Church against scandalous Persons (4 April 1705) ordained that 'after a public rebuke, the ministers and elders be at farther pains in instructing the minds of the scandalous persons, if ignorant, in endeavouring to convince their consciences, and to bring them to a due sense of their sin'. If they remained 'grossly ignorant, insensible and unreformed' they were, if the Presbytery agreed, to receive the sentence of lesser excommunication and to be refused the opportunity of public repentance 'till the session be satisfied with their knowledge, seriousness and reformation'.[32]

The fact, however, that recommendations were published for the proper imposition of Church discipline suggests that it was not always carried out in an exemplary fashion. Adam Petrie urged elders to 'shew themselves ready and willing to receive all that are truly Penitent with all Tenderness, and forgive and comfort them, with all Bowels of Love and Pity towards them.... When they inflict Censure on scandalous Persons, they must do it with Regrete. It is Matter of Grief and Sorrow, that God's Laws have been violated.... They must reprove with Calmness.'[33]

The *Form of Process*, too, enjoined 'all tenderness and caution' in taking the oath of purgation,[34] proposed that, in attempting to establish paternity, 'all along there should be private treating with him [the suspect], in all meekness, charity and seriousness'[35] and restrained retributive ardour by warning that

If a person doth voluntarily confess uncleanness, and if there be no child ... the session is to enquire what presumptions there are of the truth of the thing confest, or what may have moved the person to make that confession, whether it floweth from disquietness of mind, or from sinistrous design, as when a man suing to a woman for marriage is denied, and for revenge, or for to obtain his desire, spreads the report that he hath been guilty with her.[36]

Methods of establishing guilt could be ruthless: in 1701 a Presbytery directed that in order to ascertain the paternity of an unborn child, the mother should 'be strictly questioned in her pangs by the women who shall be present'.[37] Midwives were interrogated as to the maturity of the infant where the date of birth pointed to pre-nuptial fornication and in one case an uncooperative midwife was actually incarcerated until she had satisfactorily given evidence.[38] G. D. Henderson comments that, especially as regards sexual offences, 'Methods of enquiry seem to us unnecessarily merciless, as when at Oldhamstocks in 1699 the midwife was ordered to refuse assistance to a woman in childbirth till she declared the paternity of her child, or where no fewer than 248 females were personally examined by midwives in 1803 in the Grange area to discover the mother of a waif'.[39]

The Kirk could generally rely on the assistance of civil authority and was thus able to enforce moral discipline on those outwith her communion.[40] As far back as 1578, the *Second Book of Discipline* held it the duty of the civil magistrate 'to assist and maintain the discipline of the Kirk'.[41] In 1701 the Wigtown Session resolved, in the case of a fornicator reluctant to pay his fine, 'to pursue for the penalty befor the civill judge',[42] and the Kirk-Session of Banff, in the early eighteenth century, had the magistrates commit to prison a woman they believed was lying as to the paternity of her child. Incarceration is recorded as having brought about a man's confession of paternity and the Banff Session also requested the Provost to search the Acts of Parliament to discover what corporal punishments could be inflicted on delinquents. It was the common hangman who scourged sinners through the streets of burghs and frequently banished them from the town.[43]

Nevertheless, as Session records show, the Church was more than able to do its own sleuthing: in the case of Elspet Glover who was suspected of having named an innocent man as the father of her child, the Wigtown Session, in March 1702,

understanding that there is a *fama clamosa* of her guilt with John Carsan, a marryed person, who exercised the employment of a cooper lately in this place but now of a sudden is a fugitive, and gross presumptions of the said guilt being reported such as first, that he ... came to her when she was in bed with her children in the night time and that frequently; 2dly, when he went from this town she accompanied him a great many miles from the place; 3dly, they were seen together drinking at the Goatend where they had very unsuitable carriage one with another; 4thly, she followed him from thence to Kilcudbrigh and would have entered into the boat with him for England but was not allowed. The Session appoints their severall members to make diligent enquiry as to what proofs may be had of the foresaid presumptions. The said Elspet denying them all....[44]

Their efforts brought about Elspet's confession in November 1702 and she was ordered to appear 'in sackcloth upon the publick place of repentance' for an indefinite period. The entry for 18 July 1703 records that 'Elspet Glover, adultress, having compeared about twelve severall Sabbath days in sackcloth and rebuked every other Sabbath' applied to be absolved from censure. The Session ruled that the minister could rebuke and dismiss her, and she was required 'to pay in her penalty ... viz. five shillings Starling, she being poor'.

Wigtown seems to have been lenient, given the claim that up to twenty-six appearances for adultery were common,[45] and transgressors might be heartily thankful to be tried by Church courts: in the case, on 14 September 1699, of His Majesty's Advocate against John Murdoch and Janet Douglas, 'They were capitally indicted, upon the law of God, and the *Canon law*, for adultery, aggravated by their being married persons.... The libel was restricted to an arbitrary punishment; upon which they came in the King's will, and consented to be banished Scotland for life.'[46] Arbitrary punishment was inflicted on another couple in 1757 and in 1766 a married Church of Scotland minister found guilty of adultery with a married woman was tried at the Inverness circuit court, sentenced to imprisonment on bread and water for two months and finally 'transported to the plantations, and banished for life'.[47] As late as 1694, apparently, a man was hanged for adultery and his paramour beheaded[48] and William Creech deplored the relaxation of Church censure by 1783, although the law making adultery a capital offence was unrepealed.[49]

Fornication, as one would expect, was regarded as a less heinous sin than adultery: this was the reason for Elspet Glover's naming an unmarried and untraceable dragoon instead of the married man who was in fact the father of her child (p. 54 above). A first offender made public appearance on three consecutive Sundays, a relapse requiring appearance on six consecutive Sundays and a quadrilapse three-quarters of a year—the same punishment as a single relapse in adultery. Fifty-two Sabbaths' appearances were required for incest or murder, '"in case the magistrate do not his duty in punishing such crimes capitally"'.[50] Pre-marital fornication was least severely punished.[51] Proportional censorship is demonstrated by the Edinburgh Council's Act 'Against Adultery and Trilapse in Fornication' (12 April 1704), which in addition to enacting that guilty persons should be fined and punished according to various Acts of Parliament, also decreed that they should 'lose their Priviledge of Burgess in this Burgh and Suburbs'.[52] Fornicators themselves were eager to assert their comparative moral superiority:

> In 1732 at Alves 'the black chair being broken it is appointed that fornicators as well as adulterers stand at the west pillar foot;' but this caused a strike, and the Session were informed that 'the fornicators refused to stand at the same pillar with the adulterers,' so they were assigned a place 'at the pillar opposite to the pulpit.'[53]

The 'pillar', 'stool of repentance' or 'cutty stool' were names for the pew to one side of the pulpit, standing higher than it, to allow penitents to be openly on view. The worst offenders stood at the church door clad in sackcloth—a black sheet or gown—and were called in after the congregation had entered, to mount the stool, a practice that continued in Mauchline, for example, until as late as 1781[54] and in Arbuthnott until 1783.[55]

In this vulnerable location sinners received public rebuke. The minister of Rothesay in 1701 represented to a self-confessed fornicator

> the heinousnes of his sin and how great advantage the divel had gotten of him and how loth the divel was to part with any grip he once got and how much he now stood in need to be eminent in his repentance as he was eminent in his sin, and exhorted him seriouslie to wrestle with the Lord to see if it might please God to make his fall the occasion of his more close dependance on God and oblidge him to studie exact and sincere holines more watchfullie.[56]

Dread of public appearance was commonly believed to be a major factor in infanticide;[57] some turned to the Roman Catholic Church[58] and the Kirk's attempts to enforce public penitence until absolution was earned were sometimes thwarted by the more accommodating of the Episcopal clergy.[59] Burt records spirited defiance of public penance when friends of guilty youths stood beside them at the pillar 'so that many of the Spectators, Strangers especially, cannot distinguish *Culprit* from the rest'.[60] Characters in fiction took on various disguises, one appearing as an elderly man[61] while another came 'with two coats, one buttoned behind him, and another buttoned before him, and two wigs . . . the one over his face, and the other in the right way', evoking from the pulpit the irate reminder that 'if ye had been a' back, ye would nae hae been there this day'.[62]

Comic denunciation of Church discipline, rather than belittling its authority, emphasises its influence. In *Jockey and Maggy's Courtship*[63] neither the minister, the Kirk-Session, the treasurer, the sackcloth nor the cutty stool escape censure and the tale offers abundant insight into the sexual mores of Jockey's social stratum.

When marriage is agreed upon, Jockey looks forward eagerly to consummation, despite Maggy's restraining observation that 'it's best to keep the feast until the feast day'. Jockey, by way of apology, explains that his mother's view is 'that fouk sud ay try gin their house will haud their plenishin'[64]—one shared by the poor in rural areas well into the nineteenth century.[65] Haggis and whisky on the wedding day damp Jockey's ardour somewhat, and reminiscent of Chaucer's Troilus, when the time came to spence him and bed him with the bride, 'pale and ghostly was his face, and closed were baith his een'.[66] Revived by enthusiastic guests, he protests he is unequal to the task and refuses to lie with any woman 'if it binna heeds and thraws,[67] the way that I lay wi' my mither'.[68] The bride weeps and a battle breaks out between the relatives, under cover of which Jockey, revived, succeeds in getting not only Maggy, but his mother's servant lass 'wi' bairn'.

Jockey is called before the Session and he and his mother discuss tactics. She advises him to 'confess ye did it, but say but ance, and that it was on the terms of marriage, the way that a' our kintry bystarts is gotten'.[69] But Jockey's courage fails him and after three summonses 'the session insisted for a warrant from the justice of the peace, which was readily granted, more for diversion than justice' sake'.[70] At the summons to the Session,

Maggy's fa's a greeting, and wringing her hands; Jockey's mither fell a fliting, and he himself a rubbing his lugs, and riving his hair, saying, O gin I were but a half ell higher, I sud be a soger or it be lang, and gie me a good flail or a corn fork, I sud kill Frenchmen enew, before I gaed to face yon flyting ministers, an be set up like a warlds wonder, on their cock-stool or black stool an wha can bide the shame, when every body looks to them, wi' their sacken sarks or gowns on them, like a piece of an auld canvass prickt about a body, for naething, but what every body does amaist, or they be married as well as me.[71]

Mother provides moral support, denouncing the sackcloth and cutty stool as 'a wheen papist rites an rotten ceremonies'[72] and treating the Session to a discourse on their popish origin. But Jockey is sentenced to the stool despite his mother's vigorous defence and her protest that 'there needs na be nae mair wark about it' since 'he's gien the lazy hulke, the mither o't, baith meal and groats to maintain't ... he's a dutifu' father indeed, weel a wat, whan he feeds his bystart sae weel'.[73] Thus bolstered, Jockey refuses to make public appearance, until the minister's refusal to baptise his legitimate child breaks his spirit.

Popular superstition aided the Church's power of blackmail by fearing the theft of a newborn child by the fairies and substitution of a changeling until baptism was carried out. Traditionally an all-night vigil was kept with the aid of friends who encircled the bed and waved the Bible over the child to ward off foes.[74] Only after baptism did the child have a name 'and without a name it would possibly not be saved; for how could it in the resurrection be identified?' Until baptism, too, it remained vulnerable to the power of the evil eye and it was the custom to give visitors a piece of bread as they arrived, to ensure their good will.[75]

Baptism was thus a matter of some urgency and special sessions were held on Sundays and sometimes on certain other days of the week, to which fathers carried their infants as soon after birth as possible. Many took place on the day of birth and prior to 1780 most took place within a week.[76]

Before she was 'kirked' the mother did no work and was looked upon as unclean. She was not allowed to eat with the rest of the household and could not prepare their food. Kirking involved no ceremony, but neighbours accompanied the woman to the church, usually other than at a time of service, and she entered, then went out and circled the church to complete the ritual.[77]

Baptisms, according to John Armstrong, were times

> when warm'd with wine
> The mellow Matrons, by the midnight fire,
> Lewd *Orgies* hold.[78]

While this may be an example of over-heated male imagination, there is certainly abundant evidence of the orgiastic nature of Scottish weddings. 'Penny weddings' for which contributions were collected from the guests were particularly notorious[79] and the Church vainly tried to suppress them with a view to avoiding such errors as Jockey's. One Kirk-Session, in 1715, imposed a fine for 'promiscuous dancing' at weddings, 'betwixt young men and young women, which is most abominable, not to be practised in a land of light ... being only an inlet of lust and provocation to uncleanness'.[80] An Act of Presbytery of St Andrews in 1645 restricted numbers at penny weddings to twenty, but almost eighty years later the Session of Deskford had to be even more stringent, allowing only four guests on either side, apart from near relatives, 'William Mill ... having died of wounds he received at one'.[81]

An Act of the General Assembly of 1701 against abuses at 'lyk-wakes, penny brydalls, and promiscuous dancing' revived Acts of 1645 and 1649, yet penny weddings did not die out until the end of the eighteenth century. As late as 1761 and 1762 four couples in Deskford each forfeited £3 Scots for holding penny weddings[82] and it was in vain that Synods such as Glasgow and Ayr passed Acts 'for Reviving Piety and Suppressing Immorality' (1726), recalling the Assembly's Acts in an attempt to prevent marriages being 'the Seminaries of much Licentiousness and Debauchery'.

While riotousness at weddings was a response of one sector of Scottish society to the repressive attitude to sexuality, other outlets were found by those more outwardly respectable. The Beggar's Benison, for example, was a club founded in 1739 by the nobility and gentry of Anstruther and the surrounding districts of Fife. Records[83] indicate that most parish ministers in the region were included in the membership, though Bishop David Low, presumably mindful of his office, requested that his name be removed, an exercise that required fifty deletions.[84] Among the nobility were Sir Charles and Sir Thomas Erskine and the Earl of Kellie, and the Prince Regent himself (later George IV) was apparently delighted to be given a diploma of membership on a visit to Edinburgh, where a branch was formed in 1766.[85]

Initiations took place before the annual banquet, when the elected chief, or Sovereign (whose wig composed of 'the Privy-hairs of Royal courtezans'[86] was renowned), presided, and the 'Testing-Platter' was placed on a 'high Stool or Altar' in the middle of the room while the Novice was prepared in a closet by the Recorder and two Remembrancers. There he was made 'to propel his Penis until full erection' and was escorted forth 'with four puffs of the Breath-Horn' before the assembled company and ordered to place his genitals on the Testing-Platter. Members then processed two by two in a state of erection and touched the initiate penis to penis.

'Notes taken of the Proceedings at the Society's Half-Yearly Meetings'[87] indicate the nature of the club's preoccupations:

1733. *St. Andrew's Day.* 16 present. The engendering of Toads; The menstruation of Skate; and The gender of an Earthworm....

1734. *Candlemas.* 13 Knights present.... One Feminine Gender, 17, was hired for One Sovereign, fat and well-developed. She stripped in the Closet, nude; and was allowed to come in with face half-covered. None was permitted to speak to or touch her. She spread wide upon a Seat, first before and then behind; every Knight passed in turn and surveyed the Secrets of Nature....

1734. *Lammas.* 18 assembled, and Frigged upon the Test Platter. The origin and performance were discussed. The Platter was filled with Semen, each Knight at an average did not '*benevolent*' quite a horn spoonful.

At Candlemas 1735, elevated by 'Songs and Sights', one 'forgetful Knight had to be escorted out' and three years later strict regulations were brought in governing orderly behaviour after some of the company 'got combative' and the exhibiting girl was dismissed. The girls ranged in age from fifteen to nineteen, and sometimes appeared two at a time, dancing nude.

Housing conditions amongst the poor must have left nature few secrets, but it is possible that the better-off more seldom saw their marriage partners naked. In one comic verse tale, Dick, unable to decide which of three sisters to marry, bemoans the fact that Paris's solution of naked viewing is unacceptable:

But now such freedoms will not pass,
Tho' we with ease may find a lass,
Who will all night lie by our side,
Yet such is now the sex's pride,
That though we flatter, fawn, and beg,
The saucy thing won't shew her leg.[88]

While it could be argued that such modesty was the prerogative of the unwed, Robert Wallace, whose views, for example, on female sexuality and on masturbation can only be described as in advance of his time, nevertheless held that husband and wife should not share a bed, or even sleep in the same room 'except when the husband choosed it for the sake of a more Luscious dalliance'.[89] The sad consequences of curiosity on the part of a new husband are illustrated in 'The Keekeiad'.[90] Holding up the candle, he pleads:

> 'This Part mysterious, to my Sight, reveal,
> 'And let me gaze, transported, as I feel.'
> 'Unthinking Man,' (the Dame aghast replies,)
> For both our Sakes, restrain your curious Eyes;
> 'Cou'dst thou, unchang'd, the Gorgon's Face explore....'[91]

He proceeds boldly, however, and his insatiate gaze having devoured the feast, he has the misfortune to drop the candle and to set 'in dreadful Conflagration' the very hairs she had wished to conceal. The tale closes on a moral note:

> But as all Husbands who peruse this Tale,
> Or hear how KEEKEY's fatal Taper fell,
> Forewarn'd, will henceforth check the curious Eye,
> Nor into Love's immediate Presence spy.[92]

In sourer tone, Petrie reminds us that 'Cloaths were invented for to screen Nakedness, and a Defence of Decency; they are Badges of our Infamy and Shame'.[93] Other writers have found the relation between the shameful and the natural problematical: according to Francis Hutcheson, ' 'tis plain that bodily pleasures have none of that dignity which is the object of praise. Were the sensations never so intense, yet they all are plainly mean, and many of them shameful'.[94] Even Dr Robert Couper, who held that 'it is proper that the animal instinct, which prompts the reproduction of the species, should not be disappointed in its gratification; however brutal these sensations and ideas may appear to the purified philosopher' contrasted mere titillation 'during the gross and libidinous commerce of the sexes' with the 'nobler' end of procreation.[95] But Robert Wallace, eager though he was to see an increase in the numbers of mankind, took a more down-to-earth stance: as venery is necessary for propagation, 'nature hath not only induced both sexes, with a strong inclination' to it, 'but hath rendered the Venereal Act highly Delightfull when it is performed in obedience to nature'. He was sceptical of platonic love: 'seldom I believe can a man admire the good qualities of a fine woman's mind and conduct without a secret wish to be familiar with her person. Virtue, honour, prudence, may restrain him from any indecency, but his regard is allwayes mixed with something sensuall.'[96]

Nor had he any illusions about female delicacy:

> by a false, unnecessary, & unnaturall refinement some would deney that there is any lust in modest women & virgins, whereas every woman during certain seasons and a certain period of life is incited to lust & would gladly suffer the Venereal commerce with the other sex, unless there is something uncommon in her constitution or she is sickly and under a bad habit of body.[97]

Another minister, Daniel Maclauchlan,[98] went rather further, and was imprisoned for his publication of *An Essay upon Improving and Adding, to the Strength of Great-Britain and Ireland, by Fornication, justifying The same from Scripture and Reason. By a Young Clergyman* (London, 1735). Despite the scholarly aspiration hinted at in the latter part of the title, Maclauchlan's language alone shows him to be very much less serious-minded than Wallace (who, incidentally, had the sense to preserve his manuscript from public view). It should, argued Maclauchlan, 'be the great Business of our Lives to Plant and Propagate our Kind. To throw our Seed into every fruitful Corner. To get it vigorously into the gaping Bottom of every sweet-watered Vale. . . .'[99] Concluding a spirited case for giving in to the call of lust, he demands: 'why should the expelling these superfluous Excrements, these agreeably tormenting Humours, by the *Medium* of a pretty Girl, be a greater Sin than evacuating a distended Bladder in the middle of a clean Piss-Pot?'[100]

Wallace took a more elevated view of the female sex and of the sexual act, and his proposal that marriages should be made by renewable contract was aimed at encouraging and stabilising the married state and reducing promiscuity. He treated women with much more equality than most of his contemporaries: he would not, for example, under his proposed regime think it 'imprudent or immodest for a woman to make advances',[101] and as things were, fornication, while it should be discouraged, should be 'only gently punished. It ought not to be accounted a very great blot even upon a woman's character.'[102]

By contrast, Kames, who believed in any case that women are

'destined by nature to be obedient',[103] argued that 'With respect to matrimony, it is the privilege of the male, as superior and protector, to make a choice; the female preferred has no privilege but barely to consent or to refuse'.[104]

Adam Smith explained that the origin of punishment for fornication was to ensure that women were accustomed to chastity when they became wives, lest children of an adulterous liaison fell heir to the husband's estate.[105] For this reason, adultery was, in Kames's eyes, more heinous in the wife than in the husband, particularly as a man's occasional indulgence could result in 'little or no alienation of affection' while a wife 'does not yield, till unlawful love prevails, not only over modesty, but over duty to her husband'.[106]

Hutcheson, like Wallace, rejected the double standard, wishing that promiscuity in men were as severely condemned as in women, and promoting the idea of equality in marriage.[107] James Boswell exemplifies the current mood of confusion: while he had the grace to see the illogicality of being hurt at Mrs Dodds's 'former intrigues', in view of his own past,[108] he failed to detect male chauvinism in an incident which followed his attempt to seduce a fifteen-year-old (to the distress of his wife):

> In the evening I met an old dallying companion, now married. She willingly followed me to a field behind the Register Office. She seemed to wish to have me to press her to let me enjoy her fully, for she was big with child. But I thought it wrong, so only indulged a lesser lascivious sport; struck, however, with the insensibility to the moral doctrines of their country which some women have.[109]

The medical profession, to whom Boswell had frequent recourse when suffering the consequences of his amorous adventures, also contributed to the dampening of sexual exuberance. M. Tissot's account of the direful consequences of masturbation[110] were enthusiastically taken up by his fellow practitioners: virility, according to Robert Couper, could be reduced, if not extinguished, by premature venery or early onanism,[111] a point already made by John Armstrong, who advised would-be fathers to renounce in their youth 'The Vice of Monks recluse, the early Bane / Of rising Manhood' and warned them to

> shun the soft Embrace
> Emasculant, till twice ten years and more
> Have steel'd thy Nerves. . . .[112]

The quack Dr James Graham fanned popular fears that masturbation would result in all kinds of ailments, from deafness to insanity and even death,[113] and, like Armstrong, recommended the brothel as a healthier alternative. Possibly John Hunter alone in the medical profession believed masturbation to be less harmful than the act of intercourse itself.[114] In discussing reasons for impotence, he argued that it was too rare a complaint to be caused by such a universal habit as masturbation, whose danger was only that it might be repeated too often.[115]

An essay on 'The Male Organs of Generation' read at a meeting of the Beggar's Benison in 1813 reveals a similarly down-to-earth approach. Claiming that it is practised by three-quarters of males and females, it rejects the notion that onanism results in insanity and other ailments: it 'was not what Onan was punished for, nor can the moderate use physically cause these evils any more than the immoderate acts in the natural way'.[116]

Almost invariably, too frequent intercourse was regarded as harmful to health. Hunter claimed that the greater the degree of emotional involvement, the greater was 'the degree of debility produced, or injury done to the constitution'.[117] Dr Couper echoed the common belief that fertility in the female could be attributed to 'imprudently reiterated coition', though he pointed out that celibacy is the cause of many female ailments and that coition 'removes these and even other diseases'.[118]

But the weight of medical opinion was certainly against excess, which William Buchan cited as one of the causes of 'slow or nervous fever', inflammation of the eye, apoplexy, nervous diseases, melancholy and epilepsy.[119] Not for nothing did Boswell's friend Temple warn him against 'the "melting down" of his manhood in the arms of his Chloe'.[120]

Venereal disease was an accepted part of life: Lord Marischal Keith benignly admonished Boswell for 'getting the lassies wi' bairns, and worse to yoursel'[121] and Boswell once lost a bet that he might remain free of it for three years.[122]

It was treated with a degree of levity: 'What part of Grammar is a clap?—Sin-tax' ran a riddle of the Beggar's Benison, and the bawd Lucky Spence on her deathbed uttered the following blessing and curse:

> My bennison come on good doers,
> Who spend their cash on bawds and whores;

May they ne'er want the wale of cures
For a sair snout:
Foul fa' the quacks wha that fire smoors,
And puts nae out.

My malison light ilka day
On them that drink, and dinna pay,
But tak a snack and rin away;
May't be their hap
Never to want a gonorrhoea,
Or rotten clap.[123]

Stigma, nevertheless, was attached to the disease and the danger that, as Lucky suggests, it might be only masked and not cured was a real one: disgrace 'renders disguise necessary, and makes the patient either conceal his disorder altogether, or apply to those who promise a sudden and secret cure; but who in fact only remove the symptoms for a time, while they fix the disease deeper in the habit'.[124] Few, Buchan pointed out, were able to undergo a proper course of treatment, since, to ward off suspicion, the patient had to share the normal diet of the family.[125] He therefore included the section on venereal disease, originally omitted, in later editions of *Domestic Medicine*, believing that the good it could do would outweigh any evil consequences.[126]

According to Edward Topham the Scots may have been at a peculiar disadvantage, since the variation in climate was said by the medical profession to inhibit the effects of mercury so that it was often necessary to send the patient to England.[127]

Prostitution was an obvious source of the disease. William Creech recorded that the five or six brothels in Edinburgh in 1763 had increased twenty-fold, and the women of the town one hundred-fold by 1783.[128] Sexually repressive attitudes and the need to delay marriage for economic reasons are clearly factors in encouraging prostitution, as was the attitude to women exemplified in the following exchange between Boswell and Johnson:

I asked him if it was not hard that one deviation from chastity should so absolutely ruin a woman. JOHNSON. 'Why, no, Sir; the great principle which every woman is taught is to keep her legs together. When she has given up that principle, she has given up every notion of female honour and virtue, which are all included in chastity.'[129]

To keep her legs together was doubtless the safest method of contraception, too, though there were several to choose from. The author of the essay read to the Beggar's Benison points out that premature ejaculation has its advantages, but he is not in favour of 'French letters', even the best of which are liable to burst. Nor does he recommend alum solution syringed into the vagina after coition, which he claims is unreliable, as is the prior insertion of a sponge on a silk thread, which may, in addition, wound the penis. He gives whole-hearted support only to *coitus interruptus*, which, he argues, is perfectly safe, and which he ardently defends against the charge of unnaturalness.[130] It may be that this essay contains one of the earliest debates on the morality of contraception versus abortion: to prevent conception, the author argues, is quite different from removing an embryo. 'Before coition the seminal fluid is no more than a secretion like the saliva.... Consequently it is a total confusion of ideas to associate its loss with infanticide, as it cannot be murder to destroy that which has never existed as life.'[131]

Even into the eighteenth century superstition held that knots made by sorcerers on a cord could prevent conception and in 1705 it is recorded that two people were sentenced to death for stealing one with mischievous intent. To fend off such charms there was a tradition of loosening all knots in the clothing of the bride and groom on their wedding day.[132]

Though such customs may seem primitive, the state of medical knowledge itself was not unduly advanced: as one doctor admitted, the nature and properties of semen were as obscure in the eighteenth century as they had been in the third,[133] and Buffon's contention that females too emitted seminal fluid was currently being debated.[134] Couper concluded that fertilisation is achieved by the absorption of seminal fluid through the walls of the vagina 'into the general mass of the female' since he could see no direct communication with the uterine system.[135] He countered the claim of more enlightened authorities, that semen passed into the uterus and from there through the Fallopian tubes, arguing that the cervix became impenetrable during coition, and he even gave credence to a 'marvellous' case of the evolution of a foetus in the male scrotum.[136]

Menstrual problems in women were frequently attributed to moral causes: William Cullen, for example, traced heavy periods primarily to indolence, alcohol and excessive venery;[137] luxury was not merely a target for the economists, as hysteria, too, was put down to 'excess in venery' and 'the indolent and luxurious life'.[138]

By the end of the century urban Scotland was feeling the effects of the industrial revolution; the decline in Church discipline that might have heralded a less repressive period coincided with worsening housing conditions, an increase in prostitution, widening class division and the allied growth towards Victorian hypocrisy. 'Victorian' attitudes to sex, however, were more prevalent in eighteenth-century Scotland than might be supposed from the rollicking and robust approach popularly thought to characterise the period. Clearly a repressive attitude did not suddenly emerge during the nineteenth century, but persisted from the previous one, sustained by social change and, in the literary field, by the growing emphasis on the moral function of the artist—while the more exuberant and open approach to sexuality, with which repression had previously co-existed, declined.

NOTES

1 Edward Burt, *Letters from A Gentleman in the North of Scotland to His Friend in London* (London, 1754), I, pp. 123–4. Hereafter cited as Burt.
2 O. R. McGregor, *Divorce in England: a Centenary Study* (London, 1957), p. 14.
3 Quoted by McGregor, *ibid.*, p. 15.
4 *Letters from Edinburgh; written in the Years 1774 and 1775* (London, 1776), p. 318.
5 For marriage in Scotland, see Andrew Edgar, *Old Church Life in Scotland: Lectures on Kirk-Session and Presbytery Records* (Paisley and London, 1885–6), vol. II (second series), and Patrick Fraser, *Treatise on Husband and Wife According to the Law of Scotland*, 2nd ed. (Edinburgh, 1876–8), hereafter cited as Edgar and Fraser.
6 Edgar, II, p. 192.
7 John Erskine, *Principles of the Law of Scotland*, 21st ed. (Edinburgh, 1911), p. 64.
8 Edgar, II, p. 184n.; Fraser, I., p. 230.
9 Edgar, II, pp. 49n., 186. 'Outed ministers' were prohibited by an Act of 1695, cap. 15, from solemnising marriage. See Fraser, I, p. 235.
10 Fraser, I, p. 294.
11 *Ibid.*, pp. 322f.
12 *Ibid.*, p. 229.
13 *Ibid.*, p. 391.
14 See, e.g., F. P. Walton, *Marriages, Regular and Irregular, with Leading Cases. By an Advocate* (Glasgow, 1893), especially the Strathmore case (151ff.) and the Balbougie case (152ff.).
15 Edgar, II, pp. 200–1.

16 *Ibid.* p. 168n.
17 O. R. McGregor, *Divorce in England*, p. 17.
18 Fraser, II, p. 1139.
19 Patrick Fraser, *A Treatise on the Law of Scotland as applicable to the Personal and Domestic Relations* (Edinburgh, 1846), I, p. 652.
20 Fraser, *Treatise on Husband and Wife*, II, p. 1137.
21 *Ibid.* p. 1207.
22 Edgar, II, pp. 166–7.
23 For background to Church discipline, see Edgar, vol. I; I. M. Clark, *A History of Church Discipline in Scotland* (Aberdeen, 1929), and G. A. Henderson, *The Kirk of St. Ternan, Arbuthnott: a Scottish Heritage* (Edinburgh and London, 1962).
24 *The Form of Process In the Judicatories of the Church of Scotland* [1707] (Glasgow, 1780), p. 10 (ch. 4, sect. 1).
25 See, e.g., G. A. Henderson, *The Kirk of St. Ternan*, p. 116.
26 Burt, I, pp. 222–3 (letter IX).
27 *Ibid.* pp. 236–7 (letter IX).
28 G. A. Henderson, *The Kirk of St. Ternan*, p. 116.
29 Burt, I, p. 230 (letter IX). This is borne out by discussion between Johnson and Boswell. In reply to Johnson's assertion that 'A man is chosen Knight of the Shire not the less for having debauched ladies', Boswell claimed 'I knew in Scotland a gentleman obliged to leave it for debauching ladies'. *Boswell in Extremes 1776–1778*, ed. C. M. Weis and F. A. Pottle (New York, 1970), pp. 341–2.
30 *Wigtown Parish Records: the Session Book of Wigtown 1701–1745*, ed. Henry Paton (printed for private circulation, 1934), pp. 4–5. Hereafter cited as *Wigtown Records*. See I. M. Clark, *A History of Church Discipline*, ch. 7, for discussion of changing emphasis in Church discipline (hereafter cited as Clark) and also G. A. Henderson, *The Kirk of St. Ternan*, pp. 127ff.
31 *Wigtown Records*, pp. 126–31 (Jan.–May 1708). See also the case on p. 135 and G. D. Henderson, *The Scottish Ruling Elder* (London, [1935]), p. 117.
32 Act appended to *Form of Process* cited in n. 24, p. 44.
33 *Rules of Good Deportment for Church-Officers; or, Friendly Advices to them* (Edinburgh, 1730), pp. 114–17.
34 The oath of purgation was a solemn oath of innocence sworn before the Church court, which in Scotland was sufficient to clear a man without the addition of witnesses to testify to the trustworthiness of his oath. The oath was taken only when nothing else would remove suspicion and only on the advice of the Presbytery (*Form of Process*, ch. 4, sect. 8). There are instances of offers of oath being refused, e.g. in a case of fornication, where the process was 'laid aside till tyme discover the matter.' (*Penninghame Parish Records: the Session Book of Penninghame 1696–1724*, ed. Henry Paton (printed for private circulation, 1933), p. 203, hereafter cited as *Penninghame Records*). See

also *Rothesay Parish Records: the Session Book of Rothesay 1658–1750*, ed. Henry Paton (printed for private circulation, 1931), p. 215. Robert Wodrow illustrates superstition as to the horrid consequences of making an untruthful oath in *Analecta: or, Materials for a History of Remarkable Providences; mostly relating to Scotch Ministers and Christians* (printed for the Maitland Club, 1842–3), II, p. 187.

35 *Form of Process*, ch. 4, sect. 7.

36 *Ibid.* ch. 4, sect. 12.

37 H. G. Graham, *The Social Life of Scotland in the Eighteenth Century* (London, rpt. 1964), p. 324 n. 2.

38 *Wigtown Records*, p. 291 (1722) and pp. 294–6 (1723). On the subject of pre-marital intercourse, Wodrow records that the Commission of the General Assembly in May 1710 'agreed that a child might be born and live in the fifth moneth, which they make near six lunar moneths. On this the Commission allowed Mr Elder's oath of purgation that he was free of his wife before marriage' (*Analecta*, I, 278–9). Burt (I, p. 227) finds punishment for pre-marital intercourse extraordinary and shameful, since public dishonour might deter the father from the decent course of action, of marrying the girl.

39 G. D. Henderson, *The Scottish Ruling Elder*, pp. 108–9.

40 Clark, p. 139.

41 Quoted by Clark, p. 175, who goes on to quote a 1697 Act of Assembly which urged Presbyteries 'to pursue [a] ... negligent or refractory magistrate before the Lords of Council or Session' (p. 176).

42 *Wigtown Records*, p. 12.

43 William Cramond, *Illegitimacy in Banffshire: Facts, Figures, and Opinions* (Banff, 1888), p. 10.

44 *Wigtown Records*, p. 25.

45 See G. D. Henderson, *The Scottish Ruling Elder*, p. 116, and G. A. Henderson, *The Kirk of St. Ternan*, p. 127.

46 John Maclaurin, Lord Dreghorn, *Arguments, and Decisions, In Remarkable Cases, Before the High Court of Justiciary, and other Supreme Courts, in Scotland* (Edinburgh, 1774), p. 16. The advocate had 'strenuously maintained, That though we had no statute making simple adultery capital, yet the judges ought to inflict the last punishment; because the crime was capital by the Common law and law of Moses' (p. 733).

47 *Ibid.*, p. 732. He adds that there were very few trials for adultery during the eighteenth century.

48 Edgar, I, p. 330n.

49 *Letters, Addressed to Sir John Sinclair ... Respecting the Mode of Living, Arts, Commerce, Literature, Manners, &c. of Edinburgh, In 1763, and since that Period ...* (Edinburgh, 1793), p. 35 (letter 2).

50 G. A. Henderson, *The Kirk of St. Ternan*, p. 127.

51 See, e.g., *Wigtown Records*, p. 148 (1709), when a couple guilty of ante-nuptial fornication were 'rebuked and exhorted to repentance

and ordered to compear in publick before the congregation [once] ... and to pay in their penalty to the thesaurer'.

52 William Tait, *Magdalenism: an Inquiry into the Extent, Causes, and Consequences, of Prostitution in Edinburgh*, 2nd ed. (Edinburgh, 1842), p. 310.

53 G. D. Henderson, *The Scottish Ruling Elder*, p. 143.

54 Edgar, I, p. 293.

55 G. A. Henderson, *The Kirk of St. Ternan*, p. 135. Gradually, public repentance could be made in one's own pew if higher fines were paid (pp. 127ff.) and eventually a fine alone sufficed.

56 *Rothesay Parish Records*, p. 142.

57 Concealment of pregnancy, not calling for assistance at the birth and having no clothes ready for the child were condemned by the Church as evidence of intention to murder the child (see, e.g., *Wigtown Records*, pp. 477ff. [1735]). Wodrow had the possibility of a servant girl's pregnancy enquired into, to prevent the danger of child murder (*Analecta*, IV, 29 [1729]) and H. G. Graham, *The Social Life of Scotland*, p. 323, asserts that the cause of infanticide 'was too frequently the dread of facing the disgrace and terrible ordeals of the Church'. G. D. Henderson, however, points out that 'the charge is not substantiated by the statistics of the Privy Council Register' and draws attention to the high infanticide rate in England, as reflected in the *Guardian*, 11 July 1713 (*The Scottish Ruling Elder*, pp. 118–19).

58 Clark, p. 180, quotes Act 1704, VIII of the General Assembly, which makes this point, though Clark adds that 'the civil disabilities with which Roman Catholics were at this time visited' make it difficult to believe that the Roman Church was a serious threat.

59 See, e.g., *Wigtown Records*, p. 267 (1720). In 1718 Robert Wodrow was shocked that the Kirk tolerated baptisms at home, a fashion '"winked at lest the gentry become Episcopalians"' (H. G. Graham, *The Social Life of Scotland*, p. 299).

60 Burt, I, p. 233.

61 *Jockey and Maggy's Courtship*, in *The Collected Writings of Dougal Graham 'Skellat' Bellman of Glasgow*, ed. George MacGregor (Glasgow, 1883), II, p. 42. Hereafter cited as Graham.

62 John Galt, *Annals of the Parish*, ed. James Kinsley (London, 1972), p. 30.

63 See n. 61. The author was a pedlar and bellman in Glasgow, thought to have been born near Stirling in 1724 and who died in 1779. According to the editor, his works were regarded by nineteenth-century writers as largely authentic descriptions of eighteenth-century social life (I, p. 65).

64 Graham, II, p. 10.

65 T. C. Smout, *A History of the Scottish People 1560–1830* (1969; rpt. Fontana, 1972), p. 76; Lord Kames, in bk. I, sketch 6 of *Sketches of the History of Man*, new ed. (Edinburgh, 1813), p. 421 (first pubd. 1774),

notes that in the Highlands 'it is scarce a disgrace for a young woman to have a bastard'.

66 Graham, II, pp. 14–15.

67 Heads and tails. This draws attention to prevalent overcrowding. *Penninghame Records* reveal that harvest was a time of great temptation, as workers of both sexes lodged at close quarters under one roof (p. 114). They also record the case of a woman sleeping in the same bed as her mother having to repel an inebriated male friend who wanted to share it with them (p. 101); an enquiry in 1704 brought a denial of fornication, the man's alibi being that on the night in question 'he was in bed with a child of John Gordons' (p. 129); and an overnight guest evoked no surprise when he claimed that intercourse did not take place as a boy of ten or twelve was also in bed with him and the daughter of his host (p. 204). *Wigtown Records* allude to Elspet Glover's being in bed with her children when allegedly visited by her lover (p. 25).

68 Graham, II, p. 15.

69 *Ibid.*, p. 23.

70 *Ibid.*, p. 23.

71 *Ibid.*, pp. 20–1.

72 *Ibid.*, p. 21.

73 *Ibid.*, p. 25.

74 H. G. Graham, *The Social Life of Scotland*, p. 192.

75 *Ibid.*, p. 299.

76 Michael Flinn, ed., *Scottish Population History from the 17th century to the 1930s* (Cambridge, 1977), p. 284.

77 Thomas Pennant, *A Tour in Scotland, and Voyage to the Hebrides; MDCCLXXII* (London, 1790), II, pp. 45–6.

78 *The Oeconomy of Love: a Poetical Essay* (London, 1736), p. 6.

79 See G. A. Henderson, *The Kirk of St. Ternan*, pp. 186–7; H. G. Graham, *The Social Life of Scotland*, pp. 186–7.

80 H. G. Graham, *op. cit.*, p. 327. The Arbuthnott Session in 1703 demanded a cash pledge that excesses would not occur at penny bridals (G. A. Henderson, *op. cit.*, p. 187) and a Session in the Highlands enacted in 1725 that "'no couple be matrimonially contracted within the parish, till they give in to the Session clerk £3 Scots, or a white plaid, or any other like pennieworth, worth £3 Scots, as a pledge that they should not have pennie weddings"' (Edgar, II, p. 143n.)

81 William Cramond, *The Church and Churchyard of Deskford* (Banff, 1885), p. 20.

82 *Ibid.*, p. 22

83 *Records of The Most Ancient and Puissant Order of the Beggar's Benison and Merryland, Anstruther* (Anstruther: printed for private distribution only, 1892). The author is grateful to Professor William Beattie for this reference and to the National Library of Scotland for

their co-operation in allowing her to see this and other material used in the essay.

84 *Ibid.*, p. 12.

85 *Ibid.*, p. 12.

86 *Ibid.*, p. 8. Initiation is described on pp. 9–10.

87 In *Supplement to the Historical Portion of 'Records of the Most Ancient and Puissant Order of the Beggar's Benison and Merryland, Anstruther,' Being an Account of the Proceedings at the Meetings of the Society, together with Excerpts from the Toasts, Recitations, Stories, Bon-Mots, Speeches, and Songs Delivered Thereat* (Anstruther: printed for private distribution only, 1892), pp. 13–16.

88 *Select Poems on Several Occasions, by The Right Hon. The Earl of Harrington* [Thomas Hamilton, 6th Earl of Haddington], *to which are added, The Duke of Argyll's Levee, and some Ballads, By the late Lord Binning* (London, 1824), p. 45 (first printed *c.* 1730).

89 Norah Smith, 'Robert Wallace's "Of Venery"', *Texas Studies in Literature and Language*, 15 (1973), 442.

90 *The Keekeiad, a Poem* (London, 1760), by John Maclaurin, Lord Dreghorn (1734–96), eldest son of Colin Maclaurin. Admitted Advocate 1756; appointed Senator of the College of Justice 1788.

91 *Ibid.*, p. 20.

92 *Ibid.*, p. 27. (Undeterred, Mrs Dodds, Boswell's mistress, enchanted Boswell by allowing him 'full sight' and promised that 'Next night I'll wear black and let candles burn to keep you longer'. *Boswell in Search of a Wife 1766–1769*, ed. Frank Brady and F. A. Pottle (London, 1957), p. 33).

93 Adam Petrie, *Rules of Good Deportment, or of Good Breeding* (Edinburgh, 1720; rpt. 1835), p. 6.

94 Francis Hutcheson, *A Short Introduction to Moral Philosophy* (Glasgow, 1747), p. 44. In fairness, one must note that Hutcheson later acknowledges that 'A moderate relish for *sensual pleasures* is useful, nay necessary' (p. 93).

95 *Speculations on the Mode and Appearances of Impregnation in the Human Female; with an examination of The Present Theories of Generation. By a Physician* (Edinburgh, 1789), pp. 43 and 58. Couper, a graduate of Glasgow University, who practised in Wigtonshire and later in Morayshire, published this work a year after the birth of his elder son.

96 Norah Smith, 'Robert Wallace's "Of Venery"', pp. 433–5.

97 *Ibid.*, p. 434.

98 See Hew Scott, *Fasti Ecclesiae Scoticanae* (new ed., 1923), IV, p. 106. In 1734 charges of 'intemperance, profanity, and singing indecent songs' were found not proven and he was ordained later that year, only to desert his charge a few months afterwards. As a result he was deposed and excommunicated in 1737 and it is likely that ecclesiastical authority was also influenced by his incarceration in the King's Bench

prison on suspicion of having written this 'vile, abominable and obscene pamphlet'. The essay is satirised by Allan Ramsay in his 'Address of Thanks from the *Society of Rakes*' (1735).

99 *Essay*, p. 17.
100 *Ibid.*, p. 45.
101 Norah Smith, 'Robert Wallace's "Of Venery"', p. 441.
102 *Ibid.*, p. 439.
103 *Loose Hints upon Education, Chiefly Concerning the Culture of the Heart*, 2nd ed. (Edinburgh, 1782), p. 256.
104 *Sketches*, I, p. 406 (bk. I, sketch 6).
105 *Lectures on Justice, Police, Revenue and Arms Delivered in the University of Glasgow ... Reported by a Student in 1763*, ed. Edwin Cannan (Oxford, 1896), pp. 74 and 76.
106 *Sketches*, I, p. 453 (bk. I, sketch 6).
107 *A Short Introduction to Moral Philosophy*, pp. 259, 261–2.
108 *Boswell in Search of a Wife*, p. 36.
109 *Boswell in Extremis*, p. 107.
110 Samuel Tissot's *Tentamen de morbis ex manustrupratione*, first pubd. 1758 and translated and augmented in 1760 as *L'Onanisme, ou Dissertation physique sur les maladies produites par la masturbation*, was soon translated into English, German and Italian and remained in print well into the twentieth century.
111 *Speculations*, p. 111.
112 *The Oeconomy of Love*, (1736), ll. 104–5, 83–5.
113 *A Lecture on the Generation, Increase, and Improvement of the Human Species ...* (London, [1783]), p. 10.
114 *A Treatise on The Venereal Disease* (London, 1786), p. 200. Hunter was born in Lanarkshire, of Scots parents, but practised in London.
115 *Ibid.*, pp. 200 and 201.
116 *Supplement to ... The Beggar's Benison*, p. 34.
117 *A Treatise on the Venereal Disease*, p. 200.
118 *Speculations*, pp. 60 & 120. The author of the Beggar's Benison essay went further: 'confirmed old batchelors, like their feminine compeers, belong to a sort of sub-animal class; for to be without sexual intercourse or the heavenly passion shews a pitiable mental defect' (p. 49).
119 *Domestic Medicine: or, A Treatise on the Prevention and Cure of Diseases by Regimen and Simple Medicines ...*, 3rd ed. (London, 1774), pp. 202–3, 281, 447, 457, 463, 471. William Cullen attributes hysteria in women partly to excessive venery (*Works*, ed. John Thomson (Edinburgh and London, 1827), II, p. 502).
120 *Boswell in Search of a Wife*, p. 52n.
121 *Ibid.*, p. 110 n. 1.
122 *Ibid.*, p. 39.
123 Allan Ramsay, 'Lucky Spence's Last Advice', ll. 85–96.
124 William Buchan, *Domestic Medicine*, p. 532.
125 *Ibid.*, p. 567.

126 *Ibid.*, p. 532. It is interesting that the title page of the edition in the National Library of Scotland bears the inscription 'Susanna Harland 1774', and in another hand, 'given to her *Belle Fille* Arethusa Harland June 1804'. This would seem to indicate that V.D. was not regarded as an unsuitable subject for young women.
127 *Letters from Edinburgh*, p. 271.
128 *Letters*, p. 36. Despite this, the Edinburgh Magdalene was not opened until 1797.
129 *Boswell in Search of a Wife*, p. 167.
130 *Supplement*, pp. 46–50.
131 *Ibid.*, p. 51.
132 John Graham Dalyell, *The Darker Superstitions of Scotland, Illustrated from History and Practice* (Edinburgh, 1834), p. 302. See also Pennant, *Tour (MDCCLXXII)*, II, pp. 44–5, and I, pp. 347–8.
133 Robert Couper, *Speculations*, p. 24.
134 *Ibid.*, p. 21; *Supplement to ... The Beggar's Benison*, pp. 51–2.
135 *Speculations*, pp. 147–8.
136 *Ibid.*, pp. 24–5, 31 and 100.
137 *Works*, II, pp. 282–3. Couper also blamed heavy and frequent periods on indolence and luxury (*Speculations*, pp. 100–1).
138 Cullen, *Works*, II, pp. 502–3.

ROBERT A. ERICKSON

'The books of generation': some observations on the style of the British midwife books, 1671–1764

The British midwife books, from the sixteenth to the mid eighteenth century, have been undeservedly neglected by the student of literature. Though they abound with instructions to midwives for the safe delivery of mother and child in 'normal' and 'difficult' labours, these books are not simply about childbirth: since most of them are concerned, in one way or another, with how men and women propagate their kind, they are in part the sex manuals of their day.[1] There was controversy among these writers, nearly all of whom were male physicians, as to just how much they should be expected to show (in 'figures') and tell about the parts of generation. Theirs was the age-old problem of explaining the 'facts of life' as they understood them, but their problem was rendered more difficult in that they were not altogether sure who their auditors were. Ostensibly, they were writing for midwives, at least for those who could read, but their book might fall into the wrong hands.[2] Long before the famous 'Victorian' phobia of bringing a blush to a maiden's cheek, these authors expressed similar fears for 'modesty' and, faced with the very real threat of prosecution for indecency and immodesty, almost all of them undergo, in their ritualistic 'Prefaces to the Reader', a variety of apologetic contortions for the propriety of their language. One of my concerns in this paper then is the problem these writers faced of finding an adequate language for 'generation' and 'midwifery'.

Now the average midwife of the seventeenth and eighteenth centuries, especially the country midwife, was legendary for her ignorance and cruelty. The licensing of midwives by the Church (never a particularly adequate means of control since the midwife was required to show her 'good moral character' rather than any particular skill in her trade) waned in the eighteenth century, and the State demanded no qualification of any kind for a midwife.[3] Most of our pictures of bad midwives have been handed down to us by male practitioners, but Jean Donnison rightly points out that the bulk of midwives, ill educated and drawn from the lower class, were limited to lowly paid attendance on the poor, and 'were full of the ignorance which so often led to rash and fatal interference'.[4] The writers of midwife books profess to see all around them the misery caused by rash and ignorant midwives, yet it is these very midwives, often remarkable for the arrogant pride they took in the strenuous delivery of their women, who must be instructed in anatomy and proper methods of delivery.[5]

Beyond these obvious concerns with propriety and their proper audience, however, the authors of these emblems of mortality afford us, in vivid and highly metaphoric language, a unique glimpse of our origins and frailties. My main subject in this paper is not medical history (though I hope some of these observations will be useful in that regard) but the style and language of selected midwife books, and the attitudes toward 'Man', women, sex, and the midwife book itself embodied in this language. These writers, like many of their contemporaries, copied and paraphrased from the works of their predecessors, and I have tried to indicate when this has occurred, but much of what they wrote has an individual flavour. Though not strictly within the confines of the eighteenth century, the period 1671–1764 is useful for seeing the evolution of the midwife's language from the abundant particularity of Jane Sharp to the more measured and 'mechanical', yet humane, observations of Smellie. I have chosen to emphasise the works of Sharp and McMath on the one hand, and those of Maubray, Burton and Smellie on the other, with specific attention to metaphors of procreation, images of the midwife, and stylistic pretensions.

I

The year 1671 saw the London publication of *Paradise Regained* and *Samson Agonistes*, and of three remarkably diverse yet complementary popular books on the art of midwifery: *The Speculum Matricis* by James Wolveridge, an English surgeon at Cork; *The Midwives Book* by Mrs Jane Sharp, 'Practitioner in the Art of Midwifery above Thirty Years'; and *The Ladies Companion* by the London physician, William Sermon. Of the three, Wolveridge's book was probably written first, and it is the one most conscious of itself as a book subject to the vicissitudes of a dangerous world:

It may perhaps be wondred, why the Author should expose his Book, not only to be tossed by the impetuous waves of the Irish Seas (e're it could set foot on the English shore) but more to be admired, that he should expose it to be tumbled, and searched by the Accustomed, Ingenious Censure, and scrutiny, not only of Learned Scholars, but of Grave Matrons, and Expert Midwives.[6]

Wolveridge sees his little book under the combined aspects of an exposed infant and a young woman, clothed in 'English dress under an Irish mantle'. Immediately there is the association, to be repeated endlessly in the literature of generation, between the book and the clothing of the body. The book itself is a kind of clothes-creature. With some startling puns, Wolveridge richly enlarges the image of his book as a child into that of a small, pretty midwife whose country dress is an extension of the 'clothing' ('*Amnios*' and '*Chorion*') of the child in the womb:

Go little Book, I envy not thy hap,
Mayst thou be dandled in the Ladies lap;
I hope the Ladies will not disdain,
Th'art clean, though in a home-spun dress, and plain:
Nor mayst thou to a gaudy Garb aspire,
Thy native Idiom is thy best attire....
Beware the Press a-while,' twere better tarry,
Lest being prest too hard thou mayst miscarry....
And yet thy fringed skirt adorn'd may be
With ornaments, and by Authority.
Here's Vest and Tunick, *Amnios* and *Chorion* ...
Th'art furnish'd with a Royal Sash (withall,
N'er out of fashion) Cord, Umbilical....[7]

After a long panegyric on the 'excellency of man', an assemblage of tags from Pythagoras, Plato and others, Wolveridge invites the reader to make with him

a nearer indagnation [*sic*] and scrutiny into the formation of man ... from the first conception till the day of his birth: And then, the more we seriously weigh it, and pry into it, the more with the Psalmist, we shall admire our Creator by our creation, and bless that God that hath cover'd us in our Mother's womb, and praising him, say; We are fearfully and wonderfully made, marvellous are thy works, &c. My substance was not hid from thee when I was made in secret; and curiously wrought in the lowest parts of the Earth. Thine eyes did see my substance yet being unperfect, and in thy Book all my members were written, which in continuance were fashioned, when as yet there was none of them.[8]

Psalm 139, quoted here, is the central passage in the Old Testament on the formation of man in the womb, to be compared with Job 10: 11: 'Thou hast clothed me with skin and flesh, and hast fenced me with bones and sinews'; Psalm 22: 9–10: 'But thou art he that took me out of the womb.... Thou art my God from my mother's belly'; and Psalm 71: 6: 'thou art he that took me out of my mother's bowels'. God is seen to have his own 'Book' of generation, the prototype of all midwife books, the Hebrew counterpart to the Greek Book of Fate, and the prototype of the 'Book of Nature'—'Nature' in its etymological sense as the power that brings things to birth. God, the first sewer and knitter-up of the skin, flesh and bones of the clothes-creature man, is the original of the midwife with her scissors and thread for tying off the umbilicus, and he it is who takes this creature out of the womb-belly. Hence, in this capacity, God is the master midwife overseeing the work of midwives on earth. Behind all this is of course the traditional picture in Genesis of God as spirit and voice, the shaper of man from the dust and water of earth. Noting that the 'Original of all ... proceeds from the first Command of the great Lord of Creation, *Increase and Multiply*', and putting the words of Job and David together, the author of *Aristotle's Master Piece* says 'they make up the most accurate System of Philosophy, respecting the Generation of Man, that has ever been written'.[9]

The child is sewn in the womb and eventually clothed by the two coats of the 'Amnion' and 'Chorion', but as he moves towards the birth he must break out of this original clothing. He is like a small hero breaking his chains, overcoming the bonds and restrictive or oppressive forces of his womb-world to make for himself a breathing space, a new life, though one in which he will be far more vulnerable. It was widely held at this time that labour was initiated not by the contractions of the uterus but by the efforts of the healthy child, ripe for his freedom, to break out of the prison of the womb:

[the infant] is moved with great struglings and force in the womb, insomuch, as it breaketh the ligaments, the reins and coats in which [it] is involved ... with the other coats ... and ... fitteth it self toward the birth ... the womb open, the humors begin to flow down, of which the infant being now freed, he presently is sensible of the air, and being desirous of his life, is turn'd toward the out-let of the matrix.[10]

Wolveridge solves the problem of how best to instruct the midwife by inventing a dialogue between one '*Philadelphos*', a doctor, and 'Mrs. *Eutrapelia*'. The doctor says,

your name bespeaks you fit for the work, as being a well-bred woman; therefore give me leave to tell you what kind of person a Midwife ought to be ... The best Midwife is she that is ingenuous, that knoweth Letters, and having a good memory, is studious, neat and cleanly over the whole body, healthful, strong, and laborious, and well instructed in women's conditions ... pleasant, quiet, prudent ... like the Hebrew Midwives, such as fear God ... that the people may multiply and increase after their hands, and that the Lord may build them houses.[11]

The midwife 'knoweth Letters'. Nearly all the early midwife authors stress that the good midwife must be literate, must be mistress of her mother tongue and discreet in her employment of it, speaking or writing. Mrs Jane Sharp, the first midwife in England actually to write a book about midwifery, may not have been a Mrs Eutrapelia, but she is a remarkable representative of her calling and a fascinating writer on birth and sex. Her books went through several editions, and many impressions into the eighteenth century.[12] They were much read, partly, I suppose, because she gives a more detailed, and memorable, account of the members of generation than do Wolveridge and Sermon, one which cannot help but challenge comparison with similar formulations by the Wife of Bath, another spinner of clothes and words. Jane Sharp's main subject is 'Anatomy ... the principal Part effectually necessary for a Midwife',[13] and one too many midwives, she thinks, are ignorant of. She too quotes Exodus on God's finding favour with midwives and building them houses, and she well knew that others of her sisterhood (older midwives reputed to be bawds) put such 'houses' to questionable use. In fact, Mrs Sharp, in her uninhibited discussion of human sexual anatomy, must have run the risk of appearing like the 'merry Midwives' or 'Mother Midnights' described by Ned Ward and Daniel Defoe.[14]

She writes to and for 'the Midwives of England', her 'Sisters', and argues that it is proper for women to be of this profession because they have Biblical authority for it and are the ones most concerned with the business of birth. The art of midwifery is both '*Speculative* and *Practical*', but 'it is not hard words that perform the work, as if none understood the Art that cannot understand Greek. Words are but the shell, that we oft-times break our Teeth with them to come at the kernel, I mean our brains to know what is the meaning of them; but to have the same in our mother tongue would save us a great deal of needless labour.'[15] She feels it necessary to explain her metaphor. She seems to distrust figurative language at the same time that she employs it. Most of these early writers on midwifery make it clear that they want to be understood by the meanest capacity, usually the meanest female capacity. They want to speak plain English, unadorned with technical hard words or poetic conceits, yet they love using similes. This same concern with being plain *or* poetic continues up to John Burton. Jane Sharp gives the impression of labouring hard over the 'Speculative' side of her art, namely treatises, written by men, on anatomy and midwifery; it is as if she had forced herself to learn what she could from these books, but that her own experience and her 'mother tongue' were more important to her advancement in skill and knowledge than any book. She was up against the prejudice not only of the ignorant midwife, but a deeper one which may be inferred from *The Expert Midwife* of the authoritative Jacob Rueff, who reminds his reader that although midwives have 'ever been useful for reliefe and succour of all the daughters of *Evah*', women in general are none the less uneducated: 'women with all being universally as all men know (for the most part) unlearned, any further than to understand their own native language'.[16] In the context of midwife handbooks, 'mother tongue' takes on a fresh significance. Jane Sharp, alienated from the hidden masculine languages of Latin and other Continental tongues, as well as from professional recognition by men, can afford to purchase translations of the men's treatises, but as a woman she draws upon her mother tongue to express clearly the close relationship she feels with female Nature in aiding and describing the birth process. The mother tongue is like a mother shaping the form and style of her writing, and the midwife's language itself reflects the act of procreation and birth.

Jane Sharp's language is that of the seamstress and the gardener, the ancient spinner and sewer of men and a marvellously tactile Mother Eve, with Adam her ploughman, moving between the well-irrigated and fertile garden of the farmyard and a well-stocked country kitchen. She begins with a discussion of the members of generation: 'The Cod is as it were a purse for the stones to be kept in with the seminary Vessels'; this purse has a 'seam' running down the middle of it; the stones are 'two whole kernels like the kernels of a woman's paps, their figure is Oval, and therefore some call them Eggs . . . they feel exquisitely [i.e., their power of feeling is exquisite] . . . those that have the hottest stones are most prone to venery . . . The Yard is as it were the Plow wherewith the ground is tilled, and made fit for production of Fruit'; it is 'hollow as a sponge'.[17] Mrs Sharp's language for these descriptions is interspersed with 'wrinkles', 'seams', 'strings fast knit', 'woven networks', and 'Weavers Shuttles', and again there is a self-conscious use of the qualifier 'as it were'. She goes on to rehearse, in much detail, and seems to accept the old midwives' notion (supported by the male authority Mizaldus) of parity between the length of the umbilicus when cut and the size and operation of the privy members:

It is generally held, that the length or proportion of the Yard depends upon cutting the Navel string . . . all *Midwives* have cause to be careful to cut the Navel string long enough, that when they tye it, the Yard may have free liberty to move and extend itself . . . Midwives cut the Female Navel-string shorter than they doe the Males, for Boys privy parts must be longer than womens, but if Females are cut short they say it will make them modest, and their secrets narrower . . . *Miraldus* [*sic*] bids cut the navel string long in both sexes, for that the Instruments of Generation in both follow this proportion, if womens Navel-strings be cut too short, it will hinder their Child-bearing . . . If Nature framed the child by the Navel-string in the womb, there is no small use of it afterward.[18]

After describing the male parts of generation, Mrs Sharp turns to the female parts, 'because it is commonly maintain'd, that the Masculine gender is more worthy than the Feminine, though perhaps when men have need of us they will yield the priority to us'. Again aiming for the 'meanest capacity', she desires 'the Courteous Reader to use as much modesty in the perusal of it, as I have endeavoured to do in the writing of it'.[19]

Man in the act of procreation is the agent and tiller and sower of the Ground, Woman is the Patient or Ground to be tilled, who brings Seed also as well as the Man to sow the ground with. I am now to proceed to speak of this ground or Field which is the Woman's womb . . . we women have no more cause to be angry, or be ashamed of what Nature hath given us than men have, we cannot be without ours no more than they can want theirs . . . At the bottom of the woman's belly is a little bank called a mountain of pleasure near the well-spring . . . Under the hill is the springhead . . . The womb is covered with a sinewy Coat that it may stretch in time of copulation, and give way when the child is to be born; when it takes the Seed from Man the whole concavity moves towards the Center, and embraceth it, and toucheth it with both its sides.[20]

Even the most courteous reader cannot but be somewhat amused at the incongruity between Mrs Sharp's professed attention to 'modesty' and the uninhibited (and poignant) candour of what she actually writes.

Wolveridge and Sharp afford a vivid picture of the seventeenth-century views of the midwife, her book and the relations between the sexes. By striving to write simply and for the meanest capacity, these early authors, particularly Mrs Sharp, gave their language a directness, immediacy and vitality it might otherwise have lacked. Their style is usually a fit counterpart to the unpretentious, portable usefulness they claimed for their books. They are quite self-conscious in their efforts to find a proper style for expressing what they thought a midwife ought to know. At times, though, instead of shaping their mother tongue, they seem to let it shape them, and a curious, even ludicrous, sexual autonomy of language results. This effect is most noticeable in *The Expert Midwife* (1694) of the Scottish physician, James McMath.

In his preface, McMath, like Wolveridge, invokes the image of a frail vessel upon a raging sea, this time not the little midwife book, but the mother-to-be herself: 'The Impregnant Woman, embarques upon a Voyage so long and perilous, through such rough and rocky Seas ... that she needs all careful conduct, to save and recover her from these Rocks ...' Out of 'Modesty and Reverence to Nature', he will omit a description of a woman's genitalia, but he has 'studied ... all plainness of Speech, and the most easy simple Womanly Terms, and Words they could best understand';[21] again, this 'plainness' manifests itself as a robust candour which makes his language the masculine counterpart of Jane Sharp's vivid, homespun style.

For McMath, the most fruitful time for procreating 'plenty of most *Vigorous* and *Elegant Children*' is in the prime of menstrual activity, between eighteen and forty-five years of age, when 'the Blood of the courses ... is ... of a florid bright colour, and smelling like *Marigolds*'.[22] In sterility, 'the Orifice [of the womb] bides shut against the *Yard:* which else (while eager upon it, strenuously and naturally *Tickled*, and *Roused* therein) applyes to it, delightfully opens, and raveningly attracts the mans Seed (which is then sufficiently darted into the *Recesses* of the *Womb*) emits also her own'.[23] McMath is struck by the fecundity, 'the innate ... benign, dewy Warmth, Moisture, and vivid *Ferment* of the Womb', where 'the adventitious, irradiant, or *Influent Spirits*, [are] like the warm *Rayes of Heaven*'.[24]

The sign of conception in a woman is

her great *Itch* and *Lust* to *Coition* her most grateful and *Voluptuous Tickle* therein, without which Woman does not so readily and easily conceive: A light Shivering of the Body after, as after Pissing.[25]

Men and women hasten to the '*Genial Embrace* ... chiefly from that signal *Delite*, and enchanting *Pleasure* found therein,' 'this incredible pleasure excited in *Coition* from which the most exquisite *Sense* and *Tickle* affects the Genitals,' 'though empty and momentary, *Sadness* and *Drooping* coming instantly after, yea even during the *Pleasure* of this *Dance*.'[26]

Women get moreover, the very same *Symptoms* with men, after Coition, as Sadness, Lassitude, trouble of Sight, Dulness, Submission, Satiety, or Cessation of Lust, and the rest.[27]

McMath appears to make more of an effort to express the sexual pleasure (and melancholy) of women than perhaps any other British writer on midwifery—female or male—before him, though he traditionally stresses that 'the Mans Seed ... far excels woman's in active *Principles*, *Vertue*, and *Force* of Procreation'.[28] Doubtless a good part of McMath's apparent intensity is owing to his liberal use of italic emphasis, an effect carried to excess in much eighteenth-century expository prose; McMath also notes in passing the 'labours of these more Delicate, Tender, Feeble women', a theme which will be intensified in eighteenth-century treatises on women, and in fiction.

II

In the eighteenth century, the man-midwife came to displace his female counterpart in the practical as well as theoretical branches of obstetrics. There are corresponding changes in the midwife's depiction of his book, of 'Coition', and of the image and role of woman as sexual being and childbearer. Thirty years separate McMath from John Maubray, a London physician and man-midwife or 'Andro-Boethogynist', as he preferred to be called. His book, *The Female Physician, containing all the Diseases incident to that Sex. In Virgins, Wives, and Widows ... To which is added, The Whole Art of New Improv'd Midwifery* ... (1724), far from being a frail vessel subject to all manner of vicissitudes, has weight:

a *substantial* Work will stand securely upon its own Bottom, and make its way into the World without any *secondary Helps*, whereas a slight and

Defective Piece will fall and be quash'd, tho' it should even *strut* with *Majesty* itself in its glaring *Front*.

of late years . . . these Healing and obstetricious *Arts* are so much improv'd and advanc'd, that, they now seem to be arriv'd at their very Heights of *Perfection*.[29]

By contrasting his stolid, 'full-bottomed' volume with a strutting, flashy piece of ephemera, Maubray suggests for his book the image of the midwife as a heavy, grave matron. As the midwife treatises become more learned, advanced and 'philosophical', they become larger, weightier objects, culminating in the solid volumes of Burton and Smellie. These are not books meant to be carried around in one's pocket, like the older manuals. The pretended gravity (or 'gravidity') and congratulatory self-importance of a Maubray or a Burton may have helped to provoke Sterne's satire of mid-eighteenth-century obstetrics. Not that Maubray is unaware of the dangers of pomposity, but the more modest he tries to sound—he has written his work 'in our vernacular *Tongue*, but also in a certain middle *Style*, adapted to the Capacity of the meanest Reader'—the more glaring appear his style and his survey 'Of God, of Nature, of the Soul, of the Faculties of the Soul' and 'of the Dignity and Excellency of Man'.[30]

Maubray's book is a curious transitional mixture of early wisdom about human generation, astrological influence on birth, 'new' techniques in midwifery (though he shuns the use of instruments) and an exalted view of 'MAN' at marked variance not only with the melancholy picture of human mortality conveyed by most of the midwife literature of the eighteenth century, but also with his representation of women. Maubray advertises that his book presents the 'Whole Art of New Improv'd Midwifery', yet he retains a curious deference to the authority of the 'Ancients', 'who . . . discover'd the Natural Debility of the *Female Sex*, and that Women were not only Subject to all Diseases in common with Men, but also obnoxious to a vast many Distempers peculiarly singular to themselves'.[31] 'Women' (and here Maubray seems to have in mind particularly the 'Gentlewomen' of London) have a unique vulnerability to disease—this is in large part what it means to be the weaker vessel—and Maubray is at pains to describe and prescribe for all of these peculiarly feminine ailments, most of which arise from distempers of the womb: 'Well might the excellent *Democritus* write to his *Scholar*, the far more excelling *Hippocrates*, that the *Womb* is the Source of *Six Hundred Griefs*, and the *Spring of innumerable Sorrows to the* WOMAN.'[32] What was a fountain of delight and new life for Jane Sharp is the springhead of misery for Maubray. The case of the 'Widow' and her symptoms is instructive: 'she is still so far from being exempted from the *Morbifick Consequences* of the Natural Imbecility of her tender SEX; that she now . . . participates of the Indispositions of both [maiden and wife]'.[33] '*The First Action* of the *Womb* is, that by its *attractive Faculty*, it may allure the *Masculine Seed* infus'd by Coition into the FUND of its *Capacity*, after the same manner as a *famishing stomach* snatches at the victuals by the *Gullet* from the *Mouth* of the Eater.'[34]

This is Maubray's formulation of the old notion, rehearsed in many of the early midwife books, of how the womb attracts the man's seed as the loadstone attracts iron filings, and is not far different from 'the more 'tis fed, the more it craves' of a ubiquitous eighteenth-century 'Riddle'. But Maubray is more original, and more in the spirit of the modish man-midwife of 1724, who has certain similarities (which he would adamantly deny) with the libertine-as-natural philosopher epitomised in Richardson's Robert Lovelace, a connoisseur of feminine charms in exquisite motion,[35] when the man-midwife describes the '*Charms* of COPULATION' and 'all the . . . *Parts* in full AGITATION': 'The LABIA dilate: the Orifice swells: the NYMPHAE give way: the CLITORIS (of exquisite Sensibility) erects', and so on.[36] This description, amidst all the astrological and Galenic lore, has a modern ring, and seems the obvious correlative of a view of woman as a charming piece of mechanism, a 'tender' assemblage of working parts (with the womb as a central 'Pump'),[37] which tends to go out of order rather too often. One cause of disorder is the power of a woman's imagination to impress itself upon the womb and hence upon the unborn child:

if the *Woman* be . . . frighted at any unseemly sight, the *Humours* and *Spirits* presently retire downwards, and (as it were) abscond themselves in the *Recess* of the *Womb*: From whence immediately a strong *Imagination* of the disagreeable *Thing* . . . seizes her *Mind*; and the *Forming Faculty* (going on in the *Interim*) quickly impresses the *Imaginary Idea* of *That* thing heard off . . . upon the *Foetus*.[38]

Thus, if 'Woman', by reason of her peculiar weakness and natural subordination to man, is little better than a charming 'Imbecile' with a marvellously complex womb and a palpably active imagination, her midwife had best be a woman of considerable politic experience of the world: 'She ... ought to be a *Woman* of a good *middle Age*, or *solid Parts*, of *full Experience*, of a *healthy*, *strong*, *vigorous Body*, with clever *small hands* ... She ought to be *Grave* and *Considerate*, endued with *Resolution* and *Presence* of *Mind*, in order to foresee and prevent ACCIDENTS; *Sagacious* and *Prudent* in difficult *Cases* ...'[39] Maubray goes on to say she must be watchful, diligent, expert in all cases, and must not neglect 'improving the *critical* MINUTE'—a term dear to libertines, though in a different sense, as well as to midwives[40]—when the birth actually begins. If the lying-in woman will not follow advice, the midwife 'ought to reprimand and put her smartly in mind of her Duty'.[41] Finally, the sagacious midwife must be faithful and silent, always on her guard not to let slip an ill-advised word. If the midwife is a man, he should be especially considerate of the lying-in woman: 'HE ought to *handle* her *decently*, and treat her *gently*; considering Her as the *weaker Vessel*, whose elegant tender Body, will admit of no *rough Usage*'.[42] 'Elegant' is no longer coupled with 'vigorous' as in the case of McMath's memorable children, but with debility.

Maubray's midwife is like his book, substantial, solemn, grave, portentous, weighty, showing all the characteristics of the 'grave Matron' who in the works of Ned Ward, Daniel Defoe and Samuel Richardson invariably suggests a woman of the world experienced not only in the art of midwifery but also the arts of the bawd. For Maubray, there seem to be two kinds of women in the world, the capable and experienced (instructed by men), and the elegant and frail. His book makes an informative 'medical' backdrop to the representation of women in early eighteenth-century fiction, culminating in the novels of Richardson.

From Maubray to John Burton (Sterne's 'Dr Slop') and William Smellie ('Adrianus Smelvgot') is a large jump chronologically and obstetrically. The technical art of midwifery made great strides between 1724 and 1752, and the language by which that art was communicated gained in precision, economy and clarity. Still, the diction, emphases and tone of Burton and even Smellie betray certain affinities with the richly metaphoric style of their predecessors. Burton's *Essay Towards a Complete New System of Midwifery*, 1751—his bid to be counted in the first rank of modern English *accoucheurs*—has the same epigraph from Horace on its title-page as was used by Wolveridge to conclude his *Speculum Matricis*. More practically,

Burton adopts the same public-spirited tone, and insistence on a plain style, of most of the earlier midwife authors: 'I have been as brief as I well could ... neither have I been fond of obtruding any opinions upon the World, which I have not Grounds to believe are founded upon *Truth* and *Matters* of *Fact*, which I have here laid before the Public ... I have rather studied the *Weight* of *Matter*, then *Elegance* of *Stile*; and *Usefulness* rather than *Ornaments*.'[43] Of course this claim to brevity (the *Essay* is 391 pages long, with eighteen copper-plate engravings and an index) is as spurious as was the long-winded Maubray's, and the assumed unconcern of Burton's dismissal of the attacks of his opponents, who 'like *cowardly Enemies*, *unseen*, shoot their envenomed Darts at me, in secret Whispers, or anonymous Papers',[44] sounds even less convincing. Though Burton in his *Letter to William Smellie*, 1753, does not hesitate to accuse Smellie of copying extracts from earlier works on obstetrics, he himself takes much of his description of the female genitalia straight from the work of the eminent Irish man-midwife, Fielding Ould,[45] yet inserts some characteristic Burtonian 'particulars':

> I have been at the Pains to examine and measure the Bones of the *Pelvis* of several Female Skeletons, and having found one of a good sizable and well proportioned old Woman (whom I knew when alive) I took the just Dimensions, and wrote them down as a Standard.[46]

> An idea of the exact Shape of the *Pelvis* may be conveyed to the Reader, by resembling it to a Barber's Bason.[47]

> Tickling the Nipples occasions an agreeable Sensation in the *Clitoris*.[48]

In the Preface to his great *Treatise*, Smellie had unfortunately left himself open to Burton's peculiarly obtrusive sense of humour with a gratuitous caveat: 'Nor will the Reader, I hope, imagine ... that this treatise is cooked up in a hurry, when I inform him, that above six years ago I began to commit my lectures to paper, for publication ...'[49] 'And you likewise so far forget yourself,' says Burton, 'as you tell us, you *was* six *Years* in *cooking up this Treatise*.'[50] Smellie's analogy of the child's head, in parturition, to 'the form of a sow's back' and to a 'sugar-loaf',[51] celebrated by scientific parody in *Tristram Shandy* as an 'oblong conical piece of dough',[52] reinforced this image of the man-midwife as pastry cook, but Burton's stylistic contest with his obstetric nemesis is most amusing, with respect to the style of both writers, in his ironic attack on the propriety of Smellie's account of the pleasures of sexual intercourse:

You say ... 'In Coition, the Uterus yields three or four Inches to the Pressure of the Penis, having a free Motion upwards and downwards so that the reciprocal Oscillation ... increases the mutual Titillation and Pleasure.'

I will not here enter into any Debate with you upon the Matter of Fact or Propriety of your Expression, but shall only observe, that to move the Uterus four Inches higher than *its usual Situation*, will require a Man of *extensive Abilities*; but it requires no great capacity to know that it is the Friction on the Clitoris, that increases the Pleasure in the Female, to which this *oscillation* of the Uterus can no way contribute ...[53]

It is enough to peruse Burton's own account, in the *Essay*, of 'Titillation', or his remarks on the manipulation of the *os coccygis*,[54] to see how far he excels his opponent in 'Propriety of Expression'. It is rather poignant, however, to see Burton's consistent nasty sarcasm in his *Letter*—a deliberate stylistic achievement in itself, sustained over an interminable 250 pages—muted at one point by his dawning recognition of the difficulty of finding a proper language for the art of midwifery. He muses a bit enviously about Smellie's apparent stylistic debt to the author of *Peregrine Pickle*:

Had I the Talents of the ingenious Writer of that Book, what a pathetic Harangue might I make on the Usefulness of critical skill in Language in these cases? Some Latitude may be indeed allow'd for peculiar Graces and different Idioms, in different Languages, especially in Poetry; but in Matters of *Faith*, and Matters of *Fact* and *Experience*; a Translator's first Aim is to be, 'Fidus Interpres.' With such an *Aid de camp* I might hope to make even these Remarks very agreeable.—But plain *Sense* and *Usefulness* is all I ever desired; and I must own, I had rather find out one good Rule or Method of Practice, than be the finest Writer in the World in point of Style.[55]

The practical over the aesthetic. All through these midwife books, in varying degrees, there recurs the author's urgent concern—it can hardly be called a struggle—with propriety of expression: though paying deference to modesty and humility, these writers, in one way or another, consistently subvert that modesty through figurative language: Wolveridge indulges in 'poetic' licence to introduce his book, Jane Sharp and James McMath let their descriptive powers run riot, Maubray's elaborate pretence to elegance exalts his style over his subject. Now the friend of Smollett and the man who, with great industry, skill and far from satisfactory materials, fashioned his famous 'phantoms' or 'dolls' for representing to his students the mechanism of labour, might have agreed with Burton's pronouncement (quoted above), but he must have been ambivalent about it, because Smellie was a true artist with as deep a reverence for the truth as he saw it as that other mid-eighteenth-century master of verisimilitude, William Hogarth. The transition from Maubray's 'Imbecillic' females to Smellie's 'machines . . . contrived to resemble and represent real women and children'[56] would not appear to be great; the difference between the two writers, however, lies in their language for midwifery. Smellie achieves a language which expresses a genuinely humane attitude toward *women*, not 'elegant Females'; Maubray—for all his good intentions—fails. Smellie, moreover, showed Burton that one could 'find out'—and articulate, in lucid, sinuous language (not without the aid of Smollett)—'one good Rule', in his case, the mechanism of parturition, and still create a moral 'Style'. Volumes II and III of Smellie's treatise, made up of case histories drawn from his long practice, are literary documents of a high order, full of powerful, if melancholy, human drama. They do not lend themselves to short quotation, but the following cases are representative of their compression, compassion and understatement. In 1746

> I was called to a woman by some of her neighbours, who told me, it was not known that she was with child until she was in labour, when her mother had beaten, abused, and exasperated her to such a degree, that she had become frantic, and, in her turn, thrashed the mother, midwife and all present who had at length locked her in a room by herself: they therefore, begged I would visit her and bring my pupils along with me.
>
> We found her lying in bed, so sullen, that she would not speak when the women told her, they had brought several doctors to keep her in order. I examined as she lay, and feeling the child's head low in the *Pelvis*, waited a long time for a pain, but to no purpose, she seemed to be afraid and lay very quiet. . . . She lay quite calm and resigned while I . . . placed the blades [of the forceps] opposite to each other, and locked the handles firmly with a fillet, to prevent their slipping off the head, in case she should prove refractory.[57]

Smellie went on to perform, slowly and carefully, a safe delivery unaided by labour pains. I am struck by the modulated progression of oppositions and turn-abouts here, first between the 'frantic' girl and her tormentors, then between her and Smellie and his pupils, with the girl at first 'sullen', then 'afraid', then 'resigned', and finally the movement from 'locking' the girl in a room to Smellie's locking of the forceps over the child's head to deliver it from its room. The passage conveys a sense of gentle, patient, but firm control necessary for effecting several 'deliveries' at once from a complicated human predicament.

In the year 1747, I attended a gentlewoman, in labour of her first child, who, a few days before had been so much affected with the sudden death of her husband, that she was seized with frequent faintings and great anxiety of mind. When I arrived, her pains were very weak, and the membranes had broke even before the mouth of the womb was much dilated, and although the child's head was small, she continued three days in a kind of labour: yet, by encouraging and supporting her with cordials and nourishing things, and indulging her as much as possible with rest, she was safely delivered of a child, which seemed to have died soon after she heard the melancholy news of her husband's death.[58]

The materials here surveyed are so various and provocative in their own right that it is hazardous to draw many conclusions from them. Still, it may be said in a summary view that the midwife books from the year 1671 show a series of intertwined features: a self-conscious sense of the book as a little human companion and teacher, dressed out like the child clothed in the womb; a highly organic view of the generation of mankind, rich in images from the garden and the loom; and a philosophy of birth going back to the rich matrix of the Psalms and the Book of Job. The portrayal of sexual intercourse, including McMath's account, stresses the mutual delight (and melancholy) of men and women in the 'genial Embrace', and the remarkable vigour of this portrayal is carried over into the heroic labours of the infant breaking forth into his dangerous new world. The image of the ideal midwife which emerges from these earlier books is one of health and protean capacity: she has a wide experience of life, a wisdom of the body and all growing things, strength, tenderness and courage, and she is mistress of the arts of nurture and of language. With Maubray, however, the midwife book becomes self-conscious in a new way: the unpretentious, companionate quality of the small octavos gives way to Olympian views afforded by perfected knowledge of the mechanisms of womb, woman and proper ('decent') propagation, perfected mastery of the art of midwifery, and the 'full-bottomed' large octavo, a 'grave matron' in itself, to convey these views. Maubray's ideal midwife, though conforming in many respects to the image enunciated by Wolveridge, is a polite and sagacious creature who knows how to be 'faithful and silent'. Burton's corresponding resolution to study

'Weight of Matter' rather than 'Elegance of Style' cannot conceal the envious tone of his experiments in sarcasm, whereas Smellie's style, particularly in his account of the child's journey to birth and in his case histories, brings us back—though from a different world—to the wisdom and forthright human honesty of Jane Sharp in her best moments.

NOTES

1 Lawrence Stone, in *The Family, Sex and Marriage In England 1500–1800* (London, 1977), p. 493, does not appear to have recognised this implication. Although it is true that the midwife books do not offer the kind of specific and technical information regarding foreplay, positions in intercourse, and prolongation of pleasure provided in the Chinese manuals, several of them give plenty of consideration to such matters as the appearance and function of the genital organs, the 'just' length of the phallus, the mechanics of the sexual act, the sensual delights of intercourse, the method for propagating a male child, the signs of conception and whether a male or female has been conceived.

2 'My intentions herein are honest and just, and my labours I bequeath to all grave, modest and discreet women ... But young and raw heads, Idle serving-men, prophane fidlers, scoffers, jesters, rogues; avant, pack hence; I neither meant it to you, neither is it fit for you', Jacob Rueff, 'To all grave and modest Matrons', the preface to his *Expert Midwife or An Excellent and most necessary Treatise of the generation and birth of Man* (London, 1637). Cf. also the 'Dedication' to William Sermon's *The Ladies Companion, or The English Midwife* (London, 1671). My title for this paper comes from an account of the life and accomplishments of the most noted bawd of the Restoration, 'Mother Creswell', 'a Midwife to Love', who after mastering philosophy, astronomy and metaphysics, 'advanced to the Books of Generation', *The Whores Rhetorick* (Edinburgh, 1836; reprint of 1683 original), pp. 25–6, 20.

3 See Thomas R. Forbes, 'The Regulations of English Midwives in the Eighteenth and Nineteenth Centuries', *Medical History*, 15 (1971), 352–4, and *The Midwife and the Witch* (New Haven,Conn., 1966), ch. 8.

4 Jean Donnison, *Midwives and Medical Men: a History of Inter-Professional Rivalries and Women's Rights* (London, 1977), p. 33.

5 The following is typical of such professions: 'The serious consideration of the intollerable misery that many Women are daily incident to, occasioned chiefly by breeding and bringing forth children; and the want of help in such deplorable Conditions, by reason of the unskilfulness of some which pretend to the Art of Midwifery ... hath been one principal motive to me at this time, to undertake the

the Publication of this Treatise', Sermon, *The Ladies Companion*, the 'Dedication', n. p. To my knowledge, it has not before been noted that most of Sermon's book relating to midwifery is copied, at times verbatim, from the English translation of the French chirurgeon James Guillimeau's *Childbirth, or, The Happy Deliverie of Women* ... (London, 1612). Space does not permit a more detailed consideration of the Guillimeau–Sermon material in this essay.

6 Wolveridge, 'The Author to the Reader', n. p.

7 Wolveridge, 'The Author to his Book', n. p.

8 Wolveridge, 'The Preface', n. p.

9 *Aristotle's Compleat Master Piece: In Three Parts: Displaying the Secrets of Nature in the Generation of Man ... the Twenty-seventh Edition* (London, 1750), pp. 9–13. 'It is therefore the secret Parts of that curious Piece of Nature [i.e. Woman] that we are to lay open, which we shall do with as much Modesty and Sobriety as will consist with our speaking intelligibly: For 'tis better to say nothing than to speak so as not to be understood', p. 14. Cf. Fielding Ould, below.

10 Wolveridge, pp. 23–4. The literary associations of the heroic infant breaking his bonds are many, but this description may be of special significance for interpreting Gulliver's new birth in Lilliput by breaking the tiny ligaments which bind him to the earth. Cf. also Maubray's account of the infant's 'enlargement': '*The Infant* thus being thoroughly ripen'd, and arrived in full *Perfection* of *Maturity*, the *Hour* approaches, in which it scorns any longer *Confinement* to such narrow Bounds ... the *Animal Spirits* ... the *Vitals* ... and the *Natural Spirits* ... all concur to make a *Commotion*, and (as it were) a victorious *Revolt* or an *Effort* pushing for *Conquest* ... [the infant] makes its most vigorous *Attempts* to enlarge itself from the *Prison* of the *Womb*, into that of the *World*', *The Female Physician* ... (London, 1724), p. 228. In the popular and influential *Compleat Midwifes Practice* of 1656 it is noted that 'the narrowness of the place where the infant lies' is one of the causes of delivery, 'so that he [the infant] is forced to seek room other-where, which makes him to break the membranes wherein he was contained, pressing and constraining the mother ... to do her duty for his release [!] ... In this combate, the infant and mother suffer very much, by reason that woman is a creature delicate and timorous, and not patient, of much labour', pp. 73–4. Cf. (below) Mrs Sharp's account of the loss of male virginity, and Maubray's representation of 'elegant tender' females.

11 Wolveridge; pp. 26–7, 'Therefore God dealt well with the midwives: And the people multiplied, and waxed very mighty. And it came to pass, because the midwives feared God, that he made them houses' (Exodus 1:20–1). Wolveridge's midwife's name means 'ready wit, liveliness'.

12 The 1725 edition is entitled *The Compleat Midwife's Companion* and has 'The Fourth Edition' on the title-page (British Library); the third edition appeared in 1724 (Wellcome Medical Library).

13 'To the Midwives of England', n. p.
14 See Ward, *The Whole Pleasures of Matrimony* (London, n.d. [around 1700], pp. 56–60, and Defoe's *Moll Flanders*.
15 Sharp, p. 4.
16 Rueff, 'The Preface', n. p.
17 Sharp, pp. 10–19. Mrs Sharp also provides one of the very few discussions in the literature of generation of how a man loses his virginity: 'the Nut [glans] is fastened to the foreskin ... with a ligament or bridle, which is sometimes so streight tied, and is so strong, that it will pull the head of the Yard backwards when it stands; but it is usually broken, or gives way the first time that a man lyeth with a woman, for the combate is then so furious, that a man feels no pain of it by reason of the abundance of pleasure that takes it off, otherwise doubtless the part is so quick of feeling that no man were able to endure it', pp. 27–8.
18 *Ibid.*, pp. 22–3, 214.
19 *Ibid.*, p. 5.
20 *Ibid.*, pp. 33–5.
21 McMath, *The Expert Midwife* (Edinburgh, 1694), 'Preface', n. p. 'I have of purpose omitted a Description of the Parts in a Woman destined to Generation, not being absolutely necessar [*sic*] to this purpose, and lest it might seem execrable to the more chast and shamefast, through Bawdiness and Impurity of Words', 'Preface', n. p.
22 *Ibid.*, pp. 3–4.
23 *Ibid.*, p. 7.
24 *Ibid.*, p. 12.
25 *Ibid.*, pp. 10–17.
26 *Ibid.*, pp. 21–2.
27 *Ibid.*, p. 11.
28 *Ibid.*, p. 11.
29 Maubray, the 'Dedication', pp. iv, vii–viii.
30 *Ibid.*, 'Preface', pp. x–xi; 'I have all along consider'd this to be no Work of *Eloquence*, but of *Midwifery*, or *Physick*, or *both* together, if you please', p. x.
31 *Ibid.*, 'Preface', p. viii.
32 *Ibid.*, p. 393.
33 *Ibid.*, p. 391.
34 *Ibid.*, p. 197.
35 Lovelace describes Clarissa's 'neck, her lips, her cheeks, her forehead, and her streaming eyes, as this assemblage of beauties offered itself at once to my ravished sight ... Oh, what additional charms, as I now reflect, did her struggles give to every feature, every limb, of a person so sweetly elegant and lovely!' (*Clarissa*, Everyman edition, II, pp. 503–5).
36 Maubray, p. 185. Earlier Maubray had stipulated that for a 'successful' (i.e. procreative) 'Act of Coition', as this *Affair* is to be undertaken with a serene and contented *Mind* ... so it ought to be perform'd with

Moderation and *Decency*: Not in any *brutal Manner* or *Posture*; but according to the rational *Law* and proper *Instinct* of *Nature*', pp. 54–5.

37 'The Womb is not only the *Center* but also the *Pump* of the Body', Maubray, p. 395.

38 Maubray, p. 62.

39 *Ibid.*, p. 173.

40 Lovelace says, 'heroes have their fits of *fear* . . . and virtuous women, all but my Clarissa, their moment *critical*' (*Clarissa*, II, p. 499).

41 Maubray, p. 174.

42 *Ibid.*, p. 180.

43 Burton, *Essay*, p. 390.

44 *Ibid.*, p. xv.

45 Burton copies Ould almost word for word for eleven lines in the *Essay*, pp. 13–14. Cf. Ould, *A Treatise of Midwifery* (Dublin, 1742), pp. 8–9. Burton may also have been influenced by Ould's apology for his lack of elegance: 'The candid Reader must not expect to find, either Purity of Stile, or Elegance of Expression, in this Undertaking; and I hope he will criticise more tenderly on it, when I confess, that I spent that Time which others employ in their improvement in polite Literature, in a more laborious Manner; namely, in the Dissection of human Bodies, and a constant Application to Practice. No more must be expected from me, than what is merely intelligible . . .' (*A Treatise*, pp. 4–5).

46 Burton, pp. 2–3.

47 *Ibid.*, p. 3. One is reminded of Mambrino's helmet.

48 *Ibid.*, p. 11.

49 William Smellie, *A Treatise on the Theory and Practice of Midwifery*, 3 vols. (London, 1752–64), I, pp. iv–v.

50 Burton, *A Letter to William Smellie, M.D.* (London, 1753), p. 63. Burton himself, however, is guilty of a stale culinary metaphor in his 'Preface' to the *Essay*: 'Having now given the *Bill of Fare*, I shall not detain the Reader from his Entertainment', p. xviii.

51 'But if the forehead be nearer than the *Vertix* to the middle of the brim of the *Pelvis*, every pain will force it farther down; and, when delivered, it will rise in form of an obtuse cone or sugar-loaf, and in that case the crown of the head will be altogether flat. But if instead of the *Vertix* or forehead, the *Fontanelle* should first appear, the space from the forehead to the crown will then rise in the form of a sow's back . . . And in all laborious cases, the *Vertix* comes down and is lengthened in form of a sugar loaf, nine and forty times in fifty instances', Smellie, p. 90.

52 'It so happened that, in 49 instances out of 50, the said head was compressed and moulded into the shape of an oblong conical piece of dough, such as a pastry-cook generally rolls up in order to make a pye of', Laurence Sterne, *Tristram Shandy*, ed. J. A. Work (New York, 1940), p. 150.

53 Burton, p. 68, quoting Smellie, p. 102.

54 Burton, pp. 9 and 6.
55 Burton, *Letter*, pp. 10–11.
56 Smellie, I, 'Preface', p. i.
57 *Ibid.*, II, pp. 426–7.
58 *Ibid.*, II, p. 300.

G. S. ROUSSEAU

Nymphomania, Bienville and the rise of erotic sensibility

Michelet tells us that God changed his sex in the middle of the thirteenth century. If this is true, it is nevertheless inconceivable that Chaucer's grandparents could have told us why. Similarly although less obviously, if prurience is common to all ages, as Rémy de Gourmont contends in *The Natural Philosophy of Love* (1922; translated with a postscript by Ezra Pound), erotic sensibility is not. For erotic sensuality is a removed zone from erotic sensibility: some Greek friezes display enchanting bacchanalian scenes (Keats's fair 'Attic shape'); Boccaccio's nymphs tease their victims into unrestrained sense; Rowlandson's erotic watercolours superimpose a grotesque mould on the human anatomy with the aim of elevating the cock or clitoris of even decent gazers; and the Franco-Swedish Nils Lafrenson's sensual drawings of the eighteenth century lure the viewer, by a process of calculated sympathy, to imitate the frenzied state of carnal pleasure served up to him. Every epoch has its hedonists, its sensualists, as well as possessing an invisible dichotomy between those who actually 'live the life of sense' as opposed to those who merely daydream or write about it. Even the iconography of the mythological figure Eros renders this dichotomy patent, as Joseph Kunstmann's book *Ewige Kinder*, translated as *The Transformation of Eros* (1964), abundantly testifies. Nevertheless, what distinguishes one age from another in this regard is not the quantum of its sensual erotic activity—as if such a quantum could ever be measured—but artistic and theoretical speculation about it. I want to explore the latter in a very particular context: others writing in this volume have provided an overview of sexual beliefs and practices in the period; my aim is to distinguish the epoch from other ages by showing how its deep-seated cults of sensibility helped to establish the first scientific approach to sex.

I

Here philology is instructive. Let us consider the word *nymphomania*, so common today. According to the large *Oxford English Dictionary* the first printed appearance of the word is in 1802 in an English translation of Dr William Cullen's *Nosology*, originally published in 1769. A half century earlier Samuel Johnson did not include the term in his *Dictionary of the English Language* (1755); he may not have heard of it, although this would be surprising in view of the fact that the *Dictionary* is rather complete for common medical words. But Cullen, the prominent Scottish professor of medicine, certainly knew a good deal about nymphomania by 1755 and could have informed Johnson what it was. Cullen had written about 'a condition of nymphomania', technically known as *furor uterinus* or 'mania of the uterus' in his *Synopsis methodicae* (Edinburgh, 1769), an early taxonomy of nervous diseases. According to Cullen this mania was a common female disorder, yet he does not speculate about his use of the term. Indeed Cullen may not have been aware that he was the first writer to refer to nymphomania. Decorum possibly played some role in Cullen's silence about the history and genesis of the word; more likely, doctors had been invoking the term for several decades without committing it to print and Cullen believed it required no gloss as his main readers would be medically trained.[1]

Two years after the appearance of Cullen's *Synopsis* a little-known European doctor, Bienville, published a remarkable work entitled *La Nymphomanie, ou Traité de la fureur utérine*. Printed in Amsterdam in 1771 by the daring printer of the works of Jean-Jacques Rousseau—Marc-Michel Rey—it appeared in an octavo of 168 pages.[2] Soon after publication it was reissued in 1772 in another French edition and was shortly thereafter translated into several foreign languages. It was also published as from 'Padua, January 13, 1775' in an English translation by Dr Edward Sloane Wilmot, an obscure young Englishman resident in Italy who must not be confused with the far-better-known Edward Wilmot, M.D., King George III's Physician-in-Waiting. The title-page of this translation begins with the words *Nymphomania, or, a Dissertation concerning the Furor Uterinus* ... For almost a decade I have been using a well-marked copy of the 1771 Amsterdam edition that belonged to C. K. Ogden, the twentieth-century aesthetician who collaborated with I. A. Richards in *The Foundation of Aesthetics* (1935).

Almost nothing is known about Bienville except that he lived in Holland for most of his adult life, and even this fact is cited by Michaud and others without evidence.[3] Bienville's life is actually shrouded in such obscurity that there is little point in speculating about it since there is no evidence to confirm anything, neither letters, diaries nor private papers. He wrote several other scientific works—including two treatises defending inoculation for the smallpox—but no biographical materials have been found. As the contents of the *Traité* are technical and thereby suggest that he was medically trained, he may also have practised medicine. But thus far a biographical search has failed to produce evidence of any medical degree or any mention of Bienville's name among the annals of late-eighteenth-century French social history. Bienville seems to have played no role in the Revolution, neither before nor after heads were decapitated at the Bastille. There is a brief reference to him in Richard Hunter's and Ida Macalpine's *Three Hundred Years of Psychiatry 1535–1860* (Oxford, 1963, p. 349), but nowhere else in recent psychiatric or medical-historical literature do I find him discussed. This is a curious gap for someone who ought to have attracted more attention in two hundred years. Considering this dearth of biographical material, the student of Bienville must study the *Traité* itself.

The book opens with a discussion of a subject called *metromania*, a word capable of various etymologies—including one dealing with poetic verse and numerical measure—but whose correct etymology in this instance is related to the Greek *metra*, meaning womb. This development arises because the concept *metromania* (womb fury) has been confused with *metermania* (a rage for reciting verses). The confusion is even found in as reliable a source as Dr John Quincy's *Lexicon Physico-Medicum: or, a new physical dictionary* (London, 1719; many editions by 1811) which defines *metromania* as 'a rage for reciting verse' while failing to indicate that it is a synonym for *nymphomania*.

II

Whatever etymological confusions exist, Bienville maintains that *metromania* or *nymphomania*—and he uses the terms interchangeably—'begins with a melancholy delirium, the cause of which is found in a defective matrix' (i.e., defective uterus). He argues, however, that scrutiny shows a deeper cause than 'melancholy delirium', namely 'a mental derangement caused by the imagination'. The amplification is significant for a number of reasons, primarily because this is the first treatise on nymphomania and it sets an example ascribing great powers to the 'imagination'. Bienville considers the imagination so crucial to the development of this sexual disorder that he devotes his final section, the longest and most substantial of all the parts, to a discussion of it.[4] He even considers it necessary to set down his own philosophy of imagination. It was of course an age in which the imagination had come into its own; had come under the fine lens of a microscope, as it were. Philosophers from Locke and Hartley onwards had devoted part of virtually every learned treatise to this topic, and medical and scientific writers did not lag behind.[5] Whether the topic under discussion was time, space, infinity, or memory, genius, invention, sooner or later imagination was invoked. Bienville followed in the tradition by alleging that a medical treatise, such as his purportedly was, must take its stand on 'the vexed question of imagination'.[6]

'The imagination', he writes, 'is a mirror that reflects the things which interest man and which cause him to take action.' What definition could be broader? The imagination is at once everything and nothing. The analogy of mirror and reflection was old by the 1770s, as is his subsequent contention that 'it is the imagination that is almost always the mother of the greater part of the passions and their overflow'. The imagination, as a result of this authority, must be regarded, Bienville contends, 'as the bailiff of self-respect'. In this relationship of master and slave, the passions are also enslaved to it, not the other way around. For example, masturbation—an activity that Tissot had recently considered at great length in *L'Onanisme; ou dissertation physique sur les maladies produites par la masturbation* (Lausanne, 1760; translated by A. Hume as *Onanism; or, a Treatise upon the Disorders produced by Masturbation* in 1766, it had gone through five English editions by 1781)—masturbation is also enslaved to the imagination, even though it is not literally a 'passion'. In

Bienville's *Traité* it is enslaved to the imagination to a much greater degree than in previous writers: 'this harmful mania of masturbation, of which the imagination is the *sole* contriver ...'[7] Whereas earlier medical authors speculate about the possibility of religious causes (i.e., souls possessed of the devil), Bienville will have none of this: he is a thoroughgoing mechanist who views the operations of the imagination as strictly controlling those of the passions by means of the nervous system. He therefore recommends 'still continuing the other bodily remedies' as a cure for nymphomania; and presumably he means pills and potions. But he concludes that ultimately treatment must be of 'the imagination'.

At this point perspective is supplied by standing back somewhat from the treatise. There is nothing radical or new about Bienville's medical assumptions: only a myopic medical historian possessing little familiarity with the epoch and its literature would ascribe terrific importance to these assumptions. Even the designation of the imagination as 'sole contriver' of masturbation is not so important as all that. The place where Bienville ought to stir ears and raise eyebrows today is in his choice of subject: his isolation of and emphasis on nymphomania *for the first time* and his courage in making it the subject of a whole treatise. Just this novelty of subject matter may account for the shabby reception given to the *Traité* on its publication.[8] After all, it was one thing to write, as Tissot had, about masturbation and quite another to expend so much energy on a mere female disorder. Men—especially young men—were the backbone of every great nation. Of what use could a lengthy medical work about a radical female malady be?

On the Continent the *Traité* was barely noticed, perhaps because the title was so explicit about a medical area not yet respectable; alternatively, perhaps because of the reasons I have already suggested. When it was translated into English in 1775, it was consistently savaged by a few reviewers. The comments are worth scrutinising for the history of nymphomania as well as for the history of the reception of new medical theories, and for prejudices that arise in medicine when a sexual issue is involved. Edward Bancroft (1744–1821), the American-born naturalist and spy for Franklin, attacked the treatise mercilessly. 'Neither the theory nor the practice delivered in this performance have any share of merit; and we must therefore regret that Dr Edward Sloane Wilmot (if a man of this name and description really exists) should have been so regardless of his own reputation, and of public decency, as to promote an English impression of this worthless production.'[9] Can this estimate be trusted? Bancroft reviewed books because the *Monthly* paid him by the word and because his connection with the periodical brought him to some degree of prominence. Yet it is probable that he denounced Bienville's book because Bienville was a foreigner with no known qualifications. Moreover, Bancroft may have thought this harsh treatment would please his grub-street editors who themselves knew little about medicine. Bancroft may also have been catering to the taste of readers by offering them what he thought they wanted to hear about this impolite subject.

The anonymous reviewer of the *Critical Review* derided Bienville and *metromania* with equal zeal.[10] He challenged Bienville's obeisance to Ancient medical theories, arguing that 'the Moderns'—especially his own contemporaries in England—had overtaken all others. He denounced the idea of a geographical determination of illness, in this case the notion that nymphomania is influenced by warm climates where women bask in luxury, and he demanded to know how the deviation could proceed from 'image in the mind' to 'carnal act'. But his real objections are less abstruse. He actually declares what his counterpart at the *Monthly Review* deigned not to say: namely that Bienville has no credentials *ex cathedra*, that he is an imposter in medical publication, that he is veritably to be aligned with mountebanks and other charlatans. Yet the anonymous reviewer is far from accurate himself: he reveals his own inadequate credentials when proclaiming that 'this is not the first treatise on the Nymphomania'. It may not be the first book to *mention* the *furor uterinus* but it is certainly the first tract or book devoted *exclusively* to this condition. The reviewer's inaccuracy may even transcend such flaws; he errs further by assuming that the French version of 1771 and the English translation of 1775 are two different works.

III

If indecency of subject matter was the genuine cause of disapprobation, Bienville's book of nearly two hundred pages nevertheless contains very little material of a disreputable nature. Medically speaking, it certainly is far from disreputable. Bienville's theories are traditional, based on the medical progress of two or three generations. Bienville's medical argument embodies many of the assumptions of Dr George Cheyne's *The English Malady* (1733), a treatise about 'melancholic hysteria' which does not mention nymphomania though it glances obliquely at it in a couple of passages. Yet there are considerable differences between the two that exceed the philosophic or logical domain: each author has a different sense of the relation between cause and cure—a crucial connection in psychosomatic theory—and each approaches his implied audience differently, Cheyne by politely refusing to approach any matters except the English weather directly and Bienville by laying bare his subject at the outset and then proceeding to account analytically for the formation of its chief symptoms, in this case the all-powerful imagination. Cheyne's, to be sure, is the wittier book; better written, better informed, even something of a potboiler. But more than information is at stake here and there are, additionally, differences between the British and French reading publics: by the 1770s French society—especially Parisian readers—had abandoned much of its public refinement and was eager to learn 'the truth' about sexual customs and private taboos. Deviants such as hermaphrodites and nymphomaniacs were of especial interest.

There are other differences too, some pointing to the progress of five decades of European civilisation from the 1730s to the 1770s, others more narrowly signifying the theme about erotic sensibility I consider so pertinent here. Doubtless Cheyne and his predecessors understood very well that hysterical women crave the male phallus because their imagination is inflamed and diseased. By 1730 one could read about such cases in medical literature and even view them in serious scenes of Greek erotic art as well as comic imitations. One could read about them, moreover, in Boccaccio's tales and in Aretino's sonnets, and gaze at them in Giulio Romano's illustrations of these and many other Italian sonnets. Surely the representation and availability of this body of literature and this mass of art cannot be what distinguishes the medical sensibility of Cheyne and Bienville. Nor is theirs an awareness marked by a different reading class: for if the aristocrats and wealthy classes of the 1730s had constituted a ready market for high-class erotica, by the 1770s that class had filtered downwards to include the middle class and again expanded to incorporate less sophisticated erotica. Both groups, early and late, knew about the past, knew that the Middle Ages had been permeated with disturbed young women said to be possessed by evil demons causing them to crave for male insertion; and they had yearned to such a degree that only the rites of exorcism, when successfully administered, could salvage them and bring them back to a healthy reality. Both knew something about the anatomic disturbances of the *uterus* or matrix, even about its damage at birth; and both physicians were aware that not only accidents caused late in life but violent insertion as well and occurring at any stage could cause irrevocable harm. Both men probably could have recited ancient dogma to the effect that the damaged uterus wanders through the female body wrecking organs and tissues as it marches, even if earlier ages, the Middle Ages, could not. Ilza Veith has studied these theories of the 'wandering uterus' in a useful though limited book entitled *Hysteria: the History of a Disease* (Chicago, 1965) and her results confirm this description of information available to both groups of doctors. But what is only implicit in Cheyne is explicit in Bienville—a sense of the erotic as essentially a province of the imagination—and on this difference my whole argument about erotic sensibility depends.

Moreover, the great proliferation of treatises on venereal disease in the eighteenth century—by Boerhaave, John Douglas, Jean Astruc, John Armstrong, Jourdain de Pellerin, J. Profily, J. H. Smith and many others—influenced popular conceptions of the erotic as well as works on melancholy. Aberrant sexual conditions, although they are usually the primary subject of these treatises, are referred to over and over again. There is a sense in which that age—1700–90—was ready to consume the history of *every* disease; and every history included abundant material about other conditions. Significantly, then, Bienville does not classify his chosen condition under mania or hysteria; nor does he mention even once the rampages of the uterus as a cause of nymphomania or delineate those proverbially old wanderings. Bienville's new proximate cause is 'the imagination': therefore he staunchly classifies the condition as psychosomatic. If such classification and implicit reasoning had occurred a half century later (in 1825) it would be less significant: there is nothing radical in 1823, for example, about Dr Andrew Jacob's *An Essay on the Influence of the Imagination and Passions in the Production and Cure of Diseases.*[11] Fifty years earlier it would have been, for in Bienville's 'leap' is seen a significant theoretical difference: the attribution to 'the imagination' of a whole class of sexual disorders. Before this approximate time—the second half of the eighteenth century—the imagination was credited with certain mechanical powers, but it was not considered the agent of sexual aberrations.

For such a giant step Foucault tied ribbons around Bienville's neck two decades ago in the *Histoire de la Folie* (Paris, 1961) and, more recently, in the first volume of the *Histoire de la Sexualité* (Paris, 1976). While 'the leap' appears minimal to us it was not in the late eighteenth century, for Bienville rejects an entirely mechanistic view of the nervous system and shatters the notion that a condition such as nymphomania can arise from an anatomically damaged nervous system. He does so just at the time that a materialist science of eros—we would call the science sexology, a word unknown in Bienville's time—is becoming established. Bienville does not consider the damaged brain to be a cause of nymphomania or contend that a 'diseased imagination' confounds the physiological-anatomic brain; he rather argues that the brain and imagination influence each other in some reciprocal but unspecified way. Such a mechanistic view *manqué*, defective as it appears to a late-twentieth-century audience, may also seem ambivalent to us: is it mechanistic or not? we ask. The question is simplistic in both epochs: Bienville conceived of the imagination as a less vitalistic force than we do, and the reply he would have made is that the imagination is *both* mechanistic and vitalist at the same time, a position not radically different from our stance today.[12]

This seeming defect of logic notwithstanding, Bienville's line of reason in the *Traité* is not so consistent as I may be implying. On the one hand he is a child of the times and has been enticed into the subject—nymphomania—through a concurrent fascination for the concept of masturbation. He may even have hoped to generate his own theory of masturbation.[13] Bienville wants to correlate the male and female genital zones, and then, further correlate both to the imagination in the brain, doing this as if all three categories were of a parity. This is the point in which Bienville's logic weakens: he believes that all three are more similar than dissimilar, though he nowhere says they are identical, a position we can understand only if we comprehend to what extreme degree 'the imagination' had been mechanised by 1760 or 1770. Therefore, one of the main arguments of the *Traité* is the notion that 'external objects inflame and excite the uterus', causing it 'to masturbate as a result of its vast concentration of nerve tips'.[14] During this time the vast accumulations of nerve endings succumb, the female erotic zone craves—as if it had a mind of its own—enactment of the fantasies it has enjoyed in solitude, and by a process of repetition the habit directly leads to the aberrant condition Bienville designates as nymphomania.

Given this quasi-mechanistic view of the imagination which Bienville's successors, the Romantics, rejected in favour of a far more vitalistic and organic model, Bienville's thinking is rational but not altogether logical. Stimulation leads to action, action to habit, habit to disorder. The chain seems inevitable when viewed this way, except that the nerves are rhetorically personified and endowed with such active mental properties that they cannot help but carry out the demands of the nerves, fibres and animal spirits in the erotic zone. For Bienville the physiological nervous system of man is one vast interconnecting chain; what one part knows all the others soon will, and the reader who peruses the *Traité* need not read very far to learn that by the term 'nervous' Bienville actually means something akin to 'endowed with extraordinary mental or cognitive capabilities'. So 'nervous', for example, are the anatomic extremities of the male and female erotic zones in Bienville's conception, that he cannot conceive of any physiological or mental state in which either has no contact with the brain, although he would probably have had to concede that if the central spinal cord were destroyed communication would also be impeded. The vast nervous chain would be intercepted.

The clue, then, to Bienville's theory of nymphomania is his whole sense of the role of masturbation in human life: only by cessation of it can the physician hope to cure the patient afflicted with nymphomania. Ten years before Bienville published his *Traité*, Tissot, already mentioned, had brought out a compendium entitled *L'Onanisme; ou dissertation physique sur les maladies produites par la masturbation*,[15] an anthology demonstrating the hundreds of pernicious effects produced by this allegedly vilest of human activities. Dr Tissot attributed almost every form of sexual deviance and lunatic derangement to it. Understandably he was catering primarily, although not exclusively, to a Swiss Protestant readership who wanted to hear this position stamped by the authority of a revered medical expert. But the ascription, while reaching the masses who thoroughly endorsed it, was unoriginal. More than fifty years earlier, in 1707–8, there had appeared on the other side of the Channel an anonymous *Onania; or, the Heinous Sin of Self-Pollution, and all its Frightful Consequences, in both Sexes, Considered*.[16] This book was to be reissued in more than fifteen editions before the century wore out. Each decade in that epoch had naturally produced its own fantasies about masturbation and these vary widely. The doctors mythologised in one vein, writers of fiction in another; for satirists masturbation was the scapegoat, the ultimate sin with which to charge every deceitful knave or fool. But when Bienville discusses masturbation, it is with a difference: he views it as crucial to the development of nymphomania—as a symptom—but never considers it as the genuine cause. To cure nymphomania the imagination must be directly confronted; no substitute for this confrontation exists; no medicines, no cures. Twice Bienville suggests that even religion is of limited value when compared to the magisterial importance of curing the diseased imagination.

IV

Thus we discover in a nutshell in Bienville the essence of the first psychosomatic theory of this sexual disorder. The implications of Bienville's theory, if interpreted, are consequential for the rise of erotic sensibility in Europe; not only as a way of theoretical thinking and as a manner of informal speculation about art but as another example of the ways that science reinvigorates art.[17] What remains is to relate nymphomania to erotic sensibility; and, more properly, to connect a particular development in the history of medicine with the evolution of aesthetic thought in the eighteenth century.

Before the eighteenth century there was no science of the erotic;[18] no neurological or physiological explanation of basic drives and urges except of those observed among the brutes. But in the latter case a distinction was always being drawn between the instincts of brutes and those of mankind:[19] consciousness, especially the self-reflectiveness man possessed and with which God had endowed him for a particular reason, eternally provided man with the ability to harness his basic drives and direct them upwards to the contemplation and worship of God. In general, erotic *thinking* about man was still based on religious notions. Even much erotic art of the early eighteenth century had been religiously inspired, and the physiological revolution of the previous period—discovery of the circulation of the blood, the new brain theory, the new empiricism based on a mechanistic neurology, the innovations permitted by the use of the telescope and microscope—did not drastically alter this state of affairs. As late as the seventeenth-century *fin de siècle*, a sexually hysterical woman is still labelled 'possessed demonically', not called nymphomaniacal or discussed in physiological, neurological or other medical terms.[20] This comes later, in the second half of the eighteenth century; but in the earlier period—up to about 1740 or thereabout—she is thought to possess a sick uterus that wanders through her body in search of a healthy resting place.[21] This is why learned treatises up to this approximate period continue to be written about 'the sick mother', from Renaissance times a synonym for the hysterical female organ.[22] But there exists as yet—in the 1740s—no consensus about a 'diseased imagination' aggravated by masturbatory practices as the main cause of her ravings. This transition from a religious to a scientific explanation has profound consequences in the early eighteenth century for the theory of medical insanity; and although there are traces of the scientific explanation in the psychosomatic theories of Willis and Sydenham at the end of the seventeenth century,[23] those made in the middle of the eighteenth are more substantial and capable of launching a new science of erotic behaviour.[24]

The new thinking about nymphomania in particular and sexual aberration in general could not have been formulated before the eighteenth century for reasons primarily dependent on current theories of the imagination. For European philosophers and scientists then first began to isolate the imagination from metaphysical and theological speculation and scrutinise its operations according to the laws of mechanics.[25] For a while in the late seventeenth century the imagination was treated no differently from other organs in the body: the heart, the liver, the bowels, even the genitals. This approach, based on the belief that all operations of the mind functioned no differently from those of the body, reached a peak in the 1690s. At this time the iatromathematicians (sometimes called iatromechanists) went on a rampage and quantified virtually all motions within the body, as Newton had traced the motions of the planets in the same period in the *Principia* (1687).[26] Swift's satire on 'the mechanical operations of the spirit', first published in 1710, assumes widespread knowledge of the iatromechanists and of the even more recent mechanisation of the imagination.[27] Later on in the early eighteenth century in England, literary forms other than satire present this view of the imagination to the literate layman. Akenside's *Pleasures of Imagination* (1744), a long didactic poem written by a brilliant medical mind who was also a gifted poet of the second rank,[28] is a perfect example. Contemporaries of Descartes and Hobbes a century earlier would have concurred that the imagination was important; they never would have dreamed it could assume such proportions.

Yet I think we ought not to expect theory in one realm—metaphysical speculation about the imagination—to be automatically applied to another—that of sexual disorder. A time lag was necessary for the ideas to take hold, and thinkers who could make the necessary links had to appear. After the 1730s in England, physicians and physiologists adjusted their thinking to the trend attributing medical conditions to dysfunctions of this mechanical and now more powerful than ever imagination.[29] During the previous half century, 1690–1740, disease was ascribed to a number of disturbances ranging from chemical imbalance to malfunction of the non-naturals, as Jeremiah Wainewright had shown in his *Mechanical Account of the Non-Naturals* (1707). In the period before 1690, the tendency to supply secondary or supernatural religious causes to explain many forms of disease was widespread, if not preponderant.[30] But by the time when Bienville was forming the ideas he developed in maturity—the 1750s and 1760s—the imagination had, as it were, already enjoyed its revolution and was now considered by physicians the main cause of sexual disorder. Yet it would be wrong to believe that all physicians had been persuaded, or that medical theory in the mid eighteenth century was an isolated subject incapable of influencing other subjects.[31] To the contrary, medical theory as well as practical medicine then entered into daily life no less than it does today; it was then also influencing aesthetic thought about the emotions and passions in portrait painting as well as shaping ideas about the function of sexual energy in the act of artistic creation (as is evident in a number of key passages in *Tristram Shandy*).[32]

Even the demonstration of this connection between medical theory and aesthetic thought may not satisfy those who ask what the connection is between the medical history of nymphomania as found in Bienville's *Traité* and the formation of a science of the erotic. Despite the knowledge that ultimately any satisfactory answer must take into account a sound philosophy of intellectual history, surely more than the history of ideas is at stake here. More crucial is the acknowledgement that the cults of sensibility everywhere evident in mid-eighteenth-century literature actually touched on aspects of daily life.[33] On this development everything stands or falls, even the possibility that sexual knowledge can be codified into a science.

It is necessary then to recognise that four categories of explanation have been manufactured here: a medical condition called nymphomania, the medical history, a state of human consciousness called erotic sensibility, and the actual cults of sensibility.[34] Mid-eighteenth-century authors would have understood these categories (though they did not generate them themselves) with the possible exception of the third, for they were so close to erotic sensibility that it may not have been patent. Because the manufacture of all four categories is important for a science of sex, it is crucial to understand that Cullen, a Briton, not Bienville, generated the first scientific theory of nymphomania and, moreover, that a correlative theory for male *satyriasis* would not appear until the nineteenth century.[35] Cullen was the imaginative thinker whose intuition permitted him to recognize the cause of many nervous disorders, not merely of nymphomania;[36] yet if Bienville had not published the *Traité* in 1771, more time would have elapsed before Cullen's hypothesis about the nervous origins of nymphomania could make its way into the public domain, and perhaps even a longer time until it would filter down into popular culture. Furthermore, Cullen was a pious Christian[37] and a revered member of the Edinburgh scientific-university community; but it is one thing for a thinker without status *ex cathedra* to generate a theory about sexual disorders in a polite age and quite another for a leading university professor who is also a member of the Anglican Church. Bienville's religious predilections, unlike Cullen's, are unknown; and while he lives in a country where toleration extends to nearly everyone—Holland—his treatise is addressed primarily to the Continental medical community which was then not so receptive to a theory about the 'imaginative origins' of sexual disorders as Bienville may have liked. Finally, if Bienville was indebted to Cullen, Cullen himself was indebted in his philosophical assumptions to a long train of empirical philosophers extending downwards from Locke and Hume to the Scottish School.[38] Philosophers, rather than physicians, had evolved in the eighteenth century a concept of the autonomous and quasi-mechanical imagination, and this is why psychology grew out of philosophy and why the eighteenth century is the crucial period for the genesis of this province of learning.[39] Cullen, himself one of the most philosophical of eighteenth-century doctors, inherited from his teachers in Scotland, and later on from his wide reading in philosophy,[40] a notion of the mechanical imagination which he later applied to his theory of the origins of nervous diseases. This notion is the background and basic assumption of his concept of nervous diseases.

The relevance of medicine to erotic sensibility therefore becomes patent when the relations of medicine and philosophy in the eighteenth century are scrutinised, and when Cullen and Bienville are located in the continuum of thinking about sexual problems as medical disorders. Both are more advanced than their predecessors, not more progressive in any absolute sense—according to the notion that science, like history, moves toward a perfect end—but more advanced in their knowledge of 'the nervous origins of imagination'.[41] Both men maintain precisely what Blake will deny: that the imagination is anatomically as real and discernible as the liver or spleen, except that it is lodged in the brain and therefore incapable of being considered in isolation of it. (In one passage [42] Bienville astutely asks if we do not actually feel our imagination in our head. Some of us may try to locate it there and discover nothing, but there are others, Bienville notices, who do!) The imagination is healthy or diseased: it shares these states with other organs. The diseased state arises from circumstances ranging from physiological defect such as brain damage to poor economic conditions such as the malnutrition of paupers. When such a diseased imagination focuses its energy, Bienville argues, on external erotic images—the literature or art of pornography—the brain and its vassals the nerves carry these impressions to the whole organism. Every part of the body feels it, especially where there are large clusters of nerve endings. The greater the accumulation of nerves, the greater the sensation. Now the uterus, Bienville reasons,[43] is one of these but it is not the only one; so are other highly nervous zones in the female body, as is the tip of the penis in the male. The nymphomaniac, in contrast to less 'nervous women', exercises her uterus, according to these physicians, more than other women. It is also possible that she may have a greater number of nerve clusters to begin with, but by wedding her already nervous imagination to the most highly nervous zones of her body the nymphomaniac sets a psychological motion in process that results in unremitting sexual craving.[44]

V

Erotic sensibility, however, is nowhere to be found in Bienville's *Traité*, neither as a term or as a way of thinking, for it is not a type of medical learning or scientific knowledge but a manner of applying scientific precepts to an aesthetic domain. As such, erotic sensibility can be found in the novels of the Marquis de Sade, for example, or in the poetry of Lord Byron, but not in the medical treatises of Cullen or Bienville or any other eighteenth-century physician. Yet no one should conclude from this contrast that a terrific number of steps are required to move from the one to the other: science often paves the way for art, albeit indirectly, and then sometimes allows it (art) to view itself as a science both in theory and practice.[45] At the very least it permits the view that art is based on absolute principles of craft (Plato's *techné*) or knowledge (Da Vinci's anatomical learning), and that as a consequence its laws are scientific. In this sense erotic sensibility is the science of the artist who meditates reflectively on his images, forms and ideas. There are cases, of course, in which the chain is reversed; in which the artist paves the way for the scientist by helping him to imagine his ideas in the first place: one thinks of the representations of 'flying chariots' in the Renaissance that later formed the basis for modern aeroplanes,[46] and still later of Blake's myth about the powers of Energy that antedated the concept in physics by many decades.[47] Most commonly, though, the sequence is from science to art: as in the emerging science of the erotic during the last two centuries, or what has become known in modern parlance as sexology.

There were, to be sure, nymphomaniacs before Bienville scrutinised them; but there was no reflective meditation about them. It is possible that Bienville could have published the first treatise on nymphomania a hundred years before he did—in 1671—but it is not likely. Philosophers prepared the way in the seventeenth century; doctors complemented their speculative hypotheses in the first part of the eighteenth. Now the forest was cleared for writers like Sade—who learned, incidentally, most of what he knew about erotic activity and thought from philosophers and physicians—to write *Justine*, *Sodom* and other narratives that employ an aesthetic which for lack of a more elegant phrase I call 'erotic sensibility'. There is a good reason why Sade plundered the writings of then recent philosophers and physicians like Bienville and Cullen for whole pages at one time, often inserting them into his fiction without any apology or hesitation.[48] In Sade's estimate the narrative would not be disturbed by such wholesale intrusions; it could only be enhanced because the audience expected it and wanted to be educated by it.

A single example from *Justine* must suffice for lack of space. It occurs in the section of Part One in which Dubois explains to Justine the act of love. He has already told her why certain people are more passionate than others. Now Dubois himself turns to Justine, and compares her to himself:

> . . . Because you are weakly constituted; thus you have but small desires, faint pleasures, scanty whims. But such a mediocre grade is not permissible at all in a person constituted as I am. And if my own good fortune can continue to thrive by the calamity of others, it is only because I find in this misfortune the unique stimulant that strongly pricks my nerves. Also, after the violence of this shock, it more surely induces to pleasure the electric atoms which pass through the hollow tubes in the nerves.[49]

At this point Dubois's discourse grows more technical; the reader wonders with what aims other than didactic ones (surely it is neither ironic nor comic) Sade could have written it. The passage could be lifted from a page in Bienville; indeed it was extracted almost verbatim from d'Holbach's *Système de la Nature* (1770). I take the liberty of quoting it at length because it well illustrates how outright scientific discourse (Cullen, Bienville, d'Holbach) under the right circumstances becomes artistic narrative. Separate this passage from its context, and it could derive from a contemporary text on physiology. It is even replete with ready-made scientific sources: for example, the reference to La Martinière, Louis XV's First Surgeon-in-Charge, who himself wrote several physiological works.[50] The references to nerves, animal spirits, sensations and the five senses are better suited to Cullen's or Bienville's treatises on nervous diseases than to the most erotic tale ever composed. But Sade, a writer who controls his sources, must have believed it had a place. Though lifted from d'Holbach it is found in *Justine*, Sade's most popular novel and a work of erotic sensibility *par excellence*:

> Let us now give an analysis of the nerve. The nerve is the part of the human body which resembles a white string, sometimes round, sometimes flat. It usually begins at the brain; it issues in bundles or fascicles, symmetrically arranged in pairs. There is no part of the human body more interesting than the nerve. It is the kind of phenomenon, said La Martinière, that is the more

admirable as it appears less likely of action. Life and the body—indeed the entire harmony of the body as machine—depend on the nerves. All sensations, knowledge and ideas derive from it; it is, briefly, the centre of the whole human structure. The living soul is located in it, that is to say the principle of life. This same principle dies out among animals, or at least declines in them, and is reduced to mere matter.

The nerves are imagined to be tubes carrying the animal spirits into the organs to which they are distributed. These same nerves report to the brain the impressions of external objects on those organs.[51]

Immediately following this passage is an explanation of the necessity of nervous activity for erotic pleasure, this material also lifted from d'Holbach:

An intense inflammation of the nerves excites to an extraordinary degree the animal spirits that flow into the nerve tubes which, in turn, induces pleasure. All pleasure comes this way. If this inflammation occurs on the genitals, then the pleasure is remarkable. This also explains why we enjoy nervous activity in areas close to the genitals; and why we delight in receiving blows, stabbings, pinches or floggings. These animal spirits produce painful as well as pleasurable shocks; almost by virtue of the mental sensation one has received, and as if mind triumphed over matter. Much follows, Justine, from all this: the sphere of one's sensations can be remarkably extended, as I have already suggested. These principles are sound and philosophic; not to believe in them is to yield to antiquated notions.

Now the point to be noticed is that these passages are from Sade's *Justine*, a novel, not from one of Thomas Willis's treatises on the brain, or a French anatomist's discourse on the nervous system, or Bienville's *Traité*. The important point to be gathered, as I suggested at the outset, is that there are differences between Boccaccio's nymphs and Sade's, not patent distinctions between the figures themselves but differences in the author's narrative art: in his inclusion of certain kinds of scientific or pseudo-scientific material. Moreover, in the works of Sade brothels and bawds seem to exist only to be explained in technical language, as in the passage just cited. And something of the same principle is true in paintings in which the central erotic figure—Miss O'Murphy in François Boucher's erotic painting by this name—is diminished by more interesting surroundings. If one compares, for instance, Boucher's central figure, a rather unexciting creature, with Rubens's Andromeda in *Perseus and Andromeda*, the contrast is striking.[52] Boucher's exterior surroundings command more attention by virtue of their colours and enticing texture, than does the conventionally rotund and somewhat flaccid Miss O'Murphy.

Sex in the eighteenth century then is not so simple a subject as it seems, at least not unless the cultural historian merely wishes to document particular occurrences and instances. Sex then, as today, enjoyed certain theoretical prerogatives, though these are far less evident than the 'case histories' which the social historian can isolate and document.[53] Moreover, technology and religion also influence writers and painters whose aim is to be scientific about *eros* and erotic activity, and this is especially evident in cases in which a preponderantly secular or even atheist milieu prevails upon the artist. All of us have heard many times in the twentieth century from authors such as Georges Bataille, Herbert Marcuse, R. E. Masters, W. O. Young, K. Price, Leonard de Vries, that 'the erotic' is not merely an art but a science, and that some of its deepest secrets are intermingled in the economic domain that covers the acquisition and loss of property.[54] But a question is still begged, namely, when the idea that sex and sexuality were first thought to be capable—as were the other sciences of man—of becoming scientific: hence a *science of sex*. By gazing briefly at the very first treatise on nymphomania, I have attempted to chart out a little-known chapter in the rise of 'erotic science', a subject now deemed important enough by contemporary readers to compel bookshops everywhere to carry whole sections of this type of reading. Future students of the science of sex in cultural history who genuinely hope to study the rise of the phenomenon would be imprudent to do so without recognising its eighteenth-century origins.

NOTES

1 See William Cullen, *Synopsis nosologiae methodicae* (Edinburgh, 1769), p. 324. My aim in this essay is not to provide a summary of thinking about nymphomania in the period—others who are better acquainted than I am with the social history of the age can do that—but rather to study the conditions (philosophical, physiological, anatomic, aesthetic) under which a sexual category such as nymphomania arises. Important information about the eighteenth-century legacy of the 'mania of the uterus' is found in Jean-Marie Goulemot, 'Fureurs Utérines', *Dix-Huitième Siècle* (Paris, 1980), No. 12, special issue: *Représentations de la vie sexuelle*, 97–111. Those interested in the appearance of nymphomania and other sexual behaviour in the period will gain some sense from Anon, *The Bloody Register; a . . . collection of the most remarkable trials for murder, treason . . . and other high crimes from the year 1700 to . . . 1764, inclusive*, 4 vols. (London 1764).

2 A brief survey of the many editions is useful: two editions appeared in French in 1771, the one already mentioned and another containing 164 pages, larger print, different capitalisation and punctuation, but with an identical preface. In 1772 another edition in French was published by M. M. Rey in Amsterdam, this one containing 178 pages. In 1778 Rey printed a 'Nouvelle Edition' containing xxii pages of introduction and 179 pages of text. In 1784 yet another edition appeared in French as 'published in Mentz' [sic] and containing 203 pages of text; but the only known surviving copy of this work, in the British Library, was destroyed by bombing in the Second World War, and I have consequently been unable to inspect a copy. In 1789 another edition appeared in French as 'Printed in London', though no printer's name is given on the title-page, this recension also containing xxviii pages of introduction and 198 pages of text. This edition may have been followed by an undated version sometimes called 'the Sixth Edition' printed by 'Vanderauwera' in Brussells, containing 96 pages of text and no introduction, a copy of which is in the Bibliothèque Nationale. Two English translations of Bienville's treatise are known: one published by Bew in London in 1775, another *c.* 1840, a copy of which is in the Wellcome Library in London. In 1777 van Padderburg published a Dutch translation in Utrecht; in 1782 a German translation appeared in Vienna as published by S. Hartl, followed in the next year by an Italian translation by Graziosi in Venice. No Spanish, Hungarian or Danish translations are known. Selections from Bienville's treatise are quoted verbatim in P. Dusoulier's *Avis aux jeunes gens des deux sexes, ou l'on trouve réunies les observations ... de M. de Bienville dans son Traité de la nymphomanie* (Angers, 1810). Modern studies of nymphomania such as E. Podolsky and C. Wade, *Nymphomania* (New York, 1961), I. Wallace, *The Nympho and other Maniacs* (New York, 1971) and A. Ellis, *Nymphomania* (New York, 1964) do not mention Bienville because of the authors' ignorance of eighteenth-century theories of sexuality. A reprint of Bienville's *Traité*, with a preface by Jean-Marie Goulemot, was published by Editions Le Sycomore, Paris, in 1980.

3 L. G. Michaud, *Biographie Universelle* (Paris, 1855), entry under Bienville, and August Hirsch (ed). *Biographisches Lexicon der hervorragenden Artze* (Berlin, 1929–35), I, p. 529. Nor is Bienville listed in A. L. J. Bayle and A. Thillaye, *Biographie médicale par ordre chronologique d'aprés Daniel Leclerc, Eloy ...*, 2 vols. (Paris, 1855), or in Morel de Rubempré, *Biographie des Médecins Français vivans ...* (Paris, 1826), dictionaries of biography in which one would expect to find the author of such a popular treatise included.

4 See the 'Observations de l'Imagination par rapport à la Nymphomanie', in the first edition (1771) of the *Traité*, pp. 125–54. All English translations in this essay are my own.

5 I have documented this development in 'Science', in Pat Rogers (ed.), *The Context of English Literature: the Eighteenth Century* (London,

1978), pp. 153–207; 'Nerves, Spirits and Fibres: Towards Defining the Origins of Sensibility; with a Postscript, 1976', *The Blue Guitar*, II (1976), 125–53; and, most recently, 'Psychology', in G. S. Rousseau and Roy Porter (eds.), *The Ferment of Knowledge* (Cambridge, 1980), pp. 143–210. See also Jean Starobinski, *Histoire du Traitement de la Mélancolie des Origines à 1900* (Basel, 1960), and J. V. Baker, *The Sacred River; Coleridge's Theory of the Imagination* (Baton Rouge, La., 1957). Dozens of works written in the eighteenth century make the same point; it is impossible to provide even a partial list in the space allotted here, but for works in two different genres see Z. Mayne, *Two Dissertations concerning Sense, and the Imagination, with an Essay on Consciousness* (London, 1728), and L. P. Poulten, *Imagination; a Poem* (London, 1780). These physiological traditions culminate in J. P. Marat's *Philosophical Essay on Man*, 2 vols. (London, 1773), especially in such passages as this one (II, p. 54): 'the mechanical power of the imagination is not confined to any particular organ, it is extended over the whole body'.

6 See Bienville, *Traité*, pp. 156–7. My references, though given in my own literal translations, are to the first French edition.

7 *Ibid.*, p. 174.

8 See the three paragraphs below.

9 *Monthly Review*, LIII (September 1775), 275.

10 *Critical Review*, XXIX (March 1775), 252–3.

11 Published in Dublin by C. P. Archer. Even in the 1720s several medical works attribute physiological defect to the mechanical power of the imagination, but I have found no works that consider the imagination to be the pre-eminent cause of sexual disorder; see, for example, James Blondel, *The Power of the Mother's Imagination Examin'd* (London 1729), and Daniel Turner, *The Force of the Mother's Imagination upon her Foetus in Utero* (London, 1730).

12 Although the subject is more complicated than it seems. For discussion of blends of mechanism and vitalism in eighteenth-century medico-physiological thought, see Elizabeth Haigh, 'The Roots of the Vitalism of Xavier Bichat', *Bulletin of the History of Medicine*, XLIX (1975), 72–86. Hans Driesch's *History and Philosophy of Vitalism*, trans. C. K. Ogden (London, 1914), is now outdated but contains further useful material.

13 This was a common pastime of the period among medical thinkers. See A. Comfort, *The Anxiety Makers* (New York, 1969), *passim*; E. H. Hare, 'Masturbatory Insanity: the History of an Idea', *Journal of the History of Mental Science*, CVIII (1962), 1–25; R. H. MacDonald, 'The Frightful Consequences of Onanism', *Journal of the History of Ideas*, XXVIII (1967), 423–31. R. Hunter and I. Macalpine, *Three Hundred Years of Psychiatry 1535–1860* (London, 1963), p. 349: 'by the nineteenth century the sequence masturbation–venereal excess–venereal disease–nervous disease–insanity was firmly established not only in the lay but

also in the medical mind despite an occasional rational approach like that of John Hunter (1786) to these emotionally charged matters'.

14 Bienville, *Traité*, p. 78. Further commentary on the quantities of nerve tips in the sexual zones of the human body is found in William Rowley, *A Practical Treatise on ... the Breasts* (London, 1772). In *Deformity: an Essay*, (London, 1754), William Hay, himself a dwarf, asks if the nervous system, and also the erotic zones, of deformed persons differ from those of normal men.

15 Lausanne, 1760. Material about Tissot is found in Theodore Tarczylo, '*L'Onanisme de Tissot*', *Dix-Huitième Siècle* (Paris, 1980), No. 12, special issue: *Représentations de la vie sexuelle*, 79–96, and in J.-M. Goulemot (note 1 above).

16 This book was in a fifteenth edition by 1730 and a nineteenth by 1759. The first edition may have appeared as early as 1707/8.

17 See Wylie Sypher, *Literature and Technology: the Alien Vision* (New York, 1968); I. A. Richards, *Science and Poetry* (London, 1926); G. S. Rousseau, 'Literature and Science: the State of the Field', *Isis*, LXIX (1978), 583–91.

18 A 'science of the erotic' is necessarily subsequent to a theory of the 'natural philosophy of mind'—what we would call psychology; this subject arose precisely in the middle of the eighteenth century when the erotic dimension of human behaviour was being incorporated into it. Works that deal with the matter include: David G. Loth, *The Erotic in Literature: a Historical Survey of Pornography* (New York, 1961); David Foxon, *Libertine Literature in England 1660–1743* (New York, 1965); John A. Atkins, *Sex in Literature* (London, 1970); Phyliss Kronhausen, *Erotic Fantasies: a Study of the Sexual Imagination* (New York, 1970). Jean Hagstrum's important recent book, *Sex and Sensibility: Ideal and Erotic Love from Milton to Mozart* (Chicago, Ill., 1980), says that its 'main interest is not in sources or context but in meaning', p. 253; as a consequence the role of science in relation to the rise of sensibility is omitted (see also n. 44 below).

19 As Swift imaginatively did in *Gulliver's Travels* and as did contemporary physicians; see, for example, Thomas Morgan, *The Mechanical Practice of Physick* (London, 1735), pp. 287–8; Robert Douglas, *An Essay Concerning the Generation of Heat in Animals* (London, 1747), pp. 65–6; recent studies include E. Tuveson, 'The Origin of the "Moral Sense"', *Huntington Library Quarterly*, XI (1948), 241–59; L. C. Rosenfield, *From Beast-Machine to Man-Machine: Animal Soul in French Letters from Descartes to La Mettrie* (New York, 1941); and J. A. Passmore, 'The Malleability of Man in Eighteenth-Century Thought', in Earl Wasserman (ed.), *Aspects of Eighteenth-Century Thought* (Baltimore, Md., 1965).

20 I. Veith, *Hysteria: the History of a Disease* (Chicago, Ill., 1965), but for an example from the 1690s, see David Irish, *Levamen Infirmi: ... Concerning melancholy, frensie, and madness ...* (1700), p. 94.

21 Veith, *Hysteria*, pp. 126–47. By the time Erasmus Darwin writes about 'Erotomania' in *Zoonomia; or, the Laws of Organic Life*, 2 vols. (London, 1794–6), II, pp. 353–5, the concept of the wandering uterus has disappeared.

22 Veith, *Hysteria*, pp. 121–4.

23 See L. J. Rather, *Mind and Body in Eighteenth-Century Medicine* (London, 1965); L. King, 'Soul, Mind, and Body', in *The Philosophy of Medicine* (Cambridge, Mass., 1978), ch. 6, pp. 125–51; G. S. Rousseau, 'Psychology', in *The Ferment of Knowledge* (Cambridge, 1980), p. 169.

24 This is gleaned by comparing Bienville's treatment with Jacques Ferrand's earlier work on the same subject: *De la Maladie d'amour, ou maladie érotique* (Paris, 1623), trans. in 1640 by E. Chilmead as *Erotomania, or a Treatise discoursing of the Essence, Causes ... and Cure of Love, or Erotic Melancholy* (Oxford). Edward Synge's *Sober Thoughts for the Cure of Melancholy* (London, 1742) need not be considered in this context: whereas it deals with 'love sickness' in medical terms, its point of view is theological, not scientific.

25 The trend is seen at mid-century in Frank Nicholls, M.D., *De Anima Medica* (London, 1750), and is the thesis of my study of 'Science and the Discovery of Imagination in Enlightened England', *Eighteenth-Century Studies*, III (1969), 108–35; see also: P. Gay, 'Newtons of the Mind', *The Enlightenment: An Interpretation*, 2 vols. (New York, 1963–9), II, pp. 174–85, and R. Schofield, *Mechanism and Materialism* (Princeton, N.J., 1970), pp. 134–6. For an example of pre-mechanical thought about the imagination written by a physician, see L. J. Rather, 'Thomas Fienus' (1567–1631) Dialectical Investigation of the Imagination as Cause and Cure of Bodily Disease', *Bulletin of the History of Medicine*, XLI (1967), 349–67.

26 For an example of the application to medicine, see E. Ezat, *Apollo Mathematicus: Or the Art of Curing Diseases by the Mathematicks* (London, 1695); for the body-politic see J. T. Desaguliers, *The Newtonian System of the World, the Best Model of Government* (London, 1728); for music J. de Vaucanson, *An Account of the Mechanism of ... playing on the German-flute* (London, 1742).

27 See especially the passage beginning 'To proceed therefore upon the Phaenomenon of Spiritual Mechanism ...' in A. C. Guthkelch (ed.), *A Tale of a Tub ... by Jonathan Swift* (Oxford, 1965), p. 271.

28 The mechanical images are described in A. O. Aldridge, 'The Eclecticism of Mark Akenside's "The Pleasures of Imagination"', *Journal of the History of Ideas*, V (1944), 292–314. Robert Douglas, the scientist, considered Akenside so brilliant in poetry and medicine that he dedicated his *Essay Concerning the Generation of Heat in Animals* (London, 1747) to him.

29 But not yet to sexual disorders. See n. 11 above.

30 C. Hill, *The World Turned Upside Down: Radical Ideas During the*

English Revolution (London, 1972), pp. 287–300, and K. Thomas, *Religion and the Decline of Magic* (London, 1971), pp. 787–90.

31 J. P. Marat observes at many points in his autobiographical *Philosophical Essay on Man*, 2 vols. (London, 1773), that physiology led him to medicine, and medicine to the anthropological study of man.

32 Critics of Sterne are beginning to take account of this aspect: see F. Brady, '*Tristram Shandy*, Sexuality, Morality, and Sensibility', *Eighteenth-Century Studies*, IV (1970–1), 41–56, and James Rodgers, *Tristram Shandy and Ideas of Physiology* (Ph.D. thesis, University of East Anglia, 1979).

33 Especially in *la vie d'amour* and its medical explanations; James Adair, M.D., explains in his remarkable *Essays on Fashionable Diseases* (Bath, 1786), pp. 13–14, how the influence operated: 'Upwards of thirty years ago, a treatise on nervous diseases was published by ... Dr. Whytt. ... Before publication of this book, people of fashion had not the least idea that they had *nerves*; but a fashionable apothecary of my acquaintance, having cast his eye over the book, ... derived from thence a hint, by which he readily cut the gordian knot—"*Madam, you are nervous*;" the solution was quite satisfactory, the term became fashionable, and spleen, vapours, and hyp, were forgotten.'

34 I explain the rise of the four categories in 'Literature and Medicine: the State of the Field', *Isis*, LXXII (1981), 406–24.

35 Johnson defines the word in the *Dictionary* (1755) and quotes a passage from John Floyer's *The Preternatural State of Animal Humours* (1696), but satyriasis, the sexual condition, is not discussed in medical literature until the mid-Victorian age; see J. C. Bucknill and D. Tuke, *A Manual of Psychological Medicine: containing ... Treatment of Insanity* (London, 1858).

36 J. Thomson, *An Account of the Life, Lectures, and Writings of William Cullen, MD*, 2 vols. (Edinburgh, 1859), I, pp. 269–70, 344.

37 A. L. Donovan, *Philosophical Chemistry in the Scottish Enlightenment* (Edinburgh, 1975), pp. 277–8, has produced some evidence to doubt this assertion but perhaps not enough to prove that Cullen, like Hume, was actually a sceptic.

38 Thomson, I, pp. 279–80.

39 Rousseau, 'Psychology', in *The Ferment of Knowledge*, pp. 143–209. While eighteenth-century thinkers would have called this subject 'secular natural philosophy', there is no doubt of their awareness that they are generating a new province of learning about 'psyche-logos'. To credit the nineteenth century for the rise of psychology is to locate the development far too late.

40 Moreover, Cullen had succeeded Whytt, 'the philosopher of medicine', as Professor of Medicine at Edinburgh, and was thoroughly familiar with his theories. See Thomson, I, pp. 100–16, for documentation.

41 Anti-empirical Blake denied, of course, that imagination had anything whatsoever to do with memory or the nerves; see Blake, *Milton*, 41: 3–

5, and D. Ault, *Visionary Physics: Blake's Response to Newton* (Chicago, Ill., 1974). But Blake notwithstanding, Bienville leads to a whole series of nineteenth-century hypotheses about 'nervous artistic creation' in which the artist's nervous maladies and sexual misadjustments enable him to compose; see Bernard Straus, *Maladies of Marcel Proust* (New York, 1980), and J. E. Rivers, *Proust and the Art of Love* (New York, 1981).

42 Bienville, *Traité*, pp. 157–8.

43 Bienville, *Traité*, p. 52.

44 J. Hagstrum's *Sex and Sensibility* (n. 18 above) is excellent for its fusion of ideas about sex and sensibility, but the author overlooks the physiological connections, such as those implied in the psychology of the whore or deviant.

45 Herbert J. Muller, *Science and Criticism* (New Haven, Conn., 1964).

46 See M. H. Nicolson, *Voyages to the Moon* (New York, 1948), pp. 150–200.

47 M. D. Paley, 'The Sublime of Energy', in *Energy and the Imagination: a Study of the Development of Blake's Thought* (Oxford, 1970), pp. 1–29.

48 Important reasons are supplied by Jean Deprun in 'Sade et la philosophie biologique de son temps', in *Le Marquis de Sade* (Paris, 1966), pp. 156–93.

49 This and the following passages cited below appear in Justine, *Oeuvres Complètes de Sade* (Paris, 1966–7), VII, pp. 107–9; the intentionally literal translations are mine.

50 Germain Pichant de La Martinière (1696–1783), whose many surgical and medical works appeared in the form of 'Mémoires' sent to the King.

51 Sade, *Justine*, p. 108.

52 The erotic aspects of this painting are discussed by Sir Kenneth Clark in *The Nude: a Study in Ideal Form* (New York, 1956), p. 208.

53 L. Stone, *The Family, Sex and Marriage in England 1500–1800* (London, 1977), and R. Trumbach, *The Rise of the Egalitarian Family: Aristocratic Kinship and Democratic Relations in Eighteenth-Century England* (New York, 1978).

54 G. Bataille, *Death and Sensuality: a Study of Eroticism and the Taboo* (New York, 1962), pp. 164–96. Although the assertion is impossible to document in a brief space, Edmund Burke, the alleged prophet of conservatism, was also alive to the connection of the erotic and the economic; but his most recent biographer, I. Kramnick, may go too far in *The Rage of Edmund Burke* (New York, 1977) when he argues on p. 188 for a manically repressed Burke who was also 'paranoid and homosexual'.

PETER WAGNER

The pornographer in the courtroom: trial reports about cases of sexual crimes and delinquencies as a genre of eighteenth-century erotica

This article attempts to shed some light on the genesis and development of trial reports which were printed and read because of their erotic and obscene contents. They constitute a most peculiar genre of eighteenth-century English erotica. These reports covered a wide area, including not only cases of adultery but also the salacious combination of sex and crime, such as rape and cases of sexual perversion. In addition, there were some trials of priests charged with sexual crimes which provided material for pornographic and anti-religious writings.

Within the scope of an article it is obviously impossible to give an exhaustive survey of the whole genre. Hence, the main focus will be on the cases dealing with adultery, around which a vast literature developed, with an occasional glance at a few interesting cases of 'impotency' and rape.[1]

The genesis of this type of trial report was the result of changing relations between Church and State in the seventeenth century and the concomitant emergence of a surprisingly varied crime literature. Originally and until the late 1640s, the Church tried cases of adultery, incest, ribaldry etc. in its own hierarchy of more than 250 courts, the so-called 'bawdy courts'. Charles II abolished the Courts of High Commission and the *ex officio* oath, thus removing criminal jurisdiction from the ecclesiastical courts. Matrimonial and divorce cases were transferred to the quarter sessions and assizes. This was a remarkable judicial and social revolution which was to have consequences.[2] Not only was sin now distinguished from crime, a fact which entailed considerable intellectual and moral upheaval, but the trials were also made public. Among the people who attended the sessions of the Old Bailey, for instance, which was the court trying cases of serious crime in London and the contiguous county of Middlesex, there were some who took notes of the proceedings which were then published, more or less fully, and sometimes even before sentence had been passed. As the genre of pornographic trial reports is, in essence, an offshoot of this burgeoning crime literature, its emergence from the background of crime reporting deserves a brief look.

Although as early as Elizabethan times crime chap-books were published to gratify the desire of a public yearning for news about freshly committed crimes, it was only toward the end of the seventeenth century that a diverse crime literature appeared.[3] In the early eighteenth century, several branches of crime literature can be discerned. Apart from the still very popular chap-books—for which crime was, of course, merely one topic among many others—and similar broadsheets and pamphlets, at least three other distinct branches were vying for public attention. The first, and initially probably the most important, of these were the *Old Bailey Sessions Papers* (*OBSP*), reports about the single monthly 'sessions' of the Old Bailey which were published eight times a year. The *OBSP* survive from 1674 and in their early format are very much like the chap-books, offering sensational sucker-trap titles and a lot of moral instruction. These features gradually disappeared as the Sessions Papers underwent major changes in size, content and function, from chap-book to 'sessions newspapers' to true law reports. This last stage was reached in the early 1740s when the reports contained about forty pages and were considered as quasi-official publications.[4]

The *OBSP* were competing with a parallel series of pamphlet reports written by the prison chaplains who held the post of Ordinary of Newgate, and were thus able to increase their income substantially. The accounts which these clergymen published after—occasionally even shortly before—each hanging all bear the same title, *The Ordinary of Newgate, His Account of the Behaviour, Confession, and Dying Words of the Malefactors who were Executed at Tyburn*. Although, like the *OBSP*, the format and layout of the *Account* changed considerably in the eighteenth century, its internal structure did not. Already at the beginning of the eighteenth century the *Account* had gained a semi-official station but remained a moralising tract on the backgrounds, the criminal careers, the behaviour in prison as well as the execution of the convicts who had been condemned to death at the Old Bailey.[5]

The *OBSP* and the Ordinary's *Account* were thus two very important types of a popular crime literature catering for what has been termed a 'trans-Atlantic plebeian culture'.[6] They were competing in this market not only with each other and, later on, the newspapers, but also with the specialists who turned out pamphlets of criminal lives and with the printers and hack-writers of Grub Street.[7] To make things even tougher, a third branch of trial reporting developed in the early eighteenth century which eventually eclipsed its competitors with the notable exception of the newspapers. This branch was represented by the separately published trial reports or collections of trial reports which drew on and enlarged or 'embellished' the reports in the *OBSP* and the Ordinary's *Account*.[8] It was this branch which developed a particular kind of trial reporting which was soon to turn into pornography. Concentrating initially on cases involving crime in combination with sex, such as rape, incest or adultery followed by murder, the focus then slowly shifted to the sexual aspects in the trials. The advantage which this new branch had over its main competitors was its relative independence, which the others, given their quasi-official status, did not have. In the case of the chaplain of Newgate, it was obvious that his *Account*, albeit not devoid of luridness, was unable to compete in a market which demanded erotic or obscene details. The same was true to a lesser extent for the *OBSP*, although they put up a long fight and in the eighteenth century continued to include cases of bigamy, incest, rape and sodomy.[9] But the reporting of these cases did not differ in length or format from others, such as murder for instance. The separately published trial reports, however, were usually much longer than the *Sessions Papers*, relying on their salacity as a means to interest readers. The following pages will try to trace the development of this genre of erotica by outlining the major changes which can be discerned in the eighteenth century.

Although not an invention of the eighteenth century, the numerous so-called 'crim. con. cases', which are almost a hallmark of the era, were successfully exploited as potential pornographic material. Until the Matrimonial Causes Act was passed in 1857, a husband could bring an action for damages against his wife's paramour, an action for criminal conversation ('crim. con.'). This was a common law suit, and the damages were at times extraordinary. The new act abolished this procedure. From the time of Henry VIII, divorces attracted much attention, especially if those involved were the high and mighty and if the case had to do with criminal conversation, impotence or sexual perversion. In order to get a private divorce bill through Parliament, it became usual after the Norfolk case in 1700 to require a crim. con. judgement in the courts beforehand.[10] Around the turn of the century, public taste had already been whetted by some publishers, notably John Dunton and Edmund Curll, who had quickly noticed the existence of a section of the reading public interested in the obscene details that can be found in the trial reports of some unusual cases in the seventeenth century.[11] Without realising it, Curll found another goldmine in 1714 which he and others began exploiting soon afterwards. He published two volumes on the trial between the Marquis de Gesvres and his wife, Mademoiselle Mascranny, a case which in 1712 was 'more taken Notice of all over Europe, than any case of the same Nature hitherto known'.[12] Mademoiselle Mascranny charged the Marquis with impotence after three years of cohabitation and pleaded for nullity of the marriage. The first volume contains the plea of her ladyship, the interrogation of the spouses, the reports of the physicians searching the Marquis, as well as a few remarks on 'The Difference between a Maid and a Widow'. Medical reports in the divorce trials played an important part in the sale. Playing on the reader's prurient interest, the 'physicians's account' was frequently mentioned on the title-page and—as in this case—made obvious in the text by special print.[13] The next volume offers a similar arrangement of documents from the trial complemented by a discussion of virginity, 'artificial maidenheads' and 'Examples of some remarkable Cases of natural Impotence'. The pseudo-scientific and essentially pornographic contents of the two volumes as well as the person of the Marquis, who was descended from one of France's best families, were supposed to attract readers. The case must have appealed to the prurient for several reasons. Like many others of its kind, it highlighted the sometimes bizarre sex life of the aristocracy while at the same time exposing them to ridicule. In addition, a lady charging her husband with impotence was a rare event indeed. To make it even more attractive, this work contains quite a few blows against France's aristocracy, with two of its members (the Marquis and his father) shown as impotent and the king sharing a mistress, Madame de Maintenon, with a duke.[14]

Surprised but extremely pleased at the public response to this trial report, Edmund Curll immediately searched England's 'Law-Books and Historians, to see what adjudg'd Cases and Precedents we had of the same Nature', and then informed the public that the case of the Earl of Essex and the Lady Howard was 'the most considerable in our English History'.[15] The volumes of *The Case of Impotency* which appeared in 1715 presented the reader not only with documents from and about the Essex trial (in volume I), but also with such pertinent examples as 'The Case of John Bury, Esq. who was Divorced for want of his Testicles'. Volume II contained the trial for sodomy of the Earl of Castlehaven as well as that of his servants, and introduced a new case which had caused much talk before the turn of the century. It was that of Henry Howard, seventh Duke of Norfolk, and Lady Mordant. The Duchess had several affairs after she was married to the Duke in 1677. In 1685 he separated from her but did not succeed in divorcing her until 1700 because of the influence of her first cousin, the Earl of Peterborough.[16] These two volumes are an excellent example of the way in which partly obscene and pornographic material could be sold under the veil of legal and/or scientific documents. The arrangement of the title-page is remarkable, containing the gist of the content and promises of titillating disclosures, such as 'The Report of the Seven Matrons appointed to search the Countess'. Essentially, this publication was aiming at an audience interested in sensation and sex. *Cases of Divorce for Several Causes* which also appeared in 1715 is another collection of trials for divorce and crim. con. This book, republished in 1723, focuses on the life, affairs and divorce of Robert Feilding but also contains the cases of John Dormer, Esq. and of Sir George Downing. The last chapter is again on the famous Essex trial, containing 'Depositions in the Lady Howard's Case'. That Edmund Curll should have selected Beau Feilding's case is hardly surprising. His trial is one of the first in the eighteenth century to be exploited for its sexual matter, such as Feilding's bigamy.[17] Until Lord Hardwicke's Marriage Act of 1753, bigamy was facilitated by the fact that marriage was valid without banns or licence, at any time, at any place; not even a clergyman was required. No wonder then that a trade sprung up in alehouses and other places of ill repute. London was a paradise for fortune hunters of both sexes and incitement to bigamy as well as fictitious marriages for purposes of seduction were common. The Marriage Act put an end to this traffic.[18]

Meanwhile, Edmund Curll continued to find a sufficiently large reading public for the books on divorce trials and related material. This interest on the part of the readers is borne out by the publication in 1732 of two books, the first one a collection of treatises on adultery, divorce and polygamy, and the second one offering yet another divorce trial report. *The Cases of Polygamy* is unique in that it is one of the first works in the eighteenth century of a genre that might perhaps best be described as matrimonial or quasi-matrimonial writings, many of them published because of their discussion of sexual matters.[19] The second book to appear in 1732, *The Cases of Impotency and Virginity*, was so successful as to justify a second edition which was published the same year by John Crawford. It is mainly concerned with Catherine E. Weld, alias Aston, who, after three years of marriage, charged her husband, Edward Weld, with impotence. 'The Appendix of Parallel Cases' again exploits the well-known divorce trial of the Earl of Essex by including portions of the proceedings. In addition, the reader could study 'A collection of precedents, showing, what are the real proofs of impotency'. This section of chapter vi together with chapter iv, which presents the reports of the surgeons who inspected the couple, contain the sexual material indicating the great concern such cases must have caused to male readers. In the eighteenth century, a case in which a man found himself charged with impotence hit the very core of male pride and endangered the established hierarchical order. Although in the seventeenth and eighteenth centuries one tended to ridicule such unfortunate men, it is worth noting that in Mrs Weld's case and in others of a similar nature the text almost always includes implicit attacks on women who dared to question their husband's sexual powers. Thus, after an initial shock, the masculine pride is restored by a section in the book which attempts to prove 'that there are no certain signs of virginity in women'.[20]

Edmund Curll had thus well prepared the ground for others to follow. The reading public at the beginning of the fourth decade of the eighteenth century were more ready than ever to treat trial reports as entertainment. The publishers in turn were beginning to make changes in the presentation of their material in order to cater for and accommodate the tastes of their customers. By 1730 the eighteenth century had a great many cases of criminal conversation of its own providing the publishers with excellent sources for their purposes. One case in particular, which occurred between 1729 and 1730, caused much stir in London's polite world and was reported in all the newspapers. It was the trial of Colonel Francis Charteris. Exhibiting the prevailing attitude toward rape among the male members of the upper class, this unusual trial also yields a good picture of contemporary social mores. At the same time it provides us with an example of the leniency which noblemen could expect, even if convicted of a rape. Charteris was charged in 1729 with the rape of Ann Bond, a spinster who had been in his service only a few days when he began to make improper advances. Ann Bond told the court

That on the 10th of November, the Colonel rung a Bell and bid the Clerk of the Kitchen call the Lancashire Bitch into the Dining Room, That she going in, he bid her stir the Fire, while she was doing it, He lock'd the Door, and took her and threw her down on the Couch, which was nigh the Fire, in the farther Corner of the Room, and forced her down with Violence, and lay with her; that she shove what she could, and cry'd out as loud as she could, and he took off his Night Cap and thrust it into her Mouth, and then had carnal Knowledge of her.

The court then insisted on further details of what had happened:

Being asked whether the Prisoner had his Cloathes on? She reply'd, he was in his Night Gown. —— Being asked whether she had not her Petticoats on? She reply'd, yes; but he took them up, and held her down upon the Couch —— Being asked, whether she was sure, and how she knew he had carnal Knowledge of her? She reply'd, she was sure he had, and that he laid himself down upon her, and entered her Body. —— She was also asked how it was afterwards? She reply'd, that there was a great deal of wet.... That he endeavour'd to pacify her with Promises of a great many fine Cloaths, &c. if she would hold her Tongue, and say nothing of it.[21]

Since other servants confirmed Ann Bond's deposition, Charteris was found guilty and sentenced to death. This was quite a shock, as it was unusual for a gentleman to be punished in such a harsh way for what many contemporaries considered an act of gallantry. Bond's lawyer remarked in his opening speech that servant girls being raped by their masters 'were now-a-days made little Account of by too many Persons of Levity'.[22] Like many other upper-class males, Charteris seduced and raped a sizeable number of country girls in his service. Generally, he preferred lower-class women and girls for his sexual adventures, for it was easier that way to escape prosecution, and pregnant women could always be 'hushed up' with money. One result of this habit of upper-class males which they considered a part of their amusement and entertainment was a high rate of infanticide. The prize for what the upper class termed gallantry was thus paid by servant girls who would rather kill their own babies than face the common fate of pregnant servants, which was prostitution. If some servants rejoiced after the sentence which Charteris received, they were soon silenced, for he had friends among the aristocracy who persuaded the king to pardon him in April 1730, another proof of the dominating opinion among the nobility that raping a servant was a gallant adventure at best and a misdemeanour at worst, but certainly not a crime.[23]

By the fourth decade of the eighteenth century, newspapers had become a strong competition for the publishers of crim. con. cases and similar trial reports. For obvious reasons, the papers were hard to beat in the race for readers. More often than not, the publishers of books had to be content with commenting on or satirising affairs which had previously been exploited by the papers. As a consequence, very few trial reports appeared in book form between 1737 and 1770.[24] The case to end this long and dry spell for the publishers was reprinted because its success was guaranteed by the fact that the whole of England was talking about it. It was *The Trial of His R.H. the D. of C. July 5th, 1770 for Criminal Conversation with Lady Harriett G...r* and appeared in 1770. This trial report about the Duke of Cumberland and Lady Grosvenor went into more than five editions. The Earl of Grosvenor recovered £10,000 damages when the Duke was found guilty of criminal conversation with the Countess of Grosvenor.[25] The publisher of the trial report endeavoured to make his work more entertaining with the help of editorial comments. As a matter of fact, this publication is another big step forward toward the presentation in the last two decades of the century of trial reports as pornographic and erotic literature. 'Adultery is become so fashionable,' writes the editor in his introduction, 'and Divorces so frequent, that it may admit of some debate in the polite world whether the first is criminal or the latter dishonourable.' He then launches into a discourse 'of the punishment of adultery and the uncommon progress of that Crime', informing the reader that Lady Grosvenor's love affairs (she had had a 'familiar connexion' with the Duke of York before) were a partial consequence of the fact that her 'marriage was not a match of her own choice, but strongly recommended to her by her parents'.[26] After a few ironic remarks on the venereal diseases among the male members of the royal family and the aristocracy the actual trial report provides a detailed account of the meetings of the Duke and Lady Harriett as well as the letters between the two. The affair came to light when letters were intercepted:

> Several of Lord G——'s servants went down to St. Alban's with his lordship's brother, who, upon breaking open the door at the inn, found the D. of C. sitting on the bed-side along with Lady G——, with his waistcoat loose, and the lady with her Dress unbuttoned, and her breasts wholly exposed.[27]

In the years to follow, only cases involving well-known personalities appeared as reprints. Cases of adultery and divorce of commoners had to have an element of perversity to attract the publishers, such as the divorce in 1771 of the nymphomaniac Mrs Draper.[28] An affair of the Earl of Lauderdale was made public in 1776 under the title, *She is and she is not: a Fragment of the true History of Miss Caroline de Grosberg, alias Mrs. Potter ... Together with an Account of the Proceedings in the Process she commenced against his Lordship, and the Substance of the Evidence on both Sides*.

The genre of pornographic trial reports was fully developed in the late 1770s, a fact which is borne out by the publication in seven volumes of a special collection of interesting cases, *Trials for Adultery: or, the History of Divorces. Being Select Trials at Doctors Commons, For Adultery, Fornication, Cruelty, Impotence, &c* (London, 1779–81). These trials were recorded in shorthand, 'by a Civilian', and the collection claimed to be a 'complete History of the Private Life, Intrigues, and Amours of many Characters in the most elevated Sphere'. The editor remarks to the reader that 'conjugal infidelity is become so general that it is hardly considered as criminal; especially in the fashionable world'. In view of the many erotic and obscene prints contained in the seven volumes, the moral justifications offered in defence of the publication of the trial reports appear quite ridiculous if not hypocritical.[29] Mostly erotic but occasionally also obscene, such pictorial material now became a standard feature of trial reports for the rest of the century. The various prints and etchings indicate how far the genre had developed in a few decades. Illustrating erotic encounters of lovers accused of adultery, they are also a sign of the willingness on the part of the publishers to cater for an audience that was now demanding more stimulation than mere words. Some advertisements of the early 1780s bespeak the importance of the pictorial material in the sale of trial reports. *The Trial of Isaac Prescott ... for the most brutal and unheard of Cruelties inflicted on ... his Wife* was offered with the promise of a frontispiece. So was *The Trial of the Reverend Mr. James Altham ... for Adultery, Defamation, and Obscenity ...*, in which the frontispiece showed the Rev. Mr Altham 'in an indecent Situation, endeavouring to force Mrs. Ann Tavner', and 'an amorous Scene between him and Ann Saunders'.[30]

There was one crim. con. case which became the talk of the 1780s, producing astonishing literary activities. It was the action between Sir Richard Worseley and George M. Bisset. Sir Richard was made the laughing-stock of his age because he demanded £20,000 damages from Bisset, one of his wife's many paramours, but the trial report informs us that 'the jury ... returned with a Verdict for the Plaintiff, giving him only *One shilling Damages*'. The report also contains an incident which became very well known in the upper class. Bisset's lawyer could prove that 'at the Bath at Maidstone ... the Plaintiff ... had absolutely raised the Defendant upon his Shoulders to view his naked Wife while bathing ... on coming out ... [she] joined the Gentlemen; and they all went off together in a hearty laugh'.[31] This scene immediately appeared in etchings and became the focal point of several erotic-satirical poems some of which concentrated on Lady Worseley's love affairs and Sir Richard's habit of showing his sometimes naked wife to other gentlemen.[32]

The next years witnessed the publication of trial reports on cases with spectacular sentences. In a trial for criminal conversation Mr Foley, the plaintiff, received £2,500 damages from the Earl of Peterborough. Like the Ladies Grosvenor and Worseley, Lady Foley became one of the 'noble whores' of the century celebrated in mostly erotic poems and lampoons. Her numerous love affairs are the subject of *The Life and Amours of Lady Ann F–l–y* which also contained the juicier depositions of the crim. con. trial.[33] John Motherhill, charged with 'committing a rape on the body of Miss Catherine Wade', was acquitted in 1786, although the prosecution was able to prove that he did rape the victim; and in 1789 a Mr Cooke, accused of adultery with Mrs Walford, had to pay £3,500 damages to Mr Walford.[34] In the same year Francis Plowden published his monumental *Crim. Con. Biography* in twelve volumes which included numerous erotic prints.[35] Foreign visitors touring London before the turn of the century frequently expressed their disbelief at the popularity of crim. con. literature and related trial reports which were now sold and read as pornography. A German visitor with apparently strong moral principles

Plate I

remarked that 'the most scandalous literature in London consists of the reports of Crim.-Con. and Divorce Cases which are printed without expurgation. No book is asked for so frequently in the lending library, and the editions, reprints and extracts from them prove their popularity.'[36] Clearly, the publishers of trial reports were profiting from the increase of literacy and the concomitant interest of the middle stratum of eighteenth-century urban readers in the sexual peccadilloes of the nobility.[37]

The apogee of the development of this genre toward pornography was reached with the publication in 1793 of *The Cuckold's Chronicle*. The select trials for adultery, incest, ravishment etc. which are presented in two volumes are not merely reprinted or reported. In order to ensure that his readers received the best possible entertainment, the editor cut out 'longueurs' in speeches and in parts dealing with moral issues. Instead, he added generous comments of his own which are mostly ironic in kind. In the trial of Mrs Errington, for instance, several statements of witnesses are ridiculed by editorial remarks. Fun is also poked at a scene in which Mrs Errington and a parson were together in a bedroom. Some of the editor's comments add to the bawdiness of the publication. Describing Mrs Errington's gallant adventures with Captain Southby, he gives his own interpretation of the deposition of Molly Mitchell, a witness who confirmed that her mistress and the captain had had 'carnal knowledge of each other' at the occasion of a dinner at Mrs Errington's house. 'Mrs. Errington', writes the editor,

> paid but little attention to her dinners, when matters of more consequence were transacting. We cannot absolutely say how she was engaged while the repast was cooling, but we can give a shrewd conjecture; and Molly Mitchell appears to favour our opinion. The Captain and she, it is supposed, were taking a wet and relish together; or he might probably be instructing her in some new evolutions, with the modern methods of attack and defence. She is a woman who thirsted after knowledge, and if the Captain had any thing new to communicate, she was sure to pump it out of him. Molly Mitchell supposes the Captain discharged his musket, for, though she did not hear the report, she smelt the powder; and Mrs. Errington appeared to have been very much heated in the engagement.[38]

In addition to these comments, the trial itself contained numerous pornographic passages describing Mrs Errington's sexual adventures with her lovers. Ideally suited for the readership of the *Cuckold's Chronicle*, the trial report portrays adultery as a highly entertaining pastime very much enjoyed by the fashionable world. Many erotic and some obscene prints depiciting 'the most striking scenes' were supposed to add a little more spice to the work. It is indicative of the intentions of the *Cuckold's Chronicle* that less interesting cases with hardly any obscene material are 'pepped up', so to speak. In the trial report about the case Cooke versus Walford, in which Mr Walford's shock at the adultery of his wife is adequately expressed, the editor notes at the end that

> there has been so much morality in the course of this trial, through the channel of the counsel's speeches, and the judge's charge, that anything more of that kind would be superfluous. However, to simple readers, and those unacquainted with the law, the invalidated part of Mr. Eyre's evidence, relative to Mr. Walford's kicking up of Mrs. Walford's petticoats, is a part that, we are persuaded, must still remain a mystery.[39]

The hint about Mr Walford's 'kicking up his wife's petticoats' refers to the statement of J. Eyre in whose presence the proud Walford displayed his wife's shapely legs. This scene was selected by the *Cuckold's Chronicle* for a print, thus giving more attraction to an otherwise less interesting case.[40]

Trials for criminal conversation during that period also appeared in abbreviated form in erotic magazines which seemed to thrive on the sexual content of the cases and the accompanying obscene prints. The first number of *The Rambler's Magazine; or, The Annals of Gallantry, Glee, Pleasure, and the Bon Ton* was published in 1783 and then continued into the nineteenth century with the title of the magazine changing occasionally. Nearly every number has extracts, of varying lengths, from trials in progress or just concluded.[41] However, the most important of these predecessors of *Playboy* was *The Bon Ton Magazine; or, Microscope of Fashion and Folly*. Its first volume appeared in 1791 and contained passages from numerous trials. This pattern was kept up in all volumes until 1795.[42] *The Rambler* was followed in 1795 by *The Ranger's Magazine; or, the Man of Fashion's Companion*. Among other items, the title-page promised the reader 'the annals of gallantry, essence of trials for adultery, crim. con., seduction, doubles entendres'.[43] The number of this kind of magazine increased appreciably after 1800.[44]

One of the last trial collections of the eighteenth century appeared with the publication in 1799 of the first volume of R. Gill's *A New Collection of Trials for Adultery: or, General History of Modern*

Mrs. SKINN, with Mr. BROWN, the Attorneys Clerk at Hull in Yorkshire.

A
NEW COLLECTION
OF
TRIALS *FOR* ADULTERY:
OR,
GENERAL HISTORY
OF MODERN
GALLANTRY AND DIVORCES.

CONTAINING

A VARIETY OF THE MOST REMARKABLE TRIALS,
Heard and determined in the Courts of *Doctors' Commons*, the *King's Bench*, &c. &c. for

ADULTERY, FORNICATION, CRUELTY,

AND OTHER

CRIMINAL CONVERSATION, &c. &c.

To obtain Divorces or Damages,

FROM THE YEAR 1780, TO THE PRESENT TIME.

INCLUDING

THE EVIDENCE ON EACH CAUSE, AND THE CORRESPONDENCE BETWEEN THE AMOROUS PARTIES.

THE WHOLE FORMING

A Complete History of the Private Lives, Intrigues, and Amours, of many Characters in the most elevated and other Spheres of Life; as every Scene and Transaction, however Ridiculous, Whimsical, or Extraordinary, is faithfully represented by the Editor, who was determined not to sacrifice Truth either at the Shrine of Guilt or Folly.

Taken in Short Hand, from the *Records* of the *Courts* of *Doctors' Commons*, the *King's Bench*, &c. &c. and arranged for Publication, with impartial Reflections upon the various Cases,

By a *CIVILIAN of DOCTORS' COMMONS.*

EMBELLISHED with an ELEGANT SET of PLATES, Representing the most striking Scenes described in the Work, whether Humourous, Ridiculous, Whimsical or Amorous.

London:

Printed, for the Proprietors, and sold by J. GILL, at No. 16, in *Paternoster-Row*; and may be had of all the Booksellers, &c. in every Part of England, Wales, Scotland and Ireland.

1799.

Plate II

Gallantry and *Divorces*. Claiming to present a 'complete history of the private lives, intrigues, and amours, of many characters in the most elevated and other spheres of life', the compiler of the trial reports promised his readers 'impartial Reflections upon the various Cases ... Embellished with an Elegant Set of Plates'.[45] Like the frontispiece, these plates were all erotic or obscene depicting amorous scenes from trials between 1780 and 1799. Volume two of this collection, 'including all the most remarkable Trials from the year 1780, to the present year 1802', was published in 1802. It had three erotic prints and listed the names of the parties in the trials on the title-page.[46]

Around the turn of the century, then, crim. con. cases and similar trial reports had fully developed as a genre of erotica. Published primarily because of their frequently obscene contents, they appeared not only in books, brochures and collections; the magazines and newspapers, too, gave more or less full accounts of such cases, with the word *Crim-Con.* in large type above the actual articles.[47] With the press as well as the book publishers vying for the reader's attention with crim. con. cases, the genre took a last turn in 1830 before being finally stopped by the activities of the vice societies and the Matrimonial Causes Act of 1857.[48] On 20 November 1830 appeared the first number of *The Crim. Con. Gazette; or, Diurnal Register of the Freaks and Follies of the Present Day*.[49] Mainly, though not exclusively, concerned with the reports of trials for adultery and divorce, this publication changed into *The Bon Ton Gazette* in its eighth number and flourished until 1831.

It bespeaks the preoccupation of the eighteenth century that trial reports containing sexual material were published and read for erotic reasons. Starting as a rather slow trickle in the seventeenth century, the genre was gradually shaped after 1700 and eventually flowed as a full stream in a century virtually obsessed by sex. Several factors in the eighteenth century produced a climate of deep sexual interest which called for the production and distribution of sex literature. To begin with, many people in the upper class led a life which was marked by permissiveness if not licence and stood in sharp contrast to the behavioural patterns which were prevalent in the middle stratum of eighteenth-century society. The phase of licentious sexual behaviour among the aristocracy began at the court of Charles II where sexual promiscuity was almost a hallmark of fashion. Whether or not this astonishing 'release of the libido' in the eighteenth century is to be seen as a direct reaction against a 'Puritan ascetic morality' of the previous century is not altogether clear.[50] Of equal, if not more, importance for the increasing interest in sexual matters was the eighteenth-century habit among the aristocracy in particular to arrange marriages with a view to money and influence. The personal feelings of the parties concerned were rarely considered. As a consequence, very many men had extra-marital affairs, and an ever increasing number of women did the same. Lawrence Stone has argued that lower down in the social hierarchy, marriages were in the majority of cases 'based on prior personal affection, sexual attraction or love' and that when this 'attraction eventually dried up ... many husbands sought variety elsewhere'.[51] While this may have been so, one should not underestimate the exemplary position of the aristocracy and the attempts of the lower echelons of the nobility to imitate fashionable attitudinal or behavioural patterns. In the eighteenth century it became a common practice and eventually a status symbol for the London aristocrats to keep one or even several mistresses. This in turn had an impact on social as well as moral values. Given the frequency of extra-marital relations, a word like *adultery* almost lost its former connotation with sin. The new usage of words of love was partly influenced by French romances of seventeenth- and early eighteenth-century origin: formerly negative words were upgraded. Thus, adultery became *gallantry*, a love affair was an *amour*, and an attempt at seducing someone was labelled *intrigue*. The titles of the published divorce trials bear witness to this gradual change of usage and, in particular, to the euphemistic application of the term *gallantry* to what in essence was nothing else but adultery.[52] Other features contributing to the treatment of sex in the various genres of literature were the excesses of the beaux, rakes and libertines, and a growing wish to recognise the needs of the body—including its sexual needs. In addition, one ought to consider the amount of leisure time available to many members of the upper social stratum, who had very little, if any, sexual interest in each other. A writer of the time commented on this aspect, arguing

> It is a melancholy reflection that infidelities are much more frequent among people of elevated rank, than those of a less exalted station ... A superintendance over domestic concerns engrosses much of the time and attention of those who act in a more humble sphere, so that they have neither leisure nor inclination to ingage in any intrigue. On the other hand, the lady of

fashion abhors the idea of attending to domestic matters; she leads a life of dissipation, her hours hang heavy upon her hands, and she knows not how to kill time—An eternal round of sameness and insipidity disgusts them; and, as a refuge from *Ennui*, they form a connection with one in nearly the same insipid line. The intrigue keeps attention alive, and the parties, having a sort of business on their hands, drive on at an extraordinary rate, till, by growing too bold, they cannot escape destruction; and a trial from Crim. Con. and afterwards a divorce, as naturally follow.[53]

To be sure, there is plenty of evidence suggesting substantial differences of moral and intellectual attitudes between the aristocracy and the gentry on the one hand, and the nobility and commoners of the middle stratum on the other hand. One also has to take into account London's exceptional position which meant that attitudinal and behavioural patterns were rather different in the country. While the gentry and the middle stratum, for various reasons, may have been unwilling or unable to emulate the sexual behaviour of their social betters, we are still confronted with the phenomenon of an enormous amount of homespun English pornography in the eighteenth century (France continued to be a major supplier until the 1750s and even beyond) which was one consequence of the existing interest in sex and the needs arising from it, especially among the literate. It is quite possible that this literature served as a kind of 'ersatz' for the less fortunate people, who were trying to imagine what it would have been like to live a life of free-wheeling sexual promiscuity. The evidence of the trial reports, in particular the prefaces and the moral justification for their publication, would suggest that this sort of literature was read above all by the male literates lower down in the social hierarchy. They were admiring and possibly also hankering after the extra-marital liaisons of the rich and mighty, which they could not afford to have.

It is obvious that most members of the upper class had not as urgent a need as the lower echelons of society to be acquainted with the sexual adventures of people of their own kind. For the former did in everyday life what others were reading about. It is a moot point whether such pornographic material as the trial reports contained could satisfy the needs of a large number of people from various walks of life. There are some indications that the trial reports, for instance, did fulfil such alleviating functions. This is a rather tricky ground, however, for even today we do not know what pornography does, or if it has any consequences at all. As to the eighteenth century, its pornography was not merely a consequence of an obvious obsession with sex. It was also a prolongation of this obsession which had been created by changing attitudes and behavioural patterns, thus allowing the literate to indulge their favourite preoccupation. It is therefore also possible to detect in this pornographic literature some reflections, albeit slightly distorted, of the prevailing attitudes and ideas relating to sexual issues of a large and influential section of eighteenth-century society.

It is, of course, also true that eighteenth-century pornography, like all pornography, exploited existing human needs. Edmund Curll, for instance, cashed in on the knowledge that the topic of sex is a powerful one and would attract, time and again, even disappointed customers. Thus, the erotic and pornographic literature of eighteenth-century England remains an immensely rich and varied field with many open questions. Introducing the genre of trial reports, the present article has made an attempt to show that the field deserves to be studied. If this attempt has any success, it will perhaps spark off additional investigations which may eventually prove the significance of a literature that has been unjustly neglected.

NOTES

1 I will cover the whole genre more extensively in a study of eighteenth-century English erotica which I hope to conclude some time in 1982. ISR = Institute for Sex Research, Bloomington, Indiana (who supplied the illustrations); BL = British Library.

2 See G. R. Taylor, *Sex in History* (London, 1959), p. 146; Christopher Hill, *Society and Puritanism in Pre-Revolutionary England* (London, 1964), Ch. 8.

3 On the reporting of crime in the eighteenth century see Robert Collison, *The Story of Street Literature* (London, 1973), ch. 3; G. A. Cranfield, *The Press and Society* (London and New York, 1978), ch. 3; John H. Langbein, *Prosecuting Crime in the Renaissance: England, Germany, France* (Cambridge, Mass., 1974), especially pp. 45–54 on crime chap-books; *idem*, 'The Criminal Trial before the Lawyers', *The University of Chicago Law Review*, vol. 45, No. 2 (winter 1978), especially pp. 265–70 on the *Old Bailey Sessions Papers*; Leslie Shepard, *The History of Street Literature* (Newton Abbot, 1973); and R. M. Wiles, *Freshest Advices: Early Provincial Newspapers in England* (Cleveland, Ohio, 1965), ch. 8.

4 On the exact titles, the development and the location of the *OBSP*, see M. D. George, *London Life in the Eighteenth Century* (London, 1966),

p. 430; Gerald Howson, *Thief-Taker General: the Rise and Fall of Jonathan Wild* (New York, 1970), p. 325; and Langbein, 'The Criminal Trial'.

5 See Peter Linebaugh, 'The Ordinary of Newgate and his Accounts', in James S. Cockburn (ed.), *Crime in England: 1550–1800* (London, 1977), pp. 246–69.

6 *Ibid.*, p. 256.

7 See Philip Pinkus, *Grub Street Stripped Bare* (London, 1968), and Stanley Morison, *The English Newspaper* (Cambridge, 1932), which offers an historical survey.

8 For a list of such trial reports, see Howson, *Thief-Taker General*, pp. 321, 324–5; and Langbein, 'The Criminal Trial', p. 268 n. 24.

9 Cf. the cases cited by Langbein, pp. 267, 287, 301.

10 See Ivan Bloch, *Sexual Life in England Past and Present* (London, 1958), pp. 15, 70–9; and Roger Thompson, *Women in Stuart England and America* (London and Boston, Mass., 1974), pp. 170–1.

11 On Dunton and Curll, see Pinkus, *Grub Street*; and the list of Curll's publications in Ralph Straus, *The Unspeakable Curll* (London, 1927).

12 *The Case of Impotency*, 2 vols. (London, 1714), p. 2; ISR.

13 *Ibid.*, vol. I, p. 8.

14 *Ibid.*, see the initial Advertisement by the Translator.

15 See George Abbot, *The Case of Impotency as Debated in England ...*, 2 vols. (London, 1715), ISR; see especially the preface to vol. I.

16 *Ibid.*, vol. I; on the Earl of Essex and the Duke of Norfolk see *DNB*, V, pp. 890–1; and X, pp. 33–4. The case of sodomy of the Earl of Castlehaven, a remarkable trial of the early seventeenth century, was reprinted several times after 1700. It is adequately discussed in Caroline Bingham, 'Seventeenth-Century Attitudes Toward Deviant Sex', *Journal of Interdisciplinary History*, I (1970), 447–69.

17 *Cases of Divorce ...* (London, 1715), ISR; on Feilding see *DNB*, VI, p. 1153.

18 M. D. George, *London Life*, pp. 305–6.

19 See *The Cases of Polygamy, Concubinage, Adultery, Divorce, etc.* (London, 1732), BL; and Roger Thompson, *Unfit For Modest Ears* (London, 1979), ch. 6, on similar works of seventeenth-century origin.

20 *The Cases of Impotency and Virginity ...* (London, 1732), ISR, ch. VI, pt. 4.

21 See *Select Trials, For Murders ... Rapes, Sodomy ... At the Sessions-House in the Old-Bailey*, 2 vols. (London, 1734–5), vol. II, p. 200; ISR.

22 *Ibid.*, 199.

23 On Charteris, see *DNB*, IV, pp. 135–6; and E. B. Chancellor, *The Lives of the Rakes* (London, 1925). Several publications between 1730 and 1739 commented on his acts of 'gallantry'; most of them are in the BL.

24 The ISR has two trial reports of that period, one dated 1742, and the other—the case of Bosavern Penlez—1749. The latter is more criminal than erotic.

25 The copy in the ISR is the sixth edition (London, 1770); see also *DNB*, IX, pp. 560–1 on the Duke of Cumberland.

26 See *The Trial*, introduction, pp. iii–v.

27 *Ibid.*, p. 11.

28 On this case, see Bloch, *Sexual Life*, pp. 80–3.

29 See vol. I, 'To the Public'. There are copies of the seven volumes in the BL and ISR.

30 See the advertisements at the end of *The Life and Amours of Lady Ann F–l–y* (London, n.d.), published after 1782; ISR.

31 See *The Trial ... between the Rt. Hon. Sir Richard Worseley, Bart. ... Plaintiff and George Maurice Bissett, Esq. Defendant, for Criminal Conversation with the Plaintiff's Wife ... 1782* (London, 1782), pp. 11, 20. On Worseley, see *DNB*, XXI, pp. 951–2. A copy of the trial report is in the BL.

32 The ISR has a print in its collection, *British Political Cartoons of the Eighteenth Century*, probably by James Gillray, listed as No. 7. The affair in the bath was satirised in *The Whim* (London, 1782). Other satires in verse of the same year are *Variety, or; which is the Man?; An Epistle from L——y W——y to Sir R——d W——y*; and *The Devil Divorced*. Anecdotes about Worseley and his wife are contained in *Memoirs of Sir Finical Whimsey and his Lady* (London, 1782). All these works are bound in one volume with the trial report in the BL copy.

33 See *The Life and Amours*, p. 8.

34 See Joseph Gurney, *The Trial of John Motherhill*, 2nd ed. (London, 1786); and *The Trial of Mr. Cooke ... For the Crime of Adultery with Mrs. Walford* (London, 1789), ISR.

35 Ivan Bloch quotes this work in his *History of English Sexual Morals* p. 75. The BL has an edition of 1830.

36 See the journal *London und Paris* (Weimar, 1800), vol. 8, pp. 242–3; cited by Paul Englisch, *Geschichte der erotischen Literatur* (Stuttgart, 1927), p. 624, and translated for Bloch's *History of English Sexual Morals*, p. 76.

37 On the increase of literacy in the eighteenth century, see A. S. Collins, 'The Growth of the Reading Public in the Eighteenth Century', *Review of English Studies*, II (1926), 284–93 and 428–38; and Leslie Stephen, *English Literature and Society in the 18th Century* (London, 1904), pts. IV and V.

38 This trial is reprinted in the anthology compiled by Leonard de Vries and Peter Fryer, *Venus Unmasked ... an Eighteenth-century Anthology* (London, 1967); see especially pp. 84–5 and 94.

39 *Ibid.*, p. 172.

40 See the print in *Venus Unmasked*, p. 167, which has portions from *The Cuckold's Chronicle*.

41 See H. S. Ashbee, *Catena Librorum Tacendorum* (London, 1885), pp. 329–38.

42 *Ibid.*, pp. 321–6.

43 *Ibid.*, pp. 337–8.
44 *Ibid.*, *passim.*
45 Quoting from the title-page; ISR.
46 See *A New and Complete Collection of the most remarkable Trials for Adultery* ... (London, 1802), BL.
47 Bloch, *Sexual Morals*, p. 76.
48 On the influence of the vice societies and similar organisations, see Ford K. Brown, *Fathers of the Victorians* (Cambridge, 1961); Edward J. Bristow, *Vice and Vigilance: Purity Movements in Britain since 1700* (Dublin, 1977); Steven Marcus, *The Other Victorians* (New York, 1967); and Donald Thomas, *A Long Time Burning* (London, 1969).
49 See Ashbee, *Catena*, pp. 338–9.
50 Cf. Lawrence Stone, *The Family, Sex and Marriage in England 1500–1800* (London, 1977), pp. 538 and 543; and Edmund S. Morgan, 'The Puritans and Sex', *New England Quarterly*, 15 (1942), 591–607. Morgan argues that the Puritans are blamed for the wrong reasons and were not particularly ascetic. See also my own 'Puritan Attitudes toward Recreation in Seventeenth-Century New England', doctoral dissertation (Universität des Saarlandes, 1979).
51 See Stone, *op. cit.*, p. 544.
52 *Ibid.*, pp. 530 and 533.
53 *The Life and Amours of Lady Ann F–l–y*, p. 27.

RUTH PERRY

The veil of chastity: Mary Astell's feminism

One of the first English thinkers to consider systematically the place accorded to women in the culture was the politically conservative, devout daughter of a Newcastle coal merchant named Mary Astell (1668–1731). Her conclusions about women are inseparable from her religious faith, her belief in political authority, and her commitment to philosophical rationalism. Nevertheless, this was the first issue on which she addressed the public, the first cause which drew her into print. By 1700 she had published 570 pages on the subject.

This article is not intended to outline the intellectual sources of her feminism, her complicated allegiance to her own intelligence, to reason, or to absolute authority. Nor is it intended to spell out her attitudes towards particular men, attitudes as various as the men themselves: her unqualified admiration for Henry Dodwell, the scholarly nonjuror, her contempt for Shaftesbury and his sophisticated Deism, her comradely criticism of John Norris and of Francis Atterbury, and so on. But there is in her feminism a component of sexual disaffection, a rejection of physiological womanhood, and a satiric dismissal of men as a class, and it is the context of this attitude which this study explores. For it is not enough to recognise and label this strain in Astell's thought without also making clear how unfavourable were the conditions in her culture to the biological female. And although the energy of Astell's prose discloses something of the psychological motivation behind her solution to the problem of sexual relations with men, to a historian considering women's alternatives in that era, the choice of celibacy—however repressive it may seem to post-Freudians—has the ring of emancipation.

Jeremy Taylor, whom Astell read and admired, described chastity as 'the circumcision of the heart, the cutting off all superfluity of nautiness and a suppression of all irregular desires in the matter of sensual or carnal pleasure'. It was grace which forbade and restrained sexual excess, by which he meant 'fornication, adultery, ... voluntary pollutions ... unnatural lusts and incestuous mixtures', as well as 'all immoderate use of permitted beds; concerning which judgment is to be made, as concerning meats and drinks: there being no certain degree of frequency or intention prescribed to all persons; but it is to be ruled as the other actions of man, by proportion to the end, by the dignity of the person in the honour and severity of being a Christian....'[1] He assumed that restraint made one a better Christian because of the way the ascetic habit of self-denial loosened one's grasp on the material world and left more time to spiritual involvement, to meditation and prayer.

Mary Astell was comfortable with these intellectual conceptions of chastity, having been raised on seventeenth-century Platonism, and thought of love clarified of the flesh as the ideal—an ideal best approximated by religious feeling. Her uncle, who according to tradition directed what little formal learning she had, attended Cambridge in the 1650s, during the heyday of the 'Cambridge platonists'. Ralph Astell was first admitted as a pensioner to St John's College, but briefly emigrated to Emmanuel College, then very much under the sway of Ralph Cudworth, Benjamin Whichcote and John Worthington. These were the moral philosophers who led the attack on Hobbes's materialism by asserting the pre-eminence of absolute spiritual values which proceeded from God and governed the universe. For them, the moral life consisted in discovering these innate, immutable ideas by reason, and then trying to live by them.

Mary Astell undoubtedly imbibed some distillation of this idealism from her uncle Ralph. She, too, believed that the intellect could ascertain the moral dimensions of ordinary experience—and had responsibility to do so—not so much by identifying moral feelings as by thinking abstractly through to absolute moral ideas and judging action in terms of them. The appetites and senses had a different purpose; they were to preserve the body, and could not be trusted to assess the spiritual meaning of experience. Steady reason was the only proper instrument for measuring the foundations of true morality; the volatile estimates of passion distorted truth. In her own simple life, Mary Astell tried to minimise sensual stimulation so as to preserve the dominion of mind over body, by regular meditation and observation of the fasts and devotions of the Church of England. Because moral judgement mattered more than sensual delight in her scheme of things, relations between men and women, along with all other aspects of life, had to be analysed for their ultimate service to God rather than for any other kind of satisfaction.

Her resistance to sexuality was undoubtedly part of this intellectual commitment to rationalism; but there was a psychological dimension to it as well. Whenever she spoke of men she did not keep back her sarcasm, for she resented the conventions which valued that sex above her own, and saw male power as potentially wanton and destructive. They were that sex who 'founded Empires and overturn'd them ... make laws and continually repeal and amend them. ... Their vast minds lay Kingdoms waste, no bounds or measures can be prescribed to their Desires.' Because of their ruling position in society, men were more sensualised, more rooted in the material world, more distracted from platonic realities. All her life she appears to have resisted male attractions with no difficulty at all. She never married, disapproved of beaux as a class, and in general distrusted the intentions of men towards women. She fumed at the universal understanding that women needed husbands, were unfinished without them: 'A Husband indeed is thought by both Sexes so very valuable, that scarce a man who can keep himself clean and make a Bow, but thinks he is good enough to pretend to any Woman, no matter for the Difference of Birth or Fortune, a Husband is such a Wonderworking Name as to make an Equality....'[2]

Her first feminist tract, *A Serious Proposal to the Ladies* (1694), suggested that women should take themselves off to live without men in monastic retreats, to devote themselves to the simple pleasures of uninterrupted study, meditation, music, conversation, etc. These communal institutions were to be sanctuaries, places of shelter for women who were harassed by the slings and arrows which beset women in the world of men:

> ... here Heiresses and Persons of Fortune may be kept secure from the rude attempts of designing Men; And she who has more Money than Discretion, need not curse her Stars for being expos'd a prey to bold importunate and rapacious Vultures. She will not here be inveigled and impos'd on, will neither be bought nor sold, nor be forc'd to marry for her own quiet, when she has no inclination to it, but what the being tir'd out with a restless

importunity occasions. Or if she be dispos'd to marry, here she may remain in safety till a convenient Match be offer'd by her Friends, and be freed from the danger of a dishonourable one.[3]

One of her poems, preserved in the papers of her friend and patron Lady Elizabeth Hastings, also registers this sense of the lurking danger in relationships with men.[4] She wrote the poem in memory of a young married woman not quite fifteen years old, who died after being married only three months. The 'victim' was young Eleanor Bowes, daughter of a wealthy mineowner in the North,[5] whom Mary Astell might have known through her Newcastle connections. Only two phases of this young woman's life survive on paper: a schoolgirl's polite thank-you note written in an affected, back-slanting hand; and the anxious letter of a young bride, writing to see if her husband's absence was a reproach, if he was still angry with her from a quarrel they had had earlier that day.[6] The newspapers carried the story that wealthy and well-connected Mrs Bowes was to be laid in state in the Jerusalem Chamber of Westminster Abbey and then interred 'with great Funeral Pomp and Solemnity', in the Duke of Ormonde's vault in King Henry II's chapel.[7] Her husband, George Bowes, Esq., of Durham, 'of very great estate', 'lay very ill of a fever', ten days after his young wife's death—either prostrated by grief or infected with the disease which carried her off.[8]

Mary Astell's poem for the occasion—she was in her late fifties when she looked at this young girl's life—is written in the Augustan heroic couplets she always preferred, and frames the action with music, with singing angels and harp-plucking virgins. But at the centre is a little dumbshow of Eleanor Bowes rejecting sexuality and flying up to heaven. Astell describes the marriage as 'gross', 'low', 'vulgar', and its effect on the fine spirit of Eleanor Bowes as 'Fatal', 'poisonous'. Had she remained a virgin, Eleanor Bowes might have lived, implies Mary Astell, but she was 'Lost when the fatal Nuptial Knot was tied'. Her sweet spirit, repelled by rude physical congress, gave up the ghost and fled for more ethereal realms inhabited entirely by virgins and cherubim.

On Mrs. Bowes Death

Blossom, Fragrant Spring, Bright Morn, adieu!
Virgins shall string their Harps, and mourn for you
Lost when the fatal Nuptial Knot was tie'd,
Your Sun declin'd, when you became a Bride.

A soul refin'd, when like your's soar'd far above
The gross Amusements of low, Vulgar love.
Nor tempted by that Pois'nous Cup to stay
Tasting it scorn'd the draught and fled away.
Oh Cherubims and Seraph's Noblest string,
In Heavenly Raptures you're ordained to sing
The Immortal Spouse, in Bliss refin'd from Sense
Pure as your Mind, and Sweet as Innocence.

She begins in an earthly paradise filled with delicate and wholesome sensations: 'Fragrant Spring', 'Bright Morn', harp strings. But there is a rapid progress to disaster; she soon leaves behind these innocent delights and moves on to stronger sensual experience, to 'gross Amusements', quickly surfeiting on the 'Pois'nous Cup'. The only relief then is to escape, to soar above it all, and enjoy 'Bliss refine'd from Sense'.

Although Astell's tribute to Eleanor Bowes may strike a modern sensibility as typically rhetorical eighteenth-century verse, in fact it shows an old-fashioned touch when judged in the time it was written. Her portrait of a pure soul repelled by gross sensuality belongs more to seventeenth-century Newcastle where she was raised, beyond the influence of the licentious Restoration court, and reveals more about her particular character and choices than it does about conventional sexual attitudes among the fashionable set in eighteenth-century London.

A poem written by the celebrated Lady Mary Wortley Montagu upon the same occasion probably comes closer to the tenor of the age. (Lady Mary was twenty years Astell's junior.) Spirited Lady Mary appears to have composed her verse 'extempore upon a card, in a great deal of Company' as a kind of social game or entertainment.[9] Mary Astell knew her at this time, and her own poem may well have been a response to Lady Mary's flamboyant gesture—probably not in the same crowded room, but later in the solitude of her own lodgings. That Lady Mary was in Mary Astell's mind we know from the fact that only a few days later Mary Astell wrote a little poem to honour Lady Mary Wortley Montagu's *Turkish Letters*, in which she speaks of overcoming a 'little spirit of Rivalship' to 'gladly lay my Laurels at her Feet'. Whether Mary Astell's poem was intended as an answer, a rebuttal, of Lady Mary's performance or not, the two responses to young Mrs Bowes's death could not have been more dissimilar. Lady Mary's poem went like this:

On the Death of Mrs. Bowes.

Hail happy bride! for thou art truly blest!
Three Months of Rapture crown'd with endless Rest!
Merit, like yours, was Heav'ns peculiar Care,
You lov'd,—yet trusted Happiness sincere:
To you the Sweets of Love were only shewn,
The Sure succeeding bitter dregs unknown:
You had not the fatal Change deplor'd,
The tender Lover, for the imperious Lord;
Nor felt the Pains that jealous Fondness brings,
Nor wept that Coldness from Possession springs.
Above your Sex distinguished in your Fate,
You trusted—yet experienced no Deceit.
Soft were the Hours, and wing'd with Pleasure flew,
No vain repentance gave a Sigh to you:
And if superior Bliss, Heav'n can bestow,
With Fellow Angels you enjoy it now.

Like Mary Astell's poem, this one locates Mrs Bowes in the company of the angels. But Lady Mary's vision of the three-month marriage which preceded the girl's death is crucially different from Astell's. This wordly woman does not imagine it as being 'gross' and 'vulgar' but as 'Three Months of Rapture' filled with the 'Sweets of Love'. Sexuality did not distress Lady Mary; what she feared was the cessation of ardour. Disillusioned in her own life—Wortley had turned out to be a cold husband after a long, dramatic, epistolary courtship—the best she could wish for anyone was a romantically passionate courtship without the dampening effects of domesticity.

For both Lady Mary and for Mary Astell, young Mrs Bowes' recent marriage and sudden death had significant meaning; each woman projected her own deep-seated feelings about sexuality on to these events. For Lady Mary, fleshly passion was a kind of cheat that brought betrayal, deceit and 'fatal Changes' in its train. For Mary Astell it was a rude violation to which death was the honourable response of a 'refin'd' soul. And yet Mary Astell's attitude reflected an underlying truth, for the association between sex and death in her culture must have been strong for any woman. Mrs Bowes had not been pregnant, had not died in childbirth. But many did. And women's feelings about sexuality must have been governed to a large extent by the recognition that its consequences were often lethal.

It was a culture which made little use of prophylactics; and when they were used, it was to prevent disease with prostitutes rather than as birth control for respectable women. Defoe, in *Conjugal Lewdness, or Matrimonial Whoredom* (1727), for instance, advised married couples not to use contraception lest it pervert the true meaning of marriage. This meant that during her fifteen or so fertile years, a married woman with regular sexual conduct was likely to become pregnant ten or twelve times and to give birth six or eight times.[10] And quite aside from the dangers of prematurely terminated pregnancies—abortions and miscarriages—each time a woman underwent the ordeal of 'lying in', she risked her life. Swift writes in *Journal to Stella* of a woman come to London in 1711 to have her child: 'God send her a good time! Her death would be a terrible thing.'[11]

As it happens, there are actually some statistics on childbed mortality for Mary Astell's period and the later eighteenth century. They come from the casualties listed in the London bills of mortality, from lying-in hospitals (the first one was established in London in 1739) and from actual polls of the populace—a practice instinctively resisted by the English people, who were sure that it presaged some governmental invasion of their lives.[12] These records are not easy to interpret, for the figures are uncorrected for important variables: the total number of christenings listed annually in the bills of mortality are not adjusted for multiparous births; hospitals recorded the ages of mothers who died in childbirth but not always the number of previous deliveries, a factor which influenced the chances of a successful delivery; women who died in childbed occasionally died of causes other than haemorrhage or the physical strain of labour, and conversely, there were women who died *of* childbirth if not *in* childbirth, some time after the actual delivery. Furthermore, there are wild fluctuations in the risks calculated by different statisticians even for the same historical period. Nevertheless, a conservative average of the available figures shows that for every sixty safe deliveries in the early part of the century, one woman died. One-third as many adult lives were snuffed out on the childbed as by smallpox; childbirth was ten times as dangerous as venereal disease, yet it took its toll only on one sex. If Swift's friend was facing her first delivery, her chances were sixty to one. But since most women faced these odds six or seven times, not counting the complications of additional abortions and miscarriages, the overall chance of a fertile, married woman dying during her childbearing years was much higher. If she delivered six children she had at least a ten per cent chance of dying, and probably a much higher one.[13]

This must account, in part, for the association between death and sex in Mary Astell's poem about Mrs Bowes's premature demise. Nor was hers the only poem on the subject which took sex to be the cause of death. Another verse, this time written by a 'young gentleman', can be added to the collection of public responses to Eleanor Bowes's death. He also recognised the hazardous consequences of sexuality for a woman, but from a male point of view, with fantasies of power, and allusions to the potency of classical gods:

How blest a Life; how short its Date!
'Twas Semele's and Danae's Fate.
In golden Showers the Lover came,
Like thund'ring *Jove* he clasp'd the Dame;
The Victim of too fierce a Flame.[14]

This 'too fierce a Flame', or rather its ramifications months later, explains the greater frequency of second marriages for men among the upper classes of eighteenth-century Europe than among women of that class.[15] Lawrence Stone states that because of the 'high mortality from childbirth, at all periods from the sixteenth to the nineteenth century, in three out of four cases of all first marriages among the squirearchy that were broken by death within ten years, the cause was the death of the wife'.[16]

In time these high mortality figures came down, although whether the decrease was due to medical advances and hospitalisation or rather to general immunological adjustments in the population is still a matter of debate.[17] Certainly when lying-in hospitals were first introduced to the London scene, they were dangerous places in which to give birth, and the fatalities in them were far higher than in home deliveries.[18] But in Mary Astell's time, of course, there were no lying-in hospitals, no professional debates on the subject, and the dangers of childbearing were part of life's precarious balance, along with smallpox and gout. At that time, deliveries were generally handled by midwives, although increasingly doctors assisted at difficult labours with their dangerous forceps.[19] Probably improved diet and hygiene as much as anything account for greater safety in childbirth later in history. The dirt and infection of eighteenth-century London were a particular liability for a woman when her reproductive equipment made her regularly vulnerable, as if wounded, to a very contagious environment.[20]

Although most of the complications in childbirth were probably due to infection in this culture which washed (anything) only rarely, there was also the danger of rupture and haemorrhage. The twisted bodies of women who had grown up unhealthily in the cities were not always equal to the physical task of labour and delivery. Rickets, for example, was widespread in eighteenth-century London, because of ignorance about its cause and the adulteration of milk, one of the main sources of vitamin D.[21] Vitamin D is essential to the absorption of calcium, and without it there is malformation of the growing bone. Although possibly crippling, and even fatal in either sex, rickets has a long-range effect on childbearing, for it affects the way the pelvis grows. In developing females with rickets, the sacrum at the rear grows too close to the pubic bone, narrowing the birth canal through which some day an infant must pass.[22] The high incidence of rickets, then, must have caused an unusually high proportion of difficult deliveries, in which the mother ruptured, the baby perished, or both.[23]

But death was only the most dramatic consequence of a woman's sexual experience. Long and painful labours produced symptoms which did not kill, but caused lifelong discomfort. Torn anal sphincter muscles and lesions between the bladder or rectum and the vagina made continence impossible. The loss of iron from repeated bloody deliveries and from nursing must have meant serious widespread anaemia. Women lived on with ruptured and prolapsed uteruses, with this organ torn loose and hanging visible between the legs.[24] They suffered from all manner of vaginal infections caused by examinations with unsterilised probes. John Graunt observed in 1695 that although there were 'fourteen men to thirteen women, and that they die in the same proportion also, yet I have heard *Physicians* say, that they have two women patients to one man, which assertion seems very likely; for that women have either the *Green-sickness*, or other like Distempers, are sick of *Breedings*, *Abortions*, *Child-bearing*, *Sore-breasts*, *Whites*, *Obstructions*, *Fits of the Mother*, and the like'.[25]

Nor was the medical profession of much help, in these days of cupping and purges, for women's physiological functioning was shrouded in great ignorance. A late-eighteenth-century physician, trying to account for maternal mortality, explained the causes of 'the several diseases before and after delivery' with these odd misconceptions: 'Milk fevers, and sometimes Inflammations of the womb, Suppression or deposition of the milk on some vital part, sudden and premature suppression of the Lochial flux....'[26]

Women's reproductive equipment was a mysterious matter, with its horrifying fecundity. A number of famous doctors, among them the chief surgeons and anatomist to the king, were entirely ready to believe, for instance, that Mary Tofts, a poor woman living in Godalming in Surrey, really had given birth to rabbits—an imposture believed by half of London in 1726.[27] Even in the correspondence of learned men, one finds astounding credulity: 'There is a monstrous Birth happen'd near Cardiff in Glamorganshire', wrote one scholar to a friend in 1708, 'a Girl lately of 12 years was delivered of 11 puppyes, one with hair on lived two hours, and is by the Apothcary preserved in spirit of wine: she is supposed to have been too familiar with a little dog that lay with her....'[28] The London papers sometimes carried stories of similar monstrous births, like these reported from Lisbon in 1722: three monsters with shoulders, claws and heads like dogs were born to a rich and beautiful young lady who lay with a large water dog; babies who were monkeys down to the waist and had bushy tails issued from another woman's womb; and last and most horrifying, there was the report of a baby born dead with its back 'gnaw'd by five Serpents, which came alive into the World with it, and leap'd up and down the Room, which so frightened the Midwife and others present, as made them run out; but the Husband took courage and enter'd the Room with a Stick and destroy'd them'.[29] These tales may not have been believed literally, but they speak of helplessness and fear in the face of women's unpredictable and powerful reproductive capacities.

A fertile, married woman was likely to spend her middle years continually pregnant and bringing forth children. On the average a gentlewoman bore six live children, with a number of miscarriages and stillbirths. Only half of her live children could be expected to live past the fifth year.[30] Poorer women had slightly fewer children; deficient diet impaired their fertility, and nursing their own children, rather than sending them out to nurse, helped to space their conceptions.

Lady Fanshawe's *Memoir* gives a sobering account of the fecundity of a seventeenth-century woman: 'My dear husband had six sons and eight daughters, born and christened,' she wrote in her memoir, 'and I miscarried of six more, three at several times and once of three sons when I was about half gone my time.'[31] According to her count he had fourteen children and she had six miscarriages; but to a modern sensibility, this woman spent twenty-three years of her life pregnant, with only five children surviving from her seventeen pregnancies. Almost a century later Hester Thrale Piozzi, Dr Johnson's lively friend, told the same story—annihilating several decades in her diary with the single chilling explanation: 'for bringing babies, nursing them, and losing them, was my constant Employ'.[32]

Given these conditions of life, it is impossible to imagine a fertile woman living both as an intellectual and a sexual being. Virginia Woolf, in *A Room of One's Own*, points out that the only common quality shared by writers as diverse as the Brontë sisters, George Eliot and Jane Austen was that none of them had children. It could be said for the successful writers of Mary Astell's day that they were all widows and spinsters. Aphra Behn was a childless widow; Mary Delariviere Manley had been tricked into a false marriage and then abandoned; Eliza Haywood left her husband early; Jane Barker never married; Charlotte Lennox wrote before her marriage and after the death of her husband; Elizabeth Elstob lived with her brother; Penelope Aubin began to write when her husband died. And it is commonly held that once Fanny Burney married, she never again wrote as brilliantly.

Catherine Trotter's story gives the shape of early aspirations arrested by the onset of children. Born in 1679 to a poor but genteel family, she precociously learned French by herself very early, wrote verse, and considered the array of available religions long enough to convert to Roman Catholicism. At seventeen she wrote a successfully staged tragedy—*Agnes de Castro*—adapted from a French novel translated by Aphra Behn. Two years later her second play, *Fatal Friendship*, was produced and her third play was played the same year as she anonymously published a defence of Locke, written in response to some printed *Remarks* against his *Essay on Human Understanding*. Her philosophical piece was very well received by a number of notable philosophers, and when the author's identity was discovered, Locke thanked her with a gift of some books and the acknowledgement 'that as the rest of the world take[s] notice of the strength and clearness of your reasoning, so I cannot but be extremely sensible, that it was employed in my defence'.[33]

Already welcomed in the literary world by Hughes, Congreve,

Farquhar and Manley (who acclaimed her as the successor to Katherine Phillips and Aphra Behn, 'Nature's third start, in favour of our kind'), young Catherine Trotter now began to correspond with Leibniz and other philosophers. And then in 1708 the story is interrupted by her marriage. As her biographer, Thomas Birch, expresses it: 'Mrs. Cockburn after her marriage was entirely diverted from her studies for many years by attending upon the duties of a wife and mother and by the ordinary cares of an increasing family, and the additional ones arising from the reduced circumstances of her husband.'[34] The gap between the years 1707 and 1731 in her printed correspondence is mute testimony to these cares. Nothing more of hers was published for nineteen years, although later in life she wrote several more philosophical works.

However, Lady Fanshawe, Catherine Cockburn and Mrs Thrale coped with their fecundity, it takes no feminist perspective to recognise that too many unwanted children were brought into the world in this era. In 1695 one-third of all the children in Bristol were orphans.[35] Thomas Coram, a retired sea captain who crusaded for years to arrange the backing for London's first Foundling Hospital, was shocked into his campaign by seeing so many abandoned children—dead and alive—along the road to London. And when in 1739 his institution flung open its doors for the first time, there were 117 children waiting on the front steps to be taken in. Within six months 1800 children had been consigned to the Foundling Hospital, although many of them died because the institution was not equipped to handle such numbers.[36]

Every year numbers of children were reported 'starved at nurse' or 'overlayed'—that is, smothered by being lain on in bed; some of these fatalities may have been a kind of *post hoc* birth control. It became a capital offence merely to conceal the stillborn birth of an illegitimate child and many women suspected of killing unwanted babies were brought to the dock under this law. The records of Old Bailey tell gruesome tales of infants born secretly in 'garrets, outhouses, and under stairs'.[37] *The British Journal* of 29 September 1722, for example, carried the story of Anne Morris, 'condemn'd for throwing her Bastard Child as soon as born into a House of Ease', and who died in Newgate prison.[38]

This then was the context in which Mary Astell turned from sexuality. It is not difficult to understand her refusal once these facts are clear. Everyone in her time knew of women who had suffered and died in labour, women who were pregnant more often than they cared to be, women who were wrenched by the early death of child after child. The rate books of Chelsea, where Astell lived, are filled with records of disbursements to pay for one night's firing for some poor woman or another, just delivered of a child or just about to be, and the coach fare to ship her off to some other parish in the morning.

Although Mary Astell's rhetoric about chastity may appear old-fashioned and stilted, it is not hard to see that what she suggested had very concrete advantages for her sex. She may have promised diffuse and metaphysical rewards for the celibate life—'Virtue', 'Truth' and the 'Fruits of Paradise'—but living in sweetness and light with other women had the very real utility of sparing life and health. Only by eschewing sexuality could women be free of the biological imperatives which otherwise dominated their lives and deflected them from what Mary Astell would have called their 'higher purposes'. Only if they turned away from the age-old contest between the sexes might they come to see themselves as 'capable of Nobler things than the pitiful conquest of some worthless heart'.[39]

This lay closer to the heart of Astell's polemics than her insistence on sexual abstinence—this belief in the stifled potentialities of her sex. She herself was not tempted by heterosexuality, and so her arguments against that temptation seem borrowed rather than felt, the language stiffer than her usual ringing exposition. In a sense, her advocacy of chastity was but a veil for the protective love and ambition she felt for other women. Always, her most touching friendships and deepest loyalties were with women; she wanted them to arrange their lives so as to have more time, more intellectual autonomy and more choice than most married women had, caught as they were in their webs of social obligation and family demands.[40] 'Fain wou'd I rescue my Sex, or at least as many of them as come within my Sphere, from that Meanness of Spirit into which the Generality of 'em are sunk . . .' she wrote to Norris in 1693.[41]

In *A Serious Proposal to the Ladies* she advised women to organise themselves into communal, monastic retreats because she saw them as primarily rational and independent beings—like herself—and thought that monastic life best promoted these qualities. Nothing else was as important as this. As she wrote there, with an almost unconscious use of the female pronoun, she thought the highest human achievement was a lofty philosophical indifference to the material world—a state of mind most difficult for a married woman, quick with child year after year, anxiously scanning her living children for signs of illness. 'There is a sort of Bravery and Greatness of Soul,' wrote Mary Astell, 'which does more truly ennoble us than the highest Title, and it consists in living up to the dignity of our Natures, scorning to do a mean, unbecoming thing; in passing [in] differently thro' Good and Evil Fortune, without being corrupted by the one or deprest by the other. For she that can do so, gives evidence that her Happiness depends not on so mutable a thing as this world; but, in a due subserviency to the Almighty, is bottom'd only on her own great Mind.'[42]

NOTES

This paper, which was published in Ronald C. Rosbottom, ed., *Studies in Eighteenth-Century Culture*, vol. 9 (Madison, 1979), pp. 25–43, owes a great deal to Tillie Olsen, who always insisted upon attention to the material conditions of women's sexuality.

1 *The Whole Works of Jeremy Taylor*, 10 vols. (London, 1861), III, pp. 55–6.

2 Mary Astell, *Reflections on Marriage* (London, 1700), p. 67.

3 Mary Astell, *A Serious Proposal to the Ladies* (London, 1694), p. 146.

4 I am deeply grateful to G. H. H. Wheler of Otterden, Kent, for access to Lady Elizabeth Hastings's papers and for permission to reprint this poem.

5 Eleanor Bowes's father was the Honourable Thomas Verney, son of Lord Willoby of Broke.

6 BM Add. MSS 40747:191.

7 John Sykes, *Local Records*, 2 vols. (Newcastle, 1833), I, p. 140. See also *The British Journal*, 19 Dec. 1724.

8 *The British Journal*, 26 Dec. 1724.

9 *The Weekly Journal or British Gazetteer*, Saturday 26 Dec. 1724.

10 Lawrence Stone, *The Family, Sex and Marriage in England 1500–1800* (London, 1977), p. 63. Stone reports the recent findings of demographers that women often did not marry until about twenty-five years of age, and that the earlier onset of menopause (in the forties) further limited the period of fertility. The estimates of pregnancies and births come from Edward Shorter, 'Maternal Sentiment and Death in Childbirth: a New Agenda for Psychohistory', in Patricia Branca (ed), *The Medicine Show* (New York, 1977), pp. 67–8.

11 Jonathan Swift, *Journal to Stella*, ed. George Aitkin (London, 1901), p. 271.

12 William Wales, *An Inquiry into the Present State of Population in*

England and Wales (London, 1781), *passim.* In 1750, Mr Wales found his efforts and those of his associates resisted by threats, blows and persecutions.

13 These conclusions are based on an examination of the figures for christenings and childbed deaths given in the London bills of mortality, reprinted in William Heberden, *A Collection of the Yearly Bills of Mortality From 1657–1758 inclusive* (London, 1759). The figure one in sixty was also corroborated by a late-eighteenth-century study of twenty-four years of the London bills as well as of several county registers in England and Germany. William Black, M.D., *Observations Medical and Political on the Small-Pox ... and on the Mortality of Mankind at Every Age in City and Country* (London 1781), p. 238. See also Robert Bland, M.D., 'Some Calculations of the Number of Accidents or Deaths which happen in consequence of Parturition', *Philosophical Transactions*, LXXI (1781), pt. II, 355–71.

A woman's childbearing years were the exception to the general rule that the death rate for men exceeded that for women. From the beginnings of life, because the heads of male infants are larger than those of female infants, more died in difficult deliveries. Then too, males of all ages were more susceptible to infectious diseases—many more dying in the smallpox epidemics of the late seventeenth, early eighteenth centuries. See Joseph Clark, M.D., 'Observations on Some Causes of the Excess of Mortality of Males Above that of Females' communicated by the Rev. Richard Price, *Philosophical Transactions*, LXXV (1786), pt. II, 363–4. Men also died more violent deaths than women, in wars, duels and the like. The only exception to this rule, the only instance in which women died in numbers equal to, or greater than, those of men, appears when these mortality figures are broken down into broad age brackets. Then one sees that between the ages of twenty-five and forty—the child-bearing years—women had a higher death rate than men. See T. H. Hollingsworth, 'The Demography of the British Peerage', supplement to *Population Studies*, XVIII, No. 2, pp. 54–5, 60. See also T. H. Marshall, 'The Population Problem During the Industrial Revolution: a Note on the Present State of the Controversy', reprinted in D. V. Glass and D. E. C. Eversley, *Population in History* (London, 1965), p. 263, n. 44; Marshall quotes Price's table for Chester, 1772–81, showing female mortality exceeding male mortality between the ages of twenty-eight and thirty-six.

14 *The British Journal*, Saturday 30 Jan. 1725.

15 Sigismund Peller, 'Births and Deaths Among Europe's Ruling Families since 1500', reprinted in D. V. Glass and D. E. C. Eversley, *Population in History*, p. 97.

16 Lawrence Stone, *The Family, Sex and Marriage*, pp. 79–80.

17 G. T. Griffith, *Population Problems of the Age of Malthus* (London, 1967); T. McKeown and R. G. Brown, 'Medical Evidence Related to English Population Changes in the Eighteenth Century', *Population*

Studies, IX (1955), 119; Thomas McKeown, *The Modern Rise of Population* (London, 1976), ch. 5, 'The Medical Contribution'.

18 M. Dorothy George, *London Life in the Eighteenth Century* (New York, 1925), pp. 49, 336. See also Charles White, *A Treatise on the Management of Pregnant and Lying-In Women* (London, 1773), pp. 333–5, for instances of high mortality rates in early lying-in hospitals (i.e., one fatality in twenty-eight or thirty-nine deliveries). For the continuation of the debate, over the relative safety of home and hospital deliveries in the nineteenth century, see Robert Collins, *A Practical Treatise on Midwifery: 16,654 Births in the Dublin Lying-In Hospital from 1826–1833* (Boston, 1841); Robert Collins, *A Short Sketch of the Life and Writings of the Late Joseph Clark, Esq., M.D. formerly of Dublin Lying-in* (London, 1849); Dr E. Kennedy's speech in *Dublin Quarterly Journal of Medical Science*, XLVII (May 1869), 269–307; 'Proceedings of the Dublin Obstetrical Society', *Dublin Quarterly of Medical Science*, XLVIII (August 1869) 225–429; J. Matthews Duncan, *On the Mortality of Childbed and Maternity Hospitals* (Edinburgh, 1870).

19 In 1773, when Charles White suggested that it was safer for both child and mother to permit the shoulders of the infant to be expelled by labour, rather than forcibly pulling at the head as soon as it crowned, it was considered a significant medical innovation, although Sarah Stone, a midwife trained by her mother, had published the same advice in 1737. The purpose of her book was to encourage women to learn midwifery, for she was dismayed at the number of men who were beginning to set up in the trade: 'Tho' I have made it my Observation within these few years That more Women and Children have died by the hands of such Professors, than by the greatest imbecility and ignorance of some Women-Midwives, who never went thro', or so much as heard of, a Course of Anatomy. For, give me leave to tell those young Gentlemen pretenders, who undertake the Practice of Midwifery with only the knowledge of dissecting the Dead, that all the Living who have or shall come under their care, in any difficulty, have and may severely pay for what knowledge they attain to in the Art of Midwifery; especially such young ones as now pretend to practice: by whom (I am well assured) there are many sufferers both Mothers and Children; yea, Infants have been born alive, with their Brains working out of their heads: occasion'd by the too common use of Instruments: which I never found but little use to be made of, in all my practice.' Sarah Stone, *A Complete Practice of Midwifery* (London, 1737), Preface, xii–xiii.

20 For an eighteenth-century description of puerperal fever, see Charles White, *A Treatise on the Management of Pregnant and Lying-In Women* (London, 1773), pp. 13–17. White was one of the first doctors to argue for cleanliness and ventilation in delivery wards. In his important treatise he advised women to bathe both before and after pregnancy, to exercise, to wear loose clothes, without stays, the weight of which hung from the shoulders rather than pressing against the womb, etc. He also

recommended that patients suffering from puerperal fever be removed from the wards where there were other newly delivered mothers, that their bedding and curtains be washed thoroughly and the woodwork scrubbed with vinegar.

21 J. C. Drummond and Anne Wilbraham, *The Englishman's Food: a History of Five Centuries of English Diet* (London, 1939), p. 230. The degree of misinformation about rickets at this time cannot be overestimated.

22 Edward Shorter, 'Maternal Sentiment and Death in Childbirth', pp. 9, 10, 21.

23 William Black also refers to the 'ricketty pelvis' which made manual aid necessary in a delivery. William Black, *Observations ... on the Mortality of Mankind at Every Age in City and Country*, p. 243.

24 Edward Shorter, 'Women's Diseases Before 1900', in Mel Albin (ed.), *New Directions in Psychohistory* (Lexington, Ky., 1980), pp. 183–208.

25 John Graunt, *Natural and Political Observations Made upon the Bills of Mortality* (London, 1662), p. 49.

26 William Black, *Observations*, p. 239.

27 William Connor Sydney, *England and The English in the Eighteenth Century*, 2 vols. (Edinburgh, 1891), I, p. 293.

28 Bodleian Library, Ballard Ms. 31:48.

29 *The Weekly Journal or British Gazetteer*, Saturday 20 Oct. 1722.

30 See T. H. Hollingsworth, 'A Demographic Study of the British Ducal Families', pp. 354–78, and Thomas McKeown and R. G. Brown, 'Medical Evidence Related to English Population Changes in Eighteenth Century', pp. 285–307, reprinted in D. V. Glass and D. E. C. Eversley, *Population in History*, Robert Bland, M.D., 'Some Calculations of the Number of Accidents or Deaths which happen in Consequence of Parturition', *Philosophical Transactions*, LXXI (1781), pt. II, 355–71; Edward Shorter, 'Maternal Sentiment and Death in Childbirth'.

31 *Memories of Lady Fanshawe*, ed. Sir Nicholas Harris Nicholas (London, 1830), p. 46.

32 Houghton Library, *Hester Thrale's Diary*, I, p. 20. Mrs Thrale brought twelve live children into the world; four survived into adulthood.

33 Thomas Birch, 'The Life of Mrs. Catherine Cockburn', preface to her *Works*, 2 vols. (London, 1751), I, p. xx.

34 *Ibid.*, I, p. xxxv.

35 Lawrence Stone, *The Family, Sex and Marriage*, p. 58. Quoted from J. R. Holman, 'Orphans in Pre-Industrial Towns: The Case of Bristol', *Local Population Studies*, XV (1975).

36 David Owen, *English Philanthropy* (Cambridge, Mass., 1964), p. 53.

37 J. M. Beattie, 'The Criminality of Women in 18th Century England', *Journal of Social History*, VIII (1975), 85.

38 A 'House of Ease' was a privy.

39 Mary Astell, *A Serious Proposal to the Ladies*, pp. 14–15.

40 Hester Thrale Piozzi wrote this in her diary about the constrictions on

her time and mental energies: '... All my Friends reproach me with neglecting to write down such Things as drop from him [Samuel Johnson] almost perpetually, and often say how much I shall some Time regret that I have not done 't with diligence ever since the commencement of our Acquaintance: They say well, but ever since that Time I have been the Mother of Children, and little do these wise Men know or feel, that the Crying of a young Child, or the Perverseness of an elder, or the Danger however trifling of any one—will soon drive out of a female Parent's head a Conversation concerning Wit, Science or Sentiment, however She may appear to be impressed with it at the moment: besides that to a *Mere de famille* doing something is more necessary & suitable than even hearing something; and if one is to listen all Even' and write all Morning what one has heard; where will be the Time for tutoring, caressing, or what is still more useful, for having one's Children about one: I therefore charge all my Neglect to my young ones Account, and feel myself at this moment very miserable that I have at last, after being married fourteen Years and bringing eleven Children [of whom seven had died], leisure to write a *Thraliana* for sooth;—though the second Volume *does* begin with Mr Johnson' (*Thraliana: the Diary of Mrs. Hester Lynch Thrale, 1776–1809*, ed. Katherine Balderston, 2 vols. (Oxford, 1942), I, pp. 158).

41 Mary Astell, *Letters Concerning the Love of God* (London, 1695), p. 49.

42 Mary Astell, *A Serious Proposal to the Ladies*, pp. 168–9.

JOHN VALDIMIR PRICE

Patterns of sexual behaviour in some eighteenth-century novels

About the middle of the eighteenth century, Lady Mary Wortley Montagu wrote to her daughter, Lady Bute, about an incident that took place while she was residing in her house in Gottolengo. The wife of a neighbour, Signora Laura Bono, had been discovered *in flagrante delicto* with a 'Handsome Lad of eighteen', who was enticed into bed by the Signora apparently without difficulty. The pair were discovered by the husband, who was intent upon killing his wife, when Lady Mary was summoned by the chambermaid, and murder was averted. Lady Mary's extensive comments on this episode are memorable, particularly when the Signora swore it was the first time and that she would never do it again:

> I can not be persuaded that any Woman who had liv'd virtuous till forty ... could suddenly be endow'd with such consummate Impudence to solicite a youth at first sight, there being no probabillity, his age and station consider'd, that he would have made any attempt of that kind. I must confess I was wicked enough to think the unblemish'd reputation she had hitherto maintain'd, and did not fail to put us in mind of, was owing to a series of such Frolicks.... There wants only a very Lewd Constitution, a very bad Heart, and a moderate understanding, to make this conduct easy, and I do not doubt it has been practis'd by many prudes beside her....[1]

The affair is hushed up, the Signora's local reputation is saved (so to speak), so that she 'retains the satisfaction of insulting all her acquaintance on the foundation of a spotless Character that only She can boast in the Parish, where she is most heartily hated, from these airs of impertinent virtue, and another very essential reason, being the best dress'd Woman amongst them, thô one of the plainest in her figure'.[2]

Lady Mary's judgement and attitude reveal an instructive range of assumptions and opinions about patterns of sexual behaviour and the moral postulates upon which this behaviour was founded in the eighteenth century; they are worth noting here because they also reflect many of the uncertainties and doubts that affected both theoretical debates about ethics and, to a greater extent, practical behaviour. Lady Mary was far more concerned that the Signora was likely to be murdered than she was about the immorality of the act, an ordering of values that most of us would share. The issues that the incident raises, however, are among those that feature significantly in the eighteenth-century novel. I should like to consider some of the issues raised by Lady Mary, as well as others that grow out of these, as they occur in four representative eighteenth-century novels, *Moll Flanders*, *Joseph Andrews*, *Clarissa* and *Peregrine Pickle*.[3]

Alliance or dalliance with those of an inferior social rank was a popular theme in eighteenth-century literature, and in *Joseph Andrews*, Lady Booby's attempted dalliance with Joseph comprises many of the same assumptions found in Lady Mary's account of Signora Bono.[4] Lady Booby indulges Joseph 'in all those innocent Freedoms which Women of Figure may permit without the least sully of their Virtue'.[5] Fielding adds, that while their virtue is thus untarnished, 'yet now and then some small Arrows will glance on the Shadow of it, their Reputation' (p. 27); and Lady Booby is assumed to be having an affair with her footman. There being little point in losing a reputation because of hearsay and gossip, Lady Booby makes an overture to Joseph, which is politely repulsed. Dismissed from her Ladyship's presence, Joseph is then confronted and propositioned by Slipslop, a 'Maiden Gentlewoman of about Forty-five Years of Age, who having made a small Slip in her Youth had continued a good Maid ever since' (p. 32). Unwilling to acquiesce in the demands of either, Joseph finds himself unemployed.

Fiction and reality merge in the accounts by Fielding and Lady Mary, but it is worth noting that neither is very concerned with the moral content of the incidents. Fiction, however, stops somewhat short of reality in that Fielding's Joseph does not accept the sexual invitations, while Signora Bono's handsome teenager did not hesitate. One notices also that both Lady Booby and Slipslop act on the assumption that no man is likely to refuse an offer of sexual intercourse, an act predicated on a further assumption about the perpetual readiness of the male for sex. Both Lady Booby and Slipslop clearly feel that they have an inalienable right to be immediately offended when their sexual overtures are rejected. Thus, while Fielding satirises the idea of male chastity in his novel, he also questions the conventions that divide male and female sexuality into stereotypes of instant readiness on the one hand and unvarying irresistibility on the other. The comic dimension of the episode is, to be sure, the most conspicuous one, but Fielding is also suggesting that sexual liaisons and sexual attraction depend on far, far more than mere difference of gender. Lady Booby and Slipslop too readily assume that a man is always ready to accept an offer of sexual intercourse.

Female vanity is not much different from male vanity in this respect, but an observation made in 'The Memoirs of a Lady of Quality'[6] in *Peregrine Pickle* draws attention to an aspect of female vanity that complements male chauvinism. After various adventures, the 'Lady of Quality', Lady Vane, returns safely to Paris, where her companions express surprise to discover that she was not murdered or at least raped while she was in the company of a gang of robbers. Of the possibility of being raped, she remarks, 'As for this last species of outrage, the fear of it never once entered my head, otherwise I should have been more shocked and alarmed than I really was ... and I cannot help observing, that an homely woman is always more apt to entertain those fears, than one whose person exposes her to much more imminent danger.'[7] It would not be unreasonable to expect an attractive woman to make the latter part of that observation, but the whole view is intimately bound up with characteristic assumptions in eighteenth-century novels about female vanity and sexuality.

An assumption inherent in Lady Vane's observation, and less clearly so in those of Lady Booby and Slipslop, is that rape is invited. The fact that the possibility of being raped never entered Lady Vane's head is, she implies, the reason why she escaped. The fear of being raped communicates itself by some obscure psychological or physiological process and thus helps to induce it. The accuracy of this assumption may of course be questioned, but its practical consequences and moral efficacy remain the same. Lady Vane had indeed run a risk, 'those ruffians being familiarized to rape as well as murder' (p. 525), but her ignorance of her danger probably protected her more than she realised. In this respect, one might recall the experiences of

Moll Flanders, who is never especially worried about rape, but whose sexual experiences are otherwise diverse (to say the least).

Rape has never ceased to exercise its dangerous psychological fascination, and eighteenth-century novelists not only raised the public's consciousness of rape as a moral crime but also perhaps helped to encourage a good deal of prurient speculation among their readers. Once Clarissa Harlowe has decided to escape the tyranny of her family and goes away with Lovelace, the reader is immediately moved to wonder how long it will be before she is seduced or raped. Lady Mary Wortley Montagu remarked to her daughter about the novel, 'Any Girl that runs away with a young Fellow without intending to marry him should be carry'd to Bridewell or Bedlam the next day.'[8] The novel derives much of its considerable power and attraction from the danger that the reader shares with Clarissa. The reader both anticipates and dreads the outcome.

Clarissa is a remarkable innovation not just in the history of the novel, but in the author's exploitation narratively and fictively of human nature's most formidable psychological impulses and most deeply felt needs. It is difficult for any modern reader to believe that any girl who allows herself to be taken into the custody of a well-known rake posing as her protector is not at least ever so slightly aware that she is in danger not only of compromising her reputation, but of seduction or rape. Lady Mary's comment suggests that readers in the eighteenth century were not greatly different.

Clarissa's behaviour over her elopement/abduction is virtually impossible to analyse briefly, and indeed she can be said to be unsure herself what her intentions and expectations are regarding Lovelace and her promise to let him 'save' her from the proposed marriage with Solmes. The scene in which Clarissa is constrained to leave with Lovelace is shot through with sexual imagery and also exhibits with considerable cogency all the passions likely to be roused in a young girl in such circumstances. Clarissa unlocks the door to the garden to meet Lovelace, as arranged; she leaves it, and when she attempts to return, a threatening voice is heard within, which Lovelace interprets as her brother or uncles, or the man she is to marry, and 'frightened beyond the power of controlling',[9] she rushes away from the garden. The one man whom she sees coming out of the garden after her and Lovelace she almost immediately recognises as Lovelace's accomplice, Joseph Leman, but she continues in her flight.

It is likely that Richardson's readers, both male and female, but particularly the latter, found much to respond to in this incident, but what is of equal interest to a moral historian is Clarissa's own response to the event. She regrets her imprudence and weakness and regards herself as wicked and foolish, but she makes none of the plans to escape from Lovelace that she had previously made to collaborate with him. Having taken the risk that she dare not take, she seems prepared now to enjoy the dangers inherent in that risk. The shrewdness of Richardson's psychological insight cannot be faulted here, however dubious we may find the moral assumptions upon which he bases Clarissa's behaviour. One of the words that recurs frequently in Clarissa's vocabulary is 'violence', and it is clear that she relishes the prospect though not the actuality of violence. When she reports that she is 'frightened beyond the power of controlling', she abandons herself to Lovelace's direction, rather than return to the safety of the garden (whose mythic and symbolic significance in the novel we need not dwell on here).

Morally, and perhaps psychologically, Clarissa has a little in common with a character who would seem to be as far removed from her as possible, Moll Flanders. Though their situations are different in kind, their reactions and responses differ mostly in degree. Moll is extrusively penitent about what she regards as her transgressions of virtue, though she almost always has a justification for her actions. Both are convinced that what they are doing, or what they have done, is wrong, but they nevertheless persist in patterns of behaviour that they cannot condone. In justifying her actions under the aegis of necessity, Moll is at least attempting some gesture towards expiation and moral accountancy, though the reader almost never takes seriously these conventional nods in the direction of morality. Clarissa, having asserted that she was tricked away from Lovelace against her judgement as well as her inclination, nevertheless asserts in her letter of 11 April to her sister that she was forced into the step by the measures her family were taking against her. Like Moll, she finds it psychologically necessary to have some external reason for justifying imprudent behaviour; unlike Moll, Clarissa also finds it morally necessary.

Richardson's interest in the psychological and emotional dimensions of his characters has often reminded readers of Henry James, and indeed Richardson is conspicuous, if not unique, among the eighteenth-century novelists for his awareness of the extent to which sexual desires prompt and govern behaviour, as well as the extent to which attitudes towards sex were being revalued. Smollett and Fielding are interested in the practical consequences of sexual drives and the subsequent behaviour patterns, as well as more theoretical issues of good and evil. Defoe is interested in both the social and psychological effects, but his characters more often than not decide a moral issue in terms of its practical and economic consequences and not its moral value.

Richardson's representation of Clarissa's chastity is different from that in most other eighteenth-century novels, and different from that in *Pamela*. The ideal of chastity frequently found itself under question, often in a 'will-she-or-won't-she' form. In Clarissa's case, the possibility is never broached; that she should give up her chastity under any conditions other than those of a loving marriage is unthinkable. One of the reasons she does not want to marry Solmes is that she finds unconscionable the idea of sexual intercourse with a man whom she abominates. Clarissa is probably the first heroine in the history of English fiction to think of sex as involving reciprocal pleasure, and she endows sex with values and emotional associations that her fictional predecessors did not. In allowing herself to be abducted by Lovelace, she is closer to accepting the notion of sex without marriage but with genuine love and affection than she is to accepting its opposite. The idea of becoming Lovelace's mistress, however, would appal her, and marrying him under the circumstances she finds herself in is out of the question.

Moll Flanders, in contrast, thinks of her chastity as a 'Trifle'. When she decides to accede to the elder brother's proposition, she 'thought of nothing, but the fine Words, and the Gold; whether he intended to Marry me, or not to Marry me, seem'd a Matter of no great Consequence to me. . . .'[10] For Moll, no moral question arises over chastity, and she is one of the most sexually amoral of feminine characters in the eighteenth-century novel. Occasionally, Moll will suggest that her sexual behaviour may be immoral, but she does so in such terms and so infrequently as to be unconvincing both to the reader and to herself. Of her relationship with the Gentleman she meets in Bath, she observes that their yielding to 'mutual Inclinations' should be a 'caution to Readers of this Story; that we ought to be cautious of gratifying our Inclinations in loose and lewd Freedoms, least we find our Resolutions of Virtue fail us in the juncture when their Assistance should be most necessary' (p. 119). To resist forthrightly sexual temptation is one thing; merely to be cautious in gratifying 'Inclinations in loose and lewd Freedoms' is morally quite another, and Moll accepts without hesitation an idea of sexual libertarianism or even libertinism. To some extent, Defoe plays down Moll's sexuality and her indifference to accepted canons of sexual behaviour by the language in which she describes her affairs. Moll is never remotely salacious and reports her sexual encounters in straightforward prose, usually in terms that attribute her ready acceptance to the irresistibility of inclination. Moll can resist everything but temptation.

Clarissa and Moll thus represent a large portion of the range in patterns of sexual behaviour for heroines in the eighteenth-century novel, though one would be reluctant to label the behaviour of either extreme. To Moll, sex is part and parcel of life, and she thinks about it no more than she thinks about her employment. Sex is not romantically associated with any one person or situation, and while there is no doubt that she enjoys her sexual encounters, she is not desperate about their absence.

Clarissa's reaction to being raped is to will herself into death. The dishonour that Lovelace has brought upon her is too great to bear, but given the psychological and emotional assumptions at work in the novel, I am inclined to regard her reaction as one of disappointment. Clearly, sexual intercourse means too much to Clarissa to share it with the man whom she is to marry, Solmes. The risks of continuing to be with Lovelace after he has abducted her are manifest but not insuperable. It is difficult for a reader not to feel that, all things considered, Clarissa is waiting to be raped and that when she is the event proves both too much for her (the violence was greater than anything she had imagined) and too little (it seems most unlikely that sexual intercourse can ever provide the intense pleasure that she expected). Sex exalts neither the flesh nor the spirit, and her desire for orgasm becomes compulsively pathological.

Though Richardson is primarily interested in the behaviour of his female characters, and in representing his perception of female psychology and sexuality as accurately as he can, he is equally shrewd with his male characters.[11] After the rape, Clarissa has sunk into a stupor, and Lovelace laments, 'I had rather, methinks, she should have retained all her active powers, though I had suffered by her nails and her teeth, than that she should be sunk into such a state of absolute—insensibility (shall I call it?) as she has been in ever since Tuesday morning' (III, p. 200). Though the syntax is admittedly ambiguous here, it seems clear enough that Lovelace has both the actual moment of the rape itself in mind, as well as Clarissa's condition afterwards. For a rapist, a passive reaction somewhat blunts the point of the rape, and, as Lovelace later says, 'For a rape, thou knowest, to us rakes, is far from being an undesirable thing' (III, p. 214). The fault is, to be sure, Lovelace's, as he has drugged Clarissa in order to carry out the rape. He expects Clarissa to reconcile herself to becoming his wife, or at least his passive mistress, and thus in some sense his ultimate plans are defeated.

Clarissa's moral stature would seem to all but the sternest of moralists to be unchanged: a virgin who is drugged and then raped can hardly be said to be a willing accomplice. However, so long as Clarissa remains with Lovelace, she runs the personal risk of being raped and has already incurred the public risk of being thought his mistress. In dealing with sexuality under these unusual moral constraints, Richardson has set himself and his readers no easy problem in apportioning censure, praise and judgement. But that is the nature of moral problems where sex is concerned: there are never any easy, ready-made answers, and eighteenth-century novelists were quick to exploit this phenomenon. Richardson's perception of the uniqueness of the moral choices one faces in sexual matters makes his writings far more persuasive than those of straightforward, prescriptive moralists. Moreover, Clarissa does not take the easy way out in making her moral decisions. She rightly perceives that marriage to and sexual intercourse with a man whom she abominates would be morally more dubious than running the risks she does with Lovelace. She would share Anna Howe's emphatic condemnation of a moral code which stipulates that women are 'to be courted as princesses for a few weeks, in order to be treated as slaves for the rest of our lives' (I, p. 131).[12]

Cut-and-dried solutions to moral problems are an easier recourse both for the novelist and for those without Clarissa's moral strength. When Peregrine Pickle attempts to rape Emilia, she fends him off without much difficulty. Smollett's setting for the attempt is conventional to the point of being banal. Peregrine fortifies himself with 'two whole bottles of Burgundy' (p. 406) before taking Emilia to a 'bagnio' rather than to her uncle's house. Offering all his fortune and declaring himself then content to live on her bounty, he finds himself being laughed at. Attempting to 'obey the furious dictates of his unruly and ungenerous desire' (p. 408), he is upbraided by Emilia, who simply walks away from him. The next day, Peregrine remembers what happened with mortification and is forced to admire Emilia's spirit.

Lovelace and Peregrine thus have instructively different moral reactions to their respective attempts at rape. Lovelace succeeds, though a rapist who has to rely on drugs cannot be said to be very good at his craft, but derives neither pleasure nor a sense of triumph from the act. Instead, he finds himself drawn into an admiration of Clarissa that he had not anticipated. Her resistance to him after the rape he had not expected, and the sheer power of her moral certitude eventually overwhelms him. Peregrine's not very serious attempt also leads him into greater admiration for Emilia, while simultaneously making it less likely that he will ever marry her. In the last chapter, she and Peregrine are reconciled, of course, and Smollett has no compunction about hinting at Emilia's own amorousness. When she sees Peregrine again, she 'underwent such agitation as flushed every charm with irresistible energy: her cheeks glowed with a most delicate suffusion, and her bosom heaved with such bewitching undulation, that the cambrick could not conceal or contain the snowy hemispheres, that rose like a vision of paradise to his view' (p. 774). All this before they have even had breakfast! In fact, such is Peregrine's haste to be married and bedded that he insists on marrying that same day. After some hesitation, Emilia agrees, and they are wed before dinner-time. When Emilia appears for breakfast the next morning, she is 'blushing like Aurora or the goddess of health, and sending forth emanations of beauty unparalleled ...' (p. 780). While Smollett's descriptive powers may lack the graces of subtlety and novelty (and there is more than just a tinge of irony in his descriptions), he leaves little doubt in the reader's mind that sex is good for you.

This is an attitude that Henry Fielding certainly shared, and the eventual mating of Joseph and Fanny is described in glowing terms:

> Undressing to her was properly discovering, not putting off Ornaments: For as all her Charms were the Gifts of Nature, she could divest herself of none. How, Reader, shall I give thee an adequate Idea of this lovely young Creature! the Bloom of Roses and Lillies might a little illustrate her Complexion, or their Smell her Sweetness: but to comprehend her entirely, conceive Youth, Health, Bloom, Beauty, Neatness, and Innocence in her Bridal-Bed; conceive

all these in their utmost Perfection, and you may place the charming *Fanny's* Picture before your Eyes.

Joseph no sooner heard she was in Bed, than he fled with the utmost Eagerness to her. A Minute carried him into her Arms, where we shall leave this happy Couple to enjoy the private Rewards of their Constancy; Rewards so great and sweet, that I apprehend *Joseph* neither envied the noblest Duke, nor *Fanny* the finest Duchess that Night. [p. 343]

A few lexical shifts with words such as 'conceive', 'into', 'Couple' and 'private', not to mention 'Fanny', and the reader's imagination is rewarded as well. Fielding's parodic treatment of chastity in the novel has given way to celebration of its mutual loss.

In *Joseph Andrews*, Joseph's chastity, and his Pamela-like resistance to attempts on it, are comic, and Fielding obviously does not wish to take seriously the idea of male chastity; indeed he is sceptical about the value placed upon male or female chastity in his other writings.[13] When Joseph arrives at the inn of the Tow-wouses', the chambermaid Betty is infatuated by his appearance. A chapter is given over to Betty's previous history and the warmth of her passions, and she too makes an assault on Joseph's chastity (having lost her own some time earlier). Joseph reproves her, 'but she had gone too far to recede, and grew so very indecent, that *Joseph* was obliged, contrary to his Inclination, to use some Violence to her, and taking her in his Arms, he shut her out of the Room, and locked the Door' (p. 87). Unlike Moll, Joseph can resist his inclinations, and while Fielding continues to parody male chastity in the novel, one can nevertheless infer that Joseph is to be admired for not succumbing to inclination. Joseph regards himself as pledged to Fanny, and his loyalty to her is strong enough to over-ride the temptation of Betty. Without this loyalty to Fanny, matters might be on a quite different footing.

Fielding is thus suggesting that virtue and morality do not reside in particular acts or patterns of behaviour themselves, but in the circumstances which call them forth and the context in which they are defined. Joseph's virtue is that much more admirable because he is tempted, but he responds to a more deeply felt loyalty. Moreover, it is a loyalty not to some stuffy abstraction, but to another person. Joseph is chaste not because chastity is necessarily good, but because he wishes to remain faithful to Fanny. Equally, Fielding is sympathetic to the demands raised by the sexual impulse. After Joseph has unceremoniously shuffled Betty from his room, Mr Tow-wouse, who had attempted to seduce her on other occasions, encounters her, and 'pressed her so closely with his Kisses, that the vanquished Fair-One, whose Passions were already raised, and which were not so whimsically capricious that one Man only could lay them, though perhaps, she would have rather preferred that one: The vanquished Fair-One quietly submitted, I say, to her Master's Will ...' (p. 88). Betty, committed by no particular loyalties to one person, and in the grip of a sexual drive whose imperatives she could not easily subdue, quickly comes to terms with herself and accepts a surrogate lover. Unlike Joseph, she has no other person to whom she wishes to remain loyal.

The strength of Fielding's moral vision, a vision that is more comprehensive than Richardson's though not so finely detailed, lies in the narrative impartiality with which he represents these incidents. Fielding sensed that his readers were likely to find homologues for themselves in his characters, and that a reader who found a writer responding sympathetically and humanely to the kind of moral problem that one's sexual inclinations and passions presented almost every day was likely to be a reader whose loyalties and interest he could nourish and sustain. The elaborate panoply of the opening chapter of each book, the deliberate self-consciousness of his style, and the self-indulgence that he encourages in the reader all contribute to a subjective validity that his readers can find in their own experience.

One of the features that these novels have in common with regard to patterns of sexual behaviour is that opportunities for illicit sexual intercourse depend to a considerable extent upon serendipity. Except for Lovelace, few of the characters in these novels (and the same is true of most other eighteenth-century novels) are actively and energetically trying to create opportunities. Peregrine is always ready for the possibility of sexual intercourse and is certainly one of the more aggressive male libertines in the novel, but for the most part he is not exclusively intent upon finding sexual partners. Indeed, he seems to enjoy playing practical jokes more than anything else. Moreover, Peregrine has difficulty in distinguishing between an invitation to sexual dalliance and merely eccentric behaviour. For example, when he is in Paris, he visits the house of a 'Traiteur', whose comely wife excuses herself to 'make water' before rejoining the company. Peregrine finds this behaviour 'so wide of decency and decorum' that he follows her; she executes 'in his presence the intent of her withdrawing', and Peregrine makes advances that are stopped short of rape (p. 205).

Peregrine's mistake is common enough, not only in the eighteenth-century novel, but in 'real life'. Like most males, he carries in his head a set of assumptions about what is proper behaviour in the female sex, and deviations from his imaginary set of rules are, by a curious logical process, considered evidence of easy virtue. Lovelace is constantly on the lookout for such signs; the readiness with which Clarissa allows herself to be tricked into running away with him would be likely to be regarded as one. The range of action and response between clear-cut refusal and unmistakable invitation is vast, and Peregrine, like his counterparts in real life, has very little, if any, skill in judging correctly ambiguous behaviour.

In contrast, the signals that he transmits to the wife of an English gentleman, Mrs Hornbeck, whom he meets in Calais, are returned encouragingly, and indeed all that Mrs Hornbeck wants is a suitable opportunity. It duly presents itself at Chantilly, and 'He seized opportunity by the forelock, and bearing her in his arms to the place from whence he came, she was revenged upon the cuckold [i.e. Mr Hornbeck] for the uneasy life he had made her lead, and our hero enjoyed the luscious fruits of his conquest' (p. 202).

Convention usually creates punishment for adultery, and 'Their guilty raptures, however, were not without allay' (p. 202). Peregrine's companion, Jolter, dreams that the inn is on fire, wakes everyone up, and travellers rush from their rooms. Quick thinking prevents Peregrine and Mrs Hornbeck from being discovered, but the suspicious husband soon takes his wife away. However, the context in which all this occurs is replete with comic incident and overtone, and by placing the adultery in a comic context, Smollett obviously diminishes any serious moral implications it may have. To husbands, it was no laughing matter, but Mr Hornbeck is not so much concerned with being a cuckold as being made to look a fool. In giving Mrs Hornbeck a questionable background Smollett has forestalled the necessity of treating her adultery sympathetically. In contrast, in narrating the 'Memoirs of a Lady of Quality' (ch. 88), Smollett is at some pains to ensure that Lady Vane does not appear wicked or irremediable.

Throughout these novels, one is aware of changes taking place in the eighteenth century in attitudes towards and ideas about marriage, sex and other relationships between man and woman. Writers in an earlier century might, for example, have objected to adultery on religious or theological grounds. David Hume, though he could hardly be called the most characteristic spokesman of his age, noted that men wished to be sure that they were the fathers of the children their wives produced and therefore imposed stricter notions of chastity upon women than those they applied to their own sex. Hume merely points out that although 'all these maxims have a plain reference to generation, yet women past child-bearing have no more privilege in this respect, than those who are in the flower of their youth and beauty'.[14] Hume has, to be sure, ignored feelings of jealousy and inadequacy that ensue in cases of adultery, because he is asking by implication a far more wide-ranging and potentially divisive question about the function and value of an ethic that limits sexual intercourse to a marriage contract and which exists for the purposes of rearing children and creating a family.[15]

Because of its threat to the newly emerging ideas of family, adultery figures significantly in eighteenth-century novels as an aberration whose social and moral status had to be reconsidered. In *Peregrine Pickle*, Peregrine's conquest of Deborah Hornbeck is merely an act of 'gallantry' on his part, an attempt to spite her husband on her part. Nevertheless, her adultery is regarded as more immoral than Peregrine's so-called gallantry, perhaps for the reasons that Hume cited. Theirs is not a marriage that Mr Hornbeck is particularly proud of (she was an 'oyster-wench, who had found means to decoy him into the bands of wedlock' (p. 193)), and her commitment to chastity before marriage and to fidelity after marriage seems at best dubious. Without perhaps realising it, Smollett has characterised and caricatured what was becoming a masculine *idée fixe* about adultery in the eighteenth century, both in the novel and in domestic life. A married woman's fidelity to one man was regarded as a necessary qualification, not only because the man had to be sure that the children he was rearing were biologically his, but because it was of equal importance (if not greater) that he should not appear a cuckold. A man could not be made to look ridiculous because of his wife's behaviour.

Thus, the episode that Lady Mary Wortley Montagu writes about, and the hazy, yet emphatic strictures that were being applied to (female) adultery in the novel owe much to each other. Art is imitating life, and life, not being quite certain what its models for morality should be, imitates art. The husband of Signora Bono feels obliged to kill his wife in order to retain his sense of dignity and honour and not to appear a fool in the eyes of his neighbours, but he seems glad to be relieved of the necessity of murder. Because the incident is hushed up, he and his wife can continue as before, as could Hornbeck and his so long as she had been willing to conduct her adulterous liaisons discreetly. Appearances, as we have always known, matter at least as much as what they conceal.

It is, of course, difficult if not foolhardy to generalise on the basis of a few novels, and one or two incidents from life in the eighteenth century, and I do not intend to do so. Without generalising, however, one may nevertheless note one or two features that recur in the novels and in life, whether they be events such as that described by Lady Mary or a principle like that enunciated by Hume. Novelists, moralists and diarists are all examining and considering, rather than accepting or reacting without thinking to, instances of sexual indiscretion that cannot be summarily judged or evaluated. An interest in patterns of and models for behaviour is supplanting rigid notions about sexual propriety. Young girls were not supposed to run off with (or accept the protection of) well-known rakes. Yet once a girl has done so, as Clarissa did, what does she do? Respectable, middle-aged women were not supposed to seduce teenaged boys, but once one had done so, what does one do about it? Or what did respectable female members of the upper classes do when their handsome young footmen refused an explicitly sexual invitation? Young girls were not supposed to surrender their virginity to the sons of the family with whom they lived, but once Moll has done so, what codes of conduct should guide her in the future?

Questions such as these were not being considered, much less answered, by conventional tracts on morality. Courtesy books, sermons, theoretical treatises—none of these gave any guide to those who had transgressed the hard-and-fast rules. To know that one must not commit adultery, must not give up one's virginity outside of marriage, must not accept the 'protection' of a notorious libertine is all very well, but what does one do when those moments have passed for ever? Readers and authors alike both turned to fiction for answers to these questions.

The emergence of the novel in the eighteenth century can be, and has been, attributed to many causes, literary, historical, social and economic. The success of such novels as *Moll Flanders*, *Pamela*,

Roderick Random and *Tom Jones*, to name only a few, is a measure of the extent to which the novel was not only fulfilling a demand of the market place but answering a psychological need. Moreover, people were not simply reading novels, they were frequently discussing them and writing about them to their friends: private letters and diaries abound with allusions and references to the novels and the behaviour of the characters in these novels. The amplitude of Richardson's correspondence with his friends and admirers while he was writing and publishing *Clarissa* is astonishing in its range, complexity and implication. Many of his correspondents begged him, for example, to marry Clarissa to Lovelace, or to bring the novel to some conclusion other than the one he did. Clearly, these readers were looking to the novel in general, and Richardson's in particular, for behavioural and moral guidelines, though it is doubtful that many female readers would have found Clarissa's solution to rape a practical one.

Moll Flanders was perhaps the first novel that attempted, with limited success, to explore the range of actions open to a character whose sexual behaviour did not fit a conventional pattern. Defoe is constantly reminding the reader that Moll's exploits and activities are being related in order to warn the reader against a life such as Moll's, but he even more constantly—and persuasively—returns to a narration and continuation of the possibilities open to her. From time to time, Moll regrets the life that she is leading, but she is quick to justify it; she claims that she is punished for her sexual transgressions, but she could hardly be said to come to grief at the end of the novel. A young reader of the novel who found herself in a situation similar to Moll's at the opening of the novel, when she is willingly seduced by the older brother, might very well conclude that Moll had not fared too badly at all in her transgressions against the prevailing sexual codes.

By imposing comic overtones on the sexual escapades of their various characters, Fielding and Smollett were not only making light of many conventions about these sexual codes but enabling the reader to have doubts about the utility, not to mention the wisdom, of inflexible strictures regarding sexual behaviour. Joseph Andrews's chastity and his determined preservation of it may be comic, and it certainly leads to a number of comic episodes. Perhaps Joseph is wrong to preserve his chastity so persistently, perhaps he appears faintly ridiculous, but we would be unlikely to disapprove of or to deplore the loyalty to Fanny that prompts his determination. It is Peregrine's lack of loyalty to Emilia that disturbs the reader and makes their final reconciliation and marriage implausible. Some values must be seen to be immutable.

As the novel developed and changed in the eighteenth century, so did attitudes towards sex and patterns of sexual behaviour. The novel not only documented these changes, but also enabled its readers, particularly the newly literate, to discover other models for sexual behaviour than those prescribed by Christian theology. Many novelists did, of course, seek to accommodate Christian ideals of sexual fidelity in their novels, but the very fact that they were writing representationally and not theoretically led them to create other patterns and models of sexual behaviour. Richardson's great difficulty in getting his results to match his intentions was reflected in his readers' difficulties in matching their intentions to an appropriate model of sexual behaviour. These models were proving to have endless permutations and possibilities, and the eighteenth-century novel completely redefined the contexts in which sexual behaviour and moral issues were considered.

NOTES

1 *The Complete Letters of Lady Mary Wortley Montagu*, ed. Robert Halsband (Oxford, 1967), III, pp. 44–5.
2 *Ibid.*, p. 45.
3 In a forthcoming book on sex and the eighteenth-century novel, I write at greater length on these novels, as well as others.
4 There is possibly a pun on the name of the lady about whom Lady Mary tells the tale ('bono' = good); moreover, the name may be a false one and the incident relocated in Italy to disguise something that happened a good deal nearer home.
5 Henry Fielding, *Joseph Andrews*, ed. Martin C. Battestin (Oxford, 1967), p. 27. Page references given in text hereafter.
6 The 'Lady of Quality' was Frances Anne Hawes, who first married Lord William Hamilton, second son of James Douglas, fourth Duke of Hamilton, and after his death married, in May 1735, William Vane, second Viscount Vane.
7 Tobias Smollett, *The Adventures of Peregrine Pickle*, ed. James L. Clifford (London, 1964), p. 525. Page references given in text hereafter.
8 *Op. cit.*, III, p. 9.

9 Samuel Richardson, *Clarissa*, Everyman Edition (London, 1932), I, p. 484. Page references given in text hereafter.

10 Daniel Defoe, *The Fortunes and Misfortunes of the Famous Moll Flanders*, ed. G. A. Starr (London, 1971), p. 25. Page references given in text hereafter.

11 In his excellent study, *Adultery and the Novel* (Baltimore, Md., and London, 1979), Tony Tanner describes *Clarissa* as 'this arguably most seminal of English eighteenth-century novels' (p. 111), and I have learned a good deal from his book.

12 On Clarissa's 'sexuality' and 'sensibility', see Jean H. Hagstrum, *Sex and Sensibility: Ideal and Erotic Love from Milton to Mozart* (Chicago, Ill., and London, 1980), pp. 195–205.

13 I have discussed the sexual mores in *Tom Jones* in 'Sex and the Foundling Boy: the Problem in *Tom Jones*', *Review of English Literature*, VIII, No. 4 (October 1967), 42–52.

14 David Hume, *A Treatise of Human Nature*, ed. L. A. Selby-Bigge (Oxford, 1955), pp. 572–3.

15 On this point, see Lawrence Stone, *The Family, Sex and Marriage in England 1500–1800* (London, 1977), *passim*.

This paper first appeared in Ronald C. Rosbottom, general editor, *Studies in Eighteenth-Century Culture*, Vol. 9 (Madison: The University of Wisconsin Press; © 1979 by the American Society for Eighteenth-Century Culture), pp. 25–43.

DOUGLAS BROOKS-DAVIES

The mythology of love: Venerean (and related) iconography in Pope, Fielding, Cleland and Sterne

Shaftesbury, instructing his history painter in *A Notion of the Historical Draught or Tablature of the Judgment of Hercules* (1713), was only too aware of the temptations of Venerean Pleasure to artist and viewer alike: give her roses, myrtle, emblematic vases and plate, and drapery to form 'a kind of Bower and Couch'; but, he warned, do not 'overdo this part, and express the Affection too much to the life'. Pleasure is, after all, 'of a relish far more popular, and vulgarly ingaging, than' Minervan virtue.[1] And yet the fact remains that it is sometimes difficult for the modern reader to recognise Venus in her various eighteenth-century disguises and, despite the work of Hagstrum, Paulson and others, having recognised her, to admit that still well into the century she, and other figures from classical mythology, could be endowed with an almost Renaissance density of moral and psychological meanings.[2] I wish to offer in this essay a preliminary exploration of Venerean iconography in some English eighteenth-century poems and novels.

I

I shall begin with Milton because he is a paradigm and sometimes a source for Pope, Fielding and Cleland. Halfway through Book IV of *Paradise Lost* Eve tells Adam her memory of her first awakening. She found herself 'Under a shade of flowers' near a lake and went 'to look into the clear / Smooth lake, that to me seemed another sky' (ll. 451, 458–9).[3] Narcissus-like she admired her own image and would have 'pined with vain desire' (l. 466) had not a voice warned her to abandon the shadow of her reflection for the substance of Adam, 'Whose image thou art' and by whom she is destined to 'bear / Multitudes like [her]self' (ll. 472–4). Eve's initial reaction to Adam is unfavourable:

> back I turned,
> Thou following cried'st aloud, Return fair Eve,
> Whom fly'st thou? Whom thou fly'st, of him thou art,
> His flesh, his bone. . . . [ll. 480–3]

There is a strange and (I think) unnoticed echo here of Genesis 39: 12ff.: 'And she caught him by his garment, saying, Lie with me: and he left his garment in her hand, and fled, and got him out. And it came to pass, when she saw that he had left his garment in her hand, and was fled forth, That she called unto the men of her house . . .' This passage refers, of course, to Joseph's flight from Potiphar's wife. Adam seems to recognise that Eve's flight from him has a similar (but to him and Milton inadmissible) urgency. It is just a fleeting recognition, but an important one, and one to which I shall return in connection with Fielding.

Whatever other roles she may play, Eve is always a Venus, queen of the garden of Eden (which means 'pleasure' and was connected by the mythographers with the name Adonis), associated and even identified with flowers (IX. 432), and particularly the Venerean roses and myrtle (IX. 426, 431; cf. IV. 262). Venus, through identification with Flora, was goddess of flowers and gardens.[4] Hence, too, the reflecting lake, while recalling Narcissus, also becomes Eve's mirror (IV. 263); and a mirror is one of the commonest of Venus's attributes.[5] So Eve's initial self-love is culpable female vanity. And yet the lake—Milton says it twice (ll. 456, 459)—is heavenly, skylike; so that when Eve gazes at her reflection she might be glimpsing for a moment Venus Urania, her ideal rather than procreatively real self, the Venus Pandemos.[6] At the very least there is an acceptance by Milton here of the problems of the establishing of a sexual identity through self-love and incest (a variant of the Narcissus myth found in Pausanias says that the boy was originally in love with his twin sister).[7] Joseph flees Potiphar's wife, keeping himself intact, as it were, and leaving her the garments (the shadow of himself). Narcissus and Venus are opposite, yet complementary. Milton's exploration of Eve here echoes Spenser's elaborate exploration of the growth to sexual awareness of Britomart, Amoret and Belphoebe; and I would suggest that despite the influences of empiricism and materialism, Milton and Spenser were responsible for the continuity of the Renaissance mythological mode among many writers of the eighteenth century. As Spenserian romantic epic, hand in hand with Miltonic epic, develops into the novel, so does their mythological mode enter it, too. But it is present, first, in mock epic and the Belinda of *The Rape of the Lock* (1714) who combines within herself Eve, Venus and Narcissus.

Belinda's temptation to a regressive virginity by Ariel in a dream is also a temptation to infantile self-love. Ariel is a sylph; sylphs are metamorphosed coquettes who 'sport and flutter in the Fields of Air' (I. 66;[8] air is Venus's element; Venus is traditionally associated with the first of the four ages of man.[9] Hence Ariel's 'Some secret Truths . . . / To Maids alone and Children are reveal'd' at I. 37–8). Belinda, too, is a coquette, tempting many but fulfilling none. But, says Ariel, "Know farther yet; Whoever fair and chaste / Rejects Mankind, is by some *Sylph* embrac'd" (ll. 67–8). He is her reflection, and she is his[10] and so a mirror appears on the scene: "Late, as I rang'd the Crystal Wilds of Air, / In the clear Mirror of thy ruling *Star* / I saw, alas! some dread Event impend" (ll. 107–9). The star is presumably the planet Venus; and so the way is prepared (narcissism, mirror, Venus, Miltonic echoes) for the description of Belinda's toilette which follows on from the warning 'but most beware of Man!' (l. 114).

This description is too well known to require detailed quotation. We recall, though, that we are present at an 'unveiling' (l. 121), a revelation of divine mysteries. And in fact Belinda, confronting her mirror, is here revealing the complex depths of her Venerean being.[11] As she, Narcissus-like, 'adores', her own 'heav'nly Image in the Glass appears' (l. 125): hints, *via* Milton, of Venus Urania. But this is a passing allusion, for Belinda really controls the lower world, which offers 'unnumber'd' tributes, in a passage echoing the celebrated opening of Lucretius's *De rerum natura* on the power of the generative Venus.[12] (It is echoed, too, at II. 52 when '*Belinda* smil'd, and all the World was gay'.) And yet Belinda is, at this stage of her development, the very opposite of generative. I suspect that we must link this passage with Belinda in her barge in canto II. She stands as an emblem of England's maritime and mercantile power: to Belinda / England the world pours forth its material treasures.[13] The artifacts seem sterile if we compare them, as I think we must, with the burgeoning fertility of the opening of Lucretius, and so it is difficult to agree totally with Landa's approbation of Belinda here. What Pope is offering us is an alternative Venus: Belinda as the centre of the world's trade is a parody of the sea-born Venus, the anadyomene. This, says Pope, is what Whig mercantilism has reduced the splendid sea Venus to, she who, according to Spence, gave rise to 'the most celebrated picture in all antiquity' and on whom the eighteenth century's favourite Venus de' Medici was modelled.[14]

As Belinda continues to confront herself she achieves for a moment, and in the privacy of her closet, self-fulfilment:

> Now awful Beauty puts on all its Arms;
> The Fair each moment rises in her Charms,
> Repairs her Smiles, awakens ev'ry Grace,
> And calls forth all the Wonders of her Face.... [I. 139–42]

The awakening of the Graces is no mere vapid decorative gesture. It recalls the virtuous Venerean Graces with which Belphoebe is endowed at *Faerie Queene*, II. iii. 25: 'Upon her eyelids many Graces sate, / Under the shadow of her even browes'.[15] And I mention Belphoebe since she, like Milton's Eve, is that Venerean type known to the Renaissance and earlier as the virginal Venus, or *Venus virgo*, which has its origin in part in Venus's appearance to her son Aeneas with all the attributes of a nymph of Diana at *Aeneid*, I. 314ff.[16] A recognised mythographical variant is the armed Venus (possessing the weapons of Minerva or Mars), the *Venus armata*.[17] So that when Belinda arms herself here she is not just, surely, or even, parodying the arming of the epic hero, as the Twickenham editor suggests. She is, instead, actually becoming an armed virginal Venus; an interpretation confirmed by the tortoise and elephant that 'unite' to produce her combs (ll. 135–6), since the elephant traditionally signifies chastity, and the tortoise is an attribute of the domestic Venus.[18] Moreover, the 'keener Lightnings' that 'quicken in her Eyes' (l. 144) seem to be specifically Minervan and are echoed at IV. 93–4 where Belinda is accompanied and encouraged by a companion who is a projection of her by now not just Minervan but Amazonian self ('*Belinda* burns with more than mortal Ire, / And fierce *Thalestris* fans the rising Fire'). The culmination comes with the battle at V. 37ff. ('To Arms, to Arms! the fierce Virago cries, / And swift as Lightning to the Combate flies').[19] Belinda's initial narcissism, then, fulfils itself in the projection of a militant Venerean image which is then reflected back at her through her companions and attributes: Ariel; Thalestris; Affectation (in canto IV); the Queen of Hearts (canto III), and so on.

But the beginning of canto II shows Belinda's benevolent rather than militant Venerean characteristics. As I have suggested, when she smiles and 'all the World [is] gay', she is the creating Venus of Lucretius (and also the traditional laughing Venus).[20] And she has to appear on water accompanied by music and zephyrs (II. 51, 58) not only because she is imitating Venerean Cleopatra on the Cydnus but because she knows that Cleopatra herself is imitating the Venus anadyomene. As for her cross ('On her white Breast a sparkling *Cross* she wore, / Which *Jews* might kiss, and Infidels adore'; II. 7–8), it is not just a blasphemous overgoing of the cross of Christ. Hanging round her neck and surmounted by her head it suggests the cross and circle that constitute Venus's planetary sign, ♀, and which was, incidentally, frequently understood to represent the goddess of love's mirror of vanity.[21] Everyone adores it because *omnia vincit amor*. Complementing the emblematic cross in the first paragraph of canto II are the 'two Locks, which graceful hung behind / In equal Curls' in the second paragraph. They are there to 'insnare' men as 'Slight Lines of Hair' are set to catch fish (in the old love-poem cliché) and they reinforce the mythological connections that I have been tracing. The phrase 'Man's Imperial Race' (II. 27) reminds us of wise and contemplative Adam at *Paradise Lost*, IV. 300–1; so that Belinda's hair recalls Venerean Eve's 'wanton' and luxuriant tresses as well as the English custom that brides' hair was traditionally worn long.[22] At the end of the poem the raped lock is metamorphosed into a constellation rivalling the *Coma Berenices* (which is yellow, one of Venus's colours, and was placed in the heavens by Venus herself).[23] Significantly, at V. 135 'This, the blest Lover shall for *Venus* take'. But in addition, as Wasserman has told us, the *cut* lock brings to mind Graeco-Roman virginity rituals and the sacrifice of 'virgin locks ... to a deity of chastity'.[24] We are back with Belinda as *Venus virgo* again as well as (not inappropriately) Narcissus and Dido. For Narcissus's sisters, mourning their brother's death, cut their locks in tribute to him (*Metamorphoses*, III. 505–7). Narcissus had died because he could not possess himself (or his twin); Belinda metaphorically dies (the poem darkens quite literally with canto IV) because a part of herself has been stolen or separated off: for the two locks are perhaps to be understood as *twin* locks, reflecting each other mirror fashion ('The Sister-Lock now sits uncouth, alone'; IV. 171). With one lost, the owner of the remaining one 'dies' of grief. I see Belinda as dying with the loss of the lock because of the echoes of *Aeneid*, IV, that are present here. Pope's own note compares the opening of canto IV to the opening of Virgil's fourth book, which for a moment at least equates Belinda with Dido. Dido was traditionally lascivious;[25] abandoned by Aeneas, her love turned to anger, then despair. She kills herself at the end of *Aeneid*, IV; Pope's canto III ends with the rape. But Dido's soul cannot leave her body until the 'golden lock', consecrated to Proserpina, queen of the underworld, has been cut by Iris. The pun on death here in Pope's poem (the cutting of hair as a sign of death; death as a cant term for orgasm) is insignificant compared with the primary meaning, which is the death of Belinda's childlike self to generate, in canto IV, another, darker, self, that of the Saturnian goddess Spleen with her courtiers which reflect Belinda–Venus's court of love of canto II. In the last section of this paper I shall examine more fully the relationship between Venus and Saturn.

II

In *Joseph Andrews* (1742) the Narcissus–Venus iconography is as apparent and as important as it is in *The Rape*. Joseph's love song in II. xii, the overhearing of which by Fanny in the inn leads to the first meeting of the lovers within the narrative, refers to the separated lover's anguish and his desire for fulfilment. Stanzas II and III introduce Narcissus:

> . . . *But felt not* Narcissus *more Joy,*
> *With his Eyes he beheld his lov'd Charms?*
> *Yet what he beheld, the fond Boy*
> *More eagerly wish'd in his Arms.*
>
> *How can it thy dear Image be,*
> *Which fills thus my Bosom with Woe?*
> *Can aught bear Resemblance to thee,*
> *Which Grief and not Joy can bestow?*
> *This Counterfeit snatch from my heart. . . .*[26]

On hearing the song Fanny faints, and revives to find Joseph holding her. ' "Are you *Joseph Andrews*?" "Art thou my *Fanny*" ' they echo.[27] And with Narcissus as our clue we recall Eve's awakening to her own reflection, because Joseph and Fanny are virtually physically identical, Platonic hermaphroditic complements of each other:[28] a *motif* that becomes a little bit too much of a joke for the pair themselves (however psychologically comprehensible, and also comprehensible in terms of the variant Narcissus myth we encountered earlier, in which the boy loves his twin sister) when it is thought for a while that they are actually brother and sister (IV. xii). *Joseph Andrews* is, indeed, a novel of pairing: from its self-mirroring chiastic structure,[29] to its twin heroes and twin hero and heroine, its relationship with Richardson's *Pamela* (whose own hero and heroine appear at the end), and smaller details like Lady Booby's reflection in her ungainly maid Slipslop in their pursuit of Joseph (I. v ff.). There is the curious mirror-like reversal, too, whereby Joseph has the virtue and modesty that the women, except Fanny, have not. The reluctant beautiful male reminds us, among other parallels, of Shakespeare's and Titian's version of Venus and Adonis (Joseph is referred to as an '*Adonis*' in I. vii, p. 36);[30] though Lady Booby, lustful and recently widowed, is also widow Dido to Joseph's Aeneas as well as Venerean Pleasure to Joseph's Hercules (with Fanny as Dianan Virtue).[31] The Lady's appetitive reality, mirrored in the cow/tigress/pike Slipslop of I. vi (pp. 32–3), is countermanded by the description of Joseph at the moment when, for the second time, she confronts him in bed. Joseph's defence of his virtue calls forth this reaction:

> You have heard, Reader, Poets talk of the *Statue of Surprize*; ... but from [no one] ... could you receive such an Idea of Surprize, as would have entered in at your Eyes, had they beheld the Lady *Booby*, when those last Words issued out from the Lips of *Joseph*.—'Your Virtue! (said the Lady recovering after a Silence of two Minutes) I shall never survive it. [I. viii, pp. 40–1]

The image again confronts its reality: the youth has the virtue missing from the woman, hence the ambiguously suggested mirror at the end of the chapter ('"Have I not exposed myself to the Refusal of my Footman? I cannot bear the Reflection"'; p. 42). And perhaps the statue image directs us not just to a poetic commonplace and to acting convention[32] but specifically to Ovid's Narcissus:

> He looks in speechless wonder at himself and hangs there motionless in the same expression, like a statue carved from Parian marble. Prone on the ground, he gazes at his eyes, twin stars, and his locks, worthy of Bacchus, worthy of Apollo ... all things, in short, he admires for which he is himself admired. [*Met.*, III. 418ff.][33]

Since the Biblical analogue is Joseph and Potiphar's wife, we are finally back with Milton's Eve as I described her at the beginning:

Joseph flees (when ordered from the room) as Eve flees Adam, and his mistress is left with his image tormenting her and with his even more insubstantial self, his clothes ('*Joseph* ... having stript off his Livery ...'; I. x, p. 47). It is an aspect of the novel's own mirror structure that the tormented Lady reappears at the beginning of Book IV: as soon as she sees Joseph again 'her Cheeks glow'd with red, and immediately after became as totally pale. She had in her Surprize almost stopt her Coach ...' (IV. i, p. 277). A page later we are told that 'the Arrow had pierced deeper than she imagined', of the extent of her 'Wound', and of the 'confused horrible Dreams' that disturb her sleeep. The allegorical language here is consciously archaic, depicting her psychomachia in a way familiar from Renaissance romance. But if I am right in seeing her, in part at least, as lustful Venus opposing Fanny's Dianan virtue, then what Fielding presents us with in this chapter is yet another iconographical commonplace, that of the wounded Venus, attacked by her son Cupid with the arrows which she so readily allows him to release at others.[34]

As we have already seen, though, love and chastity and their mythological counterparts do not always have to be opposed to each other. And it is Fanny who is the chaste Venus of this novel, as Sophia is of *Tom Jones*. She is sensuously beautiful but above all virginal and modest. Indeed, long before she is described physically, her modesty is mentioned (I. ix, p. 49: 'Modesty'; 'tender and chaste Passion'). When she is described she is 'tall and delicately shaped' but also 'plump' with 'swelling Breasts' and 'a Countenance in which tho' she was extremely bashful, a Sensibility appeared almost incredible; and a Sweetness, whenever she smiled, beyond either Imitation or Description' (II. xii, pp. 152–3). In other words, she combines the characteristic tallness of Diana–Minerva with the sensual appeal of Venus; though such details as the pock 'Mark on her Chin' (p. 152) leave the portrait as a whole hovering delicately between the 'realistic' and the consciously iconographical.[35]

When he wants to, however, Fielding can utilise the iconographical mode pure and simple, as for example when Fanny is attacked by one of Didapper's servants: '... the Deity who presides over chaste Love sent her *Joseph* to her Assistance' who arrives 'just as the Ravisher had torn her Handkerchief from her Breast'. The passage describing Joseph's consequent confrontation with Fanny is worth quoting at length:

... you may remember, Reader, that the Ravisher had tore her Handkerchief from *Fanny's* Neck, by which he had discovered such a Sight; that *Joseph* hath declared all the Statues he ever beheld were ... much inferiour to it in Beauty.... This modest Creature, whom no Warmth in Summer could ever induce to expose her Charms ... had stood many Minutes bare-necked in the presence of *Joseph*, before ... [reflecting] on what concerned herself; till at last, when the Cause of her Concern had vanished, an Admiration at his Silence, together with observing the fixed Position of his Eyes, produced an Idea in the lovely Maid, which brought more Blood into her Face than had flowed from *Joseph's* Nostrils. The snowy Hue of her Bosom was likewise exchanged to Vermillion at the instant when she clapped her Handkerchief round her Neck. [IV. vii, p. 305]

Fanny is here instantly recognisable as the *Venus pudica*, in which modesty is an attribute of the chaste Venus who signifies her virtue by blushing and by placing drapery or hands over breasts and pudenda. Another characteristic of modesty is the downward gaze, beautifully captured by Harriet Hearty, Fanny's double within Wilson's interpolated tale:

... I laid gently hold on her Hand, and conveying it to my Lips, I prest it with inconceivable Ardour; then lifting up my swimming Eyes, I saw her Face and Neck overspread with one Blush; she offered to withdraw her Hand, yet not so as to deliver it from mine, tho' I held it with the gentlest Force. We both stood trembling, her Eyes cast on the ground, and mine stedfastly fixed on her. (III. iii, p. 222)[36]

III

Cleland's *Memoirs of a Woman of Pleasure* (1749)[37] is as much romance as pornography. Much of its erotic language and some of its situations derive from Renaissance commonplaces,[38] and so, not surprisingly, it is a novel of Venus. She possesses it, and gives it mythological unity. 'Fanny Hill', directly translated, means *mons Veneris*, of course; and the genital descriptions, with their 'young tendrils of ... moss' (p. 20), etc., suggest that we are with the sexual topography of Spenser's Garden of Adonis and related Venerean gardens of pleasure, including Milton's Eden. But Fanny has to learn what, at Mrs Brown's 'college' (p. 18),[39] are known as 'the mysteries of Venus' (pp. 34–5), and her initiation follows the familiar progress from homoerotic to heterosexual, again within a mythological framework. The virginally modest Fanny is handed over to aptly named Phoebe (not virginal herself, but suggesting Fanny's own virginal state), whose caresses awaken in her 'the first sparks of kindling nature, the first ideas of pollution' (p. 22). After this she is 'trick[ed] out for the market' in gaudy finery and admires herself 'in the glass' (p. 23); so that her progress is literally that from Phoebe/Diana to immodest Venus, at which point she confronts the Venerean mirror, like Belinda and like Milton's Eve.[40] There are faint hints of Narcissus, too. Fanny is eager to mention that she admires the dress rather than herself (p. 25), which, taken in conjunction with Phoebe's lesbian embraces, looks forward to Louisa's autobiographical sketch at a corresponding position in the second half of the novel where we are told: 'I gave myself up to the old insipid privy shifts of my self-viewing, self-touching, self-enjoying, *in fine*, to all the means of *self-knowledge* I could devise in search of the pleasure that fled before me ...' Her masturbation is, like Narcissus reaching out to his reflection, a mere 'grasping [of] shadows' (pp. 132–3). Louisa 'instinctively' knows, however, that 'man alone' will be her cure. Fanny's first encounter with a man, on the other hand, is with a horrifying Richardsonian grotesque 'with a yellow cadaverous hue, great goggling eyes [and] a peculiar ghastliness in his grin' (p. 25);[41] she equally instinctively rejects him, as Eve rejects Adam, and the echoes of Milton continue when Fanny spies on the again grotesque activities of Mrs Brown and her 'brawny young Horse-grenadier' (p. 35) and then, in company with Phoebe, spies on the love-making of Polly and her Genoese lover at pp. 40ff. The pair (unlike the first two) are perfectly physically matched: she with hints of *modestia* and Milton's Eve ('stark naked, ... with her black hair loose and afloat down her dazzling white neck and shoulders, whilst the deepen'd carnation of her cheeks went off gradually into the hue of glaz'd snow'; p. 41), he with hints of a sensual Adam ('tall and well-limb'd ... his hair, being too short to tie, fell no lower than his neck, in short easy curls'; p. 42). All this turns Fanny, just for the moment, into an outsider, into Satan gazing enviously at the human pair as they make their first appearance in *Paradise Lost*, IV. 285ff. Polly has found her complement; Phoebe appears not to need one. Significantly, Fanny meets hers immediately after this episode, at pp. 46ff., as she is on her way to the garden. He is sleeping, 'a fair stripling between eighteen and nineteen, ... his hair in disorder'd curls, irregularly shading a face, on which all the roseate bloom of youth and all the manly graces conspired to fix my eyes and heart'. He has 'long eyelashes' and 'a pair of vermilion lips, pouting and swelling to the touch, as if a bee had freshly stung them' (pp. 47–8). He awakens to her (recalling the awakenings into existence in *Paradise Lost*, IV and VIII), and she abandons Mrs Brown to live with him, at which point the mythological basis of the novel becomes explicit. If Fanny is Venus, then Charles is 'my *Adonis*' (p. 52), around whom she curls herself 'like the tendril of a vine' (p. 56), as the emblematic cliché has it.[42] Their idyllic lovemaking recalls Spenser's Garden of Adonis and the traditions that it draws upon, and also (in the pose of the sleeping lover) the garden's prolepsis in the Bower of Bliss, where beautiful Verdant/Adonis sleeps by Acrasia/Venus (*Faerie Queene*, II, xii. 79–80). A subsequent description of Charles conforms to the Adonis/Bacchus ideal of the 'vernal freshness of an age in which beauty is of either sex' and with 'the first down over his upper lip' (p. 58).[43] At p. 68 he is once more 'my all-perfect Adonis'; and, as with the mythological Adonis, one day 'the mortal, the unexpected blow of separation fell upon us' (p. 70). Fanny's grief (pp. 72ff.) is like that of the bereaved Venus, and even though her health is restored, she 'retain[s] an air of grief, dejection, and languor' (p. 73). Three pages later 'I continued in a state of stupidity, or melancholy despair'. When her body begins to reawaken sexually she attributes this largely to the 'mechanical' operation of her 'animal spirits' (p. 81). Love returns only with the return of Charles, as Venus blooms only with the restoration of Adonis.[44]

IV

Fanny's reawakening from despair to venery, in which Mr H. is the agent of 'dissipation' which relieves her 'from the black corroding thoughts [her] head had been a prey to ever since the absence of [her] dear Charles' (p. 83), neatly introduces my final topic, the relationship between melancholy and love, Saturn and Venus. If in Cleland's novel it has its origins in the grief and despair of the Venus and Adonis myth, in general it relates to an astrological tradition which saw Venus as antithetical to Saturn and hence as offering an antidote to the ills brought by Saturn. The scheme, ubiquitous in the Renaissance, remains common in the eighteenth century.[45] From this point of view the darkness of the Cave of Spleen that follows the cutting of Belinda's lock signifies the death of Belinda's Venerean self and her transition to a Saturnian melancholy and despair: the east wind displaces the

Venerean and sanguinic zephyrs; Ariel (Venerean air) is displaced by dark Umbriel, daemon of Saturn's element, earth.[46] In Gray's 'Ode on the Spring' the solitary melancholic poet opposes himself to Venus/ Flora's month May, and Venus's 'rosy-bosom'd Hours', music and 'Cool Zephyrs'; similarly, the Eton College ode is divided exactly between Venerean sanguinic youth[47] and the dark cares of Saturnian age. But it is in Sterne that the opposition is most apparent and most lovingly worked out. I have suggested elsewhere[48] how in *Tristram Shandy* (1759–67) Sterne is obsessed with melancholy: strongly influenced by Burton on the one hand and his own Saturnian consumption on the other, he has here produced a novel in which time, sickness and death are regarded as ubiquitous and conquerable only through Venerean laughter and love.

The climax to the theme comes at the end of volume VII at the time of the vintage (Bacchus and Venus are traditionally related) as Tristram's dance of death yields to the festive dances of chapters xxxviii (Venus is goddess of the dance; and note the mention of Venus/Flora's 'May-poles') and xliii where the dance is accompanied by singing and Saturn is banished by Venus: 'VIVA LA JOIA! FIDON LA TRISTESSA!'[49] And so Tristram dances forward into Uncle Toby's amours, which occupy volumes VIII and IX and which have begun in volume VI and so intertwine with and in a sense undo the melancholic volumes V and VII.

Toby's main problem, though, is how to reconcile his sensibility and predisposition to love with his career as a soldier (the subject of his '*apologetical oration*' at VI. xxxii). At chapter xxxv Venus with her lute possesses him, displacing 'the trumpet of war'.[50] The moral problem embodied in Toby had long been a subject for mythographical and philosophical enquiry, ever since Mars fell in love with Venus and they produced the child Harmony. The answer, with a few reservations, was simple. Although excessive venery is bad, Mars must (in moderation) yield to Venus, strife must give way to love in order to achieve concord. And along with loves goes 'laughter-loving Venus';[51] hence the comedy of *Tristram Shandy*, the rationale for which is explicitly stated at IV. xxxii as Tristram's story really 'sets out':

Was I left, like Sancho Pança, to choose my kingdom ... it should be a kingdom of hearty laughing subjects: And as the bilious and more saturnine passions, by creating disorders in the blood and humours, have as bad an

> influence, I see, upon the body politic as body natural—and as nothing but a habit of virtue can fully govern those passions, and subject them to reason—I should add to my prayer—that God would give my subjects grace to be as WISE as they were MERRY; and then should I be the happiest monarch, and they the happiest people under heaven——

Saturnian black bile is to be vanquished by the wise laughter of Venus. And this really is what Clarissa says to Pope's Belinda as she recommends 'good Humour' as the antidote to spleen (*Rape of the Lock*, V. 30).

Laughter is crucial to the traveller of *A Sentimental Journey* (1768), too, and again it arrives only with the purging of Saturn. For although Yorick affirms that he bears the French king 'no spleen' as he sets out on his travels,[52] Saturnian misanthropy is affirmed by his choice of the single-seat desobligeant which 'hit my fancy at first sight' (pp. 76–7) but is rejected when he meets a lady shortly after, so that when he nexts sees a desobligeant it is symbolically 'tatter'd' and he thinks ''twas a churlish beast into whose heart the idea could first enter, to construct such a machine . . .' (p. 109). As the lady departs the springs of love have begun to flow within him and are announced by Venerean myrtle ('I would fasten [my affections] upon some sweet myrtle' (p. 116)), the rejection of the misanthropic Smollett of the *Travels Through France and Italy*,[53] and the employing of the emblematically named La Fleur as his valet who can 'play a little upon the fiddle' (p. 125) and who is 'always in love' (p. 128). This last fact suggests 'A FRAGMENT' paraphrased from Burton in which through the power of love a political and psychological golden age is restored and Saturn's hellebore[54] and Mars's weapons are again banished: 'No pharmacopolist could sell one grain of helebore—not a single armourer had a heart to forge one instrument of death—Friendship and Virtue met together, and kiss'd each other in the street—the golden age return'd, and hung o'er the town of Abdera. . . .' (p. 131). And so Yorick travels on, until La Fleur's pursuit of his new mistress on a Sunday leads to the exclamation 'Happy people! that once a week at least are sure to lay down all your cares together; and dance and sing and sport away the weights of grievance, which bow down the spirit of other nations to the earth' (p. 248). In other words, Venerean dance versus Saturnian earth again. And this is a prelude to the recognition of the religious implications of laughter and dance to be enjoyed not only on the eternal sabbath but, more immediately, when Yorick joins 'THE

SUPPER', once more at the time of the vintage, on Mont Tarare (or, as Sterne spells it, 'mount Taurira', perhaps with the suggestion that Taurus is a sign of Venus). This 'feast of love' (p. 281) ends with music and '*Religion* mixing in the dance' (p. 284); and the music is an echo of the cosmic harmony which lies behind the philosophy of sensibility itself, with its vocabulary of 'tuning' and 'vibrations'.[55] To the sentimentalist, then, the universe was still a lute, monochord or similar stringed instrument, and the deity he worshipped was the *mater harmoniae* Venus who, Mrs Shandy contradicts her husband to announce, 'keeps peace in the world' (*Tristram Shandy*, VIII. xxxiii).

NOTES

1 Anthony Ashley Cooper, third Earl of Shaftesbury, *Characteristicks of Men, Manners, Opinions, Times*, second edn., 3 vols. (London, 1714), III, pp. 370, 386–7.

2 See J. H. Hagstrum, *The Sister Arts: the Tradition of Literary Pictorialism and English Poetry from Dryden to Gray* (Chicago, 1958); Ronald Paulson, *Emblem and Expression: Meaning in English Art of the Eighteenth Century* (London, 1975); and D. C. Allen, *Mysteriously Meant: the Rediscovery of Pagan Symbolism and Allegorical Interpretation in the Renaissance* (Baltimore, Md., and London, 1970), especially ch. X. These meanings survive the general decline of allegory and, e.g., the influential euhemerism of the Abbé Banier's *La Mythologie et les fables expliquées par l'histoire* (English transln., 4 vols. (London, 1739–40)).

3 Milton quotations are from *The Poems of John Milton*, ed. John Carey and A. D. S. Fowler (London, 1968).

4 On Eden as pleasure see, e.g., Fowler, *ed. cit.*, IV, pp. 27–8n., and John Robinson, *A Theological, Biblical, and Ecclesiastical Dictionary* (London, 1815), *s.v.* ('EDEN ... signifies *pleasure*, or *delights*'); and for Adonis/Eden, J. W. Bennett, 'Spenser's Garden of Adonis', *PMLA*, 47 (1932), 48 and n. The roses and myrtle are a commonplace (e.g., Ovid, *Fasti*, IV. 138–9), as are gardens of Venus. But for an explicit statement see Henry Cornelius Agrippa, *Three Books of Occult Philosophy*, tr. J. F. (London, 1651), I. xlviii, p. 96: among places dedicated to Venus are 'pleasant fountains, green Meadows, flowrishing Gardens'. The identification of Venus and Flora is discussed by Charles Dempsey, '*Mercurius Ver*: The Sources of Botticelli's *Primavera*', *JWCI*, 31 (1968), 251–73.

5 Meg Twycross, *The Medieval Anadyomene: a Study in Chaucer's Mythography* (Oxford, 1972), pp. 82ff., who also comments on the identification *Venus-vanitas* (e.g., p. 85).

6 The Platonic and Neoplatonic distinction was still alive for the early to middle eighteenth century, as Joseph Spence's *Polymetis* (London,

1747), p. 102, testifies: '... there was a Venus, which they called the Venus Cœlestis ...' (see also p. 68). In one of the latest discussions of the Milton passage J. H. Hagstrum still sees it as offering a temptation to culpable narcissism pure and simple: *Sex and Sensibility: Ideal and Erotic Love from Milton to Mozart* (Chicago and London, 1980), pp. 44–5.

7 Pausanias, *Description of Greece*, IX. xxxi. 8. In the English transln. of Banier, the passage is quoted as follows: '... there is another Tradition, less known indeed, but which wants not however its Partisans and Authors. We are told that *Narcissus* had a Twin-Sister who perfectly resembled him; she had the same Air of Face, the same Hair, they often dressed like one another, and hunted together. *Narcissus* fell in love with his Sister, but had the Misfortune to lose her. After this Disaster, abandoning himself to Melancholy, he frequented the Banks of a Fountain, whose Water was like a Mirrour, and there he took Pleasure in contemplating himself ...' (*The Mythology and Fables of the Antients, Explained from History*, IV (1740), pp. 365–6). Biblical authority for the incest idea comes from Song of Solomon 4: 9 ('Thou hast ravished my heart, my sister, my spouse'); and cf. Ephesians 5 quoted in n. 10 below.

8 Quotations from *The Rape* are from the one vol. Twickenham edn., ed. John Butt (London, 1965).

9 Venus is 'queen of th'ayre' at *Faerie Queene*, IV. x. 47, and, together with Jupiter, rules over the first age in four-ages-of-man schemes which is also identified with the sanguinic temperament. Henry Peacham's 'Aierie *Sanguine*', youthful, lustful and delighted by flowers (*Minerva Britanna* (London, 1612), p. 127), makes the point, which is expounded at length in Raymond Klibansky, Erwin Panofsky and Fritz Saxl, *Saturn and Melancholy* (London, 1964). It is also present in Spence's *Polymetis*, pp. 191–2: Ver (the season and the first age of man) 'is infantile, and tender'; and Venus 'accompanies the Spring'. With his multi-coloured wings Ariel is also Cupid to Belinda's Venus.

10 The myth of Narcissus and his twin is relevant here, as is Addison's *Spectator*, 128 (Friday 27 July 1711), which suggests that 'the Passion of an ordinary Woman for a Man, is nothing else but Self-love diverted upon another Object: She would have the Lover a Woman in every thing but the Sex' (ed. D. F. Bond, 4 vols. (Oxford, 1965), II, p. 10). See F. A. Nussbaum's perceptive comments on this and other matters in 'Pope's "To a Lady" and the Eighteenth-Century Woman', *PQ*, 54 (1975), 444–56. But the notion had Biblical sanction from Ephesians 5: 28 ('So ought men to love their wives as their own bodies. He that loveth his wife loveth himself') which appears towards the end of the Anglican marriage service. Alongside the Miltonic notion that sylphs can change their sex (*The Rape*, I. 69–70) we should place Spence's assertion that the 'aerial nymphs: what the Romans called, Auræ; and what we call, Sylphs' (*op. cit.*, p. 207) are female.

11 Hagstrum, *The Sister Arts*, pp. 221–2, relates the passage to paintings of Venus by Titian and Rubens but does not go into details. My Venerean reading of Belinda has been partly anticipated too by A. W. Hoffman's fascinating 'Spenser and *The Rape of the Lock*', *PQ*, 49 (1970), 530–46. The common view of Belinda as a solar deity is, of course, equally valid (see R. P. Parkin, 'Mythopoeic Activity in the *Rape of the Lock*', *ELH*, 21 (1954), 30–8, and T. E. Maresca, *Epic to Novel* (Cleveland, Ohio, 1974), pp. 82ff.). I go into the implications of these allusions and their political meanings more fully in a forthcoming book.

12 'Life-giving Venus, it is your doing that under the wheeling constellations of the sky all nature teems with life.... For you the inventive earth flings up sweet flowers.... When first the day puts on the aspect of spring, when in all its force the fertilizing breath of Zephyr is unleashed, then, great goddess, the birds of air give the first intimation of your entry ... you alone are the guiding power of the universe ...': *On the Nature of the Universe*, tr. R. E. Latham, Penguin Classics (Harmondsworth, 1973), p. 27.

13 L. A. Landa, 'Pope's Belinda, The General Emporie of the World, and the Wondrous Worm', *South Atlantic Quarterly*, 70 (1971), 215–35, observing that 'the mere mention of these objects of the toilette would have provoked a pleasing mercantile image in the minds of many contemporary readers' (p. 217).

14 *Polymetis*, pp. 219–20 (and on Venus and the Venus de' Medici in general, Dialogue VII, pp. 65ff.). The Venus anadyomene is frequently parodied by Swift: e.g., 'The Goddess' Celia whose '"Secrets of the hoary deep"' Strephon discovers in 'The Lady's Dressing Room' (1730); and Venerean Chloe's urgent need to urinate on her wedding night ('Strephon and Chloe' (1731), ll. 163ff.); in *The Poems of Jonathan Swift*, ed. Harold Williams, 3 vols. (Oxford, second edn., 1958), II. Compare the supposed origin of the Yahoos 'from the ooze and froth of the sea' (*Gulliver's Travels*, IV. ix), and see C. J. Rawson, 'The Nightmares of Strephon: Nymphs of the City in the Poems of Swift, Baudelaire, Eliot', in M. E. Novak, (ed.), *English Literature in the Age of Disguise* (Berkeley, Cal., 1977), p. 79.

15 Compare E. K.'s gloss on line 25 of the June eclogue of *The Shepheardes Calender*, justifying the multiplicity of Graces 'in respect of many gyftes of bounty'. Similarly, on Eve 'as queen / A pomp of winning graces waited still' (*Paradise Lost*, VIII. 60–1).

16 On Belphoebe, see A. D. S. Fowler, *Spenser and the Numbers of Time* (London, 1964), pp. 83–4; J. T. Nohrnberg, *The Analogy of 'The Faerie Queene'* (Princeton, N. J., 1976), pp. 461–2 and 466–70; and Douglas Brooks-Davies, *Spenser's 'Faerie Queene': A Critical Commentary on Books I and II* (Manchester, 1977), pp. 130–2; for Eve, see Fowler's notes to *Paradise Lost*, IV. 262, 263–6 and 266–8, and IX. 387–92 and 426–31 (*ed. cit.*). Venus is a follower of Diana at *Metamorphoses*, X. 535ff., and the composite deity is discussed by Edgar Wind, *Pagan*

Mysteries of the Renaissance, rev. edn. (Harmondsworth, 1967), pp. 75ff.

17 Wind notes that the 'Diana-like Venus ... is but a variant of the *Venus armata*' (*op. cit.*, p. 92), and see Rudolf Wittkower, 'Transformations of Minerva in Renaissance Imagery', *JWCI*, 2 (1938–9), esp. pp. 199ff. Minerva is traditionally awesome (Spence, *Polymetis*, p. 59, can be our eighteenth-century authority: 'This goddess, as the antients used to represent her, is ... apt to strike one with awe and terror'); hence 'Now awful Beauty puts on all its Arms' at I. 139.

18 Guy de Tervarent, *Attributs et symboles dans l'art profane 1450–1600*; Travaux d'Humanisme et Renaissance, 29 (Geneva, 1958), cols. 154–5 (citing Pliny, Solinus and Aristotle) and 383 (citing Pausanias and Plutarch). Clearly, if Belinda had stayed at home, she would not have lost her hair! E. R. Wasserman's brilliant insight ('the elephant mounted on the tortoise [is] the Hindu emblem of the world') stands as a valuable complementary reading: see 'The Limits of Allusion in *The Rape of the Lock*', *JEGP*, 65 (1966), 435. The comb, too, is an emblem of Venus: Twycross, *Medieval Anadyomene*, pp. 70ff.

19 In describing virginal Virtue, however, Shaftesbury does not care to distinguish between Minervan and Amazonian: *Judgment of Hercules*, *ed. cit.*, III, 363. Spence, p. 63, citing Virgil and others, notes that 'Minerva is sometimes represented ... as dealing out the thunderbolts of Jove'; and on p. 60 reports: 'The poets do not only speak of a certain ferocity and threatening turn in the eyes of Minerva; but the very colour of them too, it seems, was adapted to this character of terror.... Virgil, in speaking of the Palladium, ... describes a certain fury and motion to the eyes of that figure in a very particular manner ...'

20 E.g., Hesiod, *Theogony*, l. 989; Spence, p. 68 ('Venus certainly was represented smiling, in many of her figures of old').

21 On the mirror, see Twycross, *op. cit.*, pp. 82ff. The association of Venus, spring, and the spring wind of youth, Zephyrus, is a commonplace: e.g., Spence, p. 192, citing Lucretius; and Catullus, LXVI. 57, where Zephyrus attends Venus. Venus is invariably associated with music: she is '*Harmoniae mater*', e.g., in Martianus Capella's *De nuptiis Philologiae et Mercurii*, ed. A. Dick (Leipzig, 1925), sec. 737, p. 372.

22 E.g., Arthur Wilson's description of the Princess Elizabeth at her wedding in 1613: '... her hair dishevil'd, hanging down her back at length, an *Ornament* of *Virginity*' (*The History of Great Britain* (London, 1653), p. 64; cit. René Graziani, 'The "Rainbow Portrait" of Queen Elizabeth I and its Religious Symbolism', *JWCI*, 35 (1972), 258n.; and see his text, pp. 258–9). After marriage the hair was worn up.

23 On the *Coma Berenices*, its colour and the connection with Venus, see R. H. Allen, *Star Names: their Lore and Meaning* (New York, 1963), pp. 168–9. For yellow and Venus, see Ptolemy, *Tetrabiblos*, II, ix; Loeb edn, tr. and ed. F. E. Robbins (London and Cambridge, Mass., 1971), p. 193. Wasserman, 'The Limits of Allusion', pp. 441–2, draws attention

to the echoes of Catullus's lock of Berenice: '"Do new brides really hate Venus?"' (*Poems*, LXVI. 15).

24 Wasserman, *ibid*., pp. 428–9.

25 See D. D. Carnicelli, 'The Widow and the Phoenix: Dido, Carthage, and Tunis in *The Tempest*', *Harvard Library Bulletin*, 27 (1979), 398ff., who also notes the tradition of her chastity. As Carnicelli (p. 402) remarks, Dido's 'original name was Elissa, but to Virgil she is *virgo* because, as Servius was to observe, the Carthaginians gave her the name Dido, the Punic word for *virago*'. On her first appearance in the *Aeneid*, Dido is compared to Diana (I. 496ff.).

26 Quotations are from the Wesleyan *Joseph Andrews*, ed. M. C. Battestin (Oxford, 1967). I include page numbers for ease of reference.

27 Fielding has Fanny *hear* Joseph first because he is hinting at the tradition, found in George Chapman's *Ovids Banquet of Sence* (1595), that the order of the senses appealed to in the lover is hearing, smell, sight, taste, touch. But there were other traditions, and the pattern in *Joseph Andrews* is hearing, seeing, touching, tasting (i.e., kissing). When Joseph imprints 'numberless Kisses' on Fanny here, he alludes slyly to the Renaissance tradition of *counting* kisses: e.g., Ben Jonson, *Volpone*, III. vii. 234–5 (I follow the Yale Ben Jonson text, ed. A. B. Kernan (New Haven, Conn., 1965)); Shakespeare's *Venus and Adonis*, ll. 22, 209–10, 522, etc.; and earlier, Joannes Secundus, *Basia* VII (in I. D. McFarlane, ed., *Renaissance Latin Poetry* (Manchester and New York, 1980), pp. 52–5).

28 Compare their descriptions at I. viii (pp. 38–9) and II. xii (pp. 152–3). M. C. Battestin offers biographical insights into Fielding's obsession with incest in 'Henry Fielding, Sarah Fielding, and "the dreadful Sin of Incest"', *Novel: a Forum on Fiction*, (1979–80), pp. 6–18.

29 I examined this in ch. IV of *Number and Pattern in the Eighteenth-Century Novel* (London and Boston, Mass., 1973).

30 See, as well as Shakespeare's poem, Douglas Bush, *Mythology and the Renaissance Tradition in English Poetry* (Minneapolis, Minn., and London, 1932), pp. 84 and 143–5; and Katherine Duncan-Jones, 'Sidney and Titian', in *English Renaissance Studies Presented to Dame Helen Gardner in Honour of her Seventieth Birthday* (Oxford, 1980), p. 11.

31 I draw attention to this in the Oxford English Novels/World's Classics '*Joseph Andrews' and 'Shamela*' (Oxford, 1970), Introduction, pp. xii–xiii.

32 See *ibid*., Introduction, p. xvii, and pp. 35 n. 1 and 237 n. 3.

33 Loeb edn., tr. F. J. Miller, 2 vols. (London and New York, 1916), I. 153–5.

34 On the *motif*, see W. Keach, 'Cupid Disarmed, or Venus Wounded? An Ovidian Source for Michelangelo and Bronzino', *JWCI*, 41 (1978), 327–31, offering a source in *Met*., X. 525–8, and with illustrations (plates 50 a–d) showing Cupid aiming his arrows at Venus's genitals, breasts, etc.

This is the answer to J. E. Evans, who cannot understand why Cupid should torment a Venerean Lady Booby, and suggests that she must be modelled on the Calypso of Fénelon's *Télémaque* instead ('Fielding's Lady Booby and Fénelon's Calypso', *Studies in the Novel* (North Texas State University), 8 (1976), 210–13). The parallels are valid; but Calypso herself is, of course, a manifestation of Venerean Pleasure, which is why she takes '*Telemachus* aside into a Grove of Myrtles' at the beginning of Book VII (Ozell's transln., 2 vols. (London, 1735), I, 133).

35 Shaftesbury comments on the familiar notion of Diana–Minerva's tallness: 'PALLAS may fitly serve as a Model for [Virtue]. . . . The Historian whom we follow, represents VIRTUE to us as a lady of goodly Form, tall and majestick' (*Judgment of Hercules*, III, 364), and Spence, *Polymetis*, p. 67, emphasises the modesty of the Venus de' Medici. Chapter VI of R. P. Utter and G. B. Needham, *Pamela's Daughters* (London, 1937), remains a useful introduction to the iconography of the heroine, while omitting consideration of Venus. Sean Shesgreen's *Literary Portraits in the Novels of Henry Fielding* (DeKalb, Ill. 1972) is disappointingly unadventurous, and takes us no further than Utter and Needham.

36 See Edgar Wind, *Pagan Mysteries*, pp. 131–2, and Spence, p. 67 and plate V and p. 146 on veiled and chaste *Pudicitia* (also plate XXI, fig. 10). Modesty became an independent female virtue but seems always to have related to the Venerean archetype, as with the blushing and downward-looking Shamefastness of *Faerie Queene*, II. ix. 40–3. The acting convention is represented in James Burgh, *The Art of Speaking* (London, 1761), p. 16: '*Modesty*, or submission, bends the body forward; *levels* the *eyes* to the breast, if not to the feet, of the superior character. The *voice low;* the *tone submissive;* and *words few.*' Compare Mentor (the disguised Minerva) at the beginning of Book I of the *Télémaque: 'Mentor* with down-cast Eyes and modest Silence followed' (*ed. cit.*, I, 5). Modesty is the prerequisite of maidenliness in the courtesy books, as Dr Gregory was eager to point out in *A Father's Legacy to his Daughters*: 'One of the chief beauties in a female character, is that modest reserve, that retiring delicacy which avoids the public eye, and is disconcerted even at the gaze of admiration. . . . When a girl ceases to blush, she has lost the most powerful charm of beauty . . .' (London, 1789 edn., pp. 26–7). Cleland's *Memoirs of a Woman of Pleasure*, incidentally, which places considerable emphasis on modesty, has Emily as a *Venus pudica*: '. . . she stood fairly naked . . . a blush at this overspread her lovely face, and her eyes downcast to the ground. . . . Then gently removing her hand, which in the first emotion of natural modesty, she had carried thither . . .' (Mayflower Books edn. (St Albans, 1976), p. 144).

37 Quotations, with page references, are from the Mayflower Books edn., cited in n. 36.

38 As John Hollander writes in what is still one of the best essays on this novel: 'The Old Last Act: Some Observations on *Fanny Hill*', *Encoun-*

ter, 21 (1963), 74. The best essay is now Janet Todd's in her *Women's Friendship in Literature* (New York, 1980), pp. 69–100.

39 There are suggestions of Rabelais's Venerean Abbey of Theleme here (*Gargantua and Pantagruel*, I. lii ff.); and see Hollander, *art. cit.*, p. 75, for the influence on the novel of the 'widely-translated *L'Académie des Dames*'.

40 B. Slepian and L. J. Morrissey, 'What is *Fanny Hill?*', *E. in C.*, 14 (1964), 67, note that it 'is a novel about the loss of innocence and the gaining of knowledge through experience'; and at p. 138 there is a quotation from *Paradise Lost*, IX. 1039 (Adam and Eve after the Fall), when Louisa is 'led ... to the couch "nothing loath"' by 'a cornet of horse'.

41 Echoing Richardson's Colbrand: 'He has great staring eyes ... vast jaw-bones sticking out ... a monstrous wide mouth; blubber lips, long yellow teeth, and a hideous grin' (*Pamela*, introd. M. Kinkead-Weekes, Everyman, 2 vols. (London and New York, 1962), I, p. 145).

42 For the cliché (symbolising friendship), see Arthur Henkel and Albrecht Schöne, *Emblemata: Handbuch zur Sinnbildkunst des XVI. und XVII. Jahrhunderts* (Stuttgart, 1967), cols. 259–60. At *Faerie Queene*, III. vi. 45–6, we are led through homosexuality (Phoebus and Hyacinthus) and Narcissus before being allowed to encounter Venus and Adonis. It is another love cliché that Cupid either is a bee (*Polymetis*, p. 70, n. 33); is stung by a bee (Anacreontic IV added to Spenser's *Amoretti*); or that the beloved's lips have been stung by a bee/Cupid, as in *Fanny Hill* and in Fielding's description of Sophia in *Tom Jones*, IV. ii, quoting Suckling's 'A Ballade. Upon a Wedding', ll. 61–3.

43 As a vegetation god Adonis is inevitably youthful and assimilated into the traditionally young Bacchus (*Met.*, IV. 18); Spenser's Verdant (on whom, briefly, see Brooks-Davies, *Spenser's 'Faerie Queene'*, pp. 195–6) is described as a 'young man sleeping', a 'goodly swayne of honorable place', with a 'well proportioned face, / And on his tender lips the downy heare / Did now but freshly spring, and silken blossomes beare' (II. xii. 79; *Variorum Spenser*, ed. E. Greenlaw *et al.* (Baltimore, Md., 1933)); and cf. Shakespeare's Adonis (*Venus and Adonis*, ll. 127ff.). In Ovid, *Met.*, X. 515–16, Adonis has a Cupid-like beauty. It is noteworthy that in Cleland's *Memoirs of a Coxcomb* the lover hunts (London: Fortune Press edn., 1926, pp. 4–5, 55, etc.) and that there seems to be a tendency, as in *Fanny Hill*, to identify the one true beloved with Venus (in this case Lydia is 'Venus in her innocence, when newborn of the sea'; p. 9). She, too, is modest (p. 10, 'with looks modestly declined', etc.) and at p. 13 is queen of paradise ('I should now have looked on every earthly paradise with indifference or contempt, that was not dignified and embellished with the presence of this new sovereign of all the world to me').

44 On the mechanistic physiology of the novel, see Leo Braudy's '*Fanny Hill* and Materialism', *ECS*, 4 (1970), 21–40. It might be mythologically significant that Charles has been sent off to sea by his father and that he

returns from it to Fanny's love (pp. 71, 213); for as Banier, citing Lucian, remarks of the Adonis festival: '... the *Egyptians* exposed upon the Sea a Basket of Osier, which being carried by a favourable Wind, arrived of it self upon the Coasts of *Phenicia*, where the Women of *Byblos*, who waited for it with Impatience, carry'd it into the City; and then it was that the publick Sorrow ended, and the Festival was concluded with Transports of universal Joy' (*The Mythology and Fables of the Ancients*, II (London, 1740), p. 15).

45 See Klibansky, Panofsky, Saxl, *Saturn and Melancholy*, *passim*. It was readily available to the eighteenth century in the opposition of Milton's *L'Allegro* to his *Il Penseroso*, or in Burton's *Anatomy of Melancholy*, II. ii. 3 and II. ii. 4; and compare Agrippa, *Three Books of Occult Philosophy* (London, 1651), I. xvii, p. 38: 'all besides *Saturne* love *Venus*'. J. H. Hagstrum, *Sex and Sensibility*, p. 145, notes 'that *Tatler* 47 prescribed marriage as a cure for the spleen' but does not relate the idea to its astrological basis.

46 For melancholy in *The Rape*, Lawrence Babb's 'The Cave of Spleen', *RES*, 12 (1936), 165–176, remains definitive, though it does not recognise the opposition of Venus and Saturn. L. P. Curtis notes that '*The Country Magazine* (Nov. 1786, 170) reports an anecdote, frequently reprinted, of Sterne's once hiring a boy to scale the cupola of Skelton Castle and tie down the weather-cock with the result that the hypochondriacal Hall[-Stevenson], having taken to his bed because of an east wind, at once rose to enjoy what he believed to be the beneficial west wind' (*Letters of Laurence Sterne*, ed. Curtis (Oxford, 1965), p. 141).

47 Gray's Etonians play rather like the Cupids depicted on Polymetis's drawing 'where you see some of them driving a hoop or playing with quoits' (Spence, *op. cit.*, p. 71).

48 *Number and Pattern in the Eighteenth-Century Novel*, pp. 173ff.

49 *Tristram Shandy* quotations are from the Penguin edn., introd. Christopher Ricks, ed. Graham Petrie (Harmondsworth, 1967).

50 Mars's trumpet is opposed by Venus's 'lyre' in Claudian's *Epithalamium*, X. 195ff., and Venus's lute accompanies the lover in the frontispiece to Burton's *Anatomy* and emblems of Venerean sanguinic youth: e.g., Peacham, *Minerva Britanna* (1612), p. 127; Cesare Ripa, *Iconologia* (Rome, 1603), pp. 76–7. Keats's Lycius begins to move away from Venerean Lamia at the sound of trumpets (*Lamia* (1819), II. 28). He addresses her as the morning and evening star (i.e. Venus) at *ibid.*, 48. Toby's 'oration' itself comes from Burton: see H. J. Jackson, 'Sterne, Burton, and Ferriar: Allusions to the *Anatomy of Melancholy* in Volumes Five to Nine of *Tristram Shandy*', *PQ*, 54 (1975), 464.

51 On Mars and Venus see *Metamorphoses*, IV. 171ff.; Wind, *Pagan Mysteries*, pp. 86ff., 95–6, and plates 74–9; and Erwin Panofsky, *Studies in Iconology* (New York, 1962), pp. 162ff. Compare the mock epithalamium in Swift's 'Strephon and Chloe' where the bride is 'by the tender Graces drest' and the bridegroom 'by *Mars*, in Scarlet Vest' (ll. 59–60;

Poems, ed. Williams, II, p. 586). Spence, *Polymetis*, p. 73 and n. 54, notes how common the Venus–Mars motif was; and the myth rapidly turned bawdy at the hands of the pornographers: Roger Thompson, *Unfit for Modest Ears* (London, 1979), pp. 182–3. For Venus and laughter, see n. 20 above.

52 Quotations are from *A Sentimental Journey through France and Italy*, ed. G. D. Stout, Jr (Berkeley, Cal., 1967). Page references are given in parenthesis.

53 Significantly, Sterne objects to Smollett's reservations about the Venus de' Medici in *Travels*, letter XXVIII (*Sentimental Journey*, p. 117).

54 La Fleur was apparently not the valet's real name: see Stout's edn., Appendix E, pp. 342–3. For Saturnian 'Hellebor' see Agrippa, *Three Books*, I. xxv, p. 56. Probably also from Burton is the contrast between grave, black, solitary Yorick and 'all the world in yellow, blue, and green' (pp. 155–6) at Paris: cf. *Anatomy*, II. ii. 3: 'Of colours it is good to behold green, red, yellow, and white ... for though melancholy persons love to be dark and alone, yet darkness is a great increaser of the humour'.

55 E.g., p. 270, 'La Fleur, whose heart seem'd only to be tuned to joy'; p. 278, 'great SENSORIUM of the world! which vibrates, if a hair of our heads but falls upon the ground ...' Addison's *Spectator*, 381 (Saturday 17 May 1712), talks about the religious implications of 'Chearfulness', while leaving its Venerean overtones implicit.

ARTHUR H. CASH

The birth of Tristram Shandy: Sterne and Dr Burton

Imagine to yourself a little, squat, uncourtly figure of a Doctor *Slop*, of about four feet and a half perpendicular height, with a breadth of back, and a sesquipedality of belly, which might have done honour to a serjeant in the horse-guards. [p. 104][1]

The citizens of York in 1759 recognised in this grotesque caricature Dr John Burton, founder and quondam surgeon of the York Public Hospital, man-midwife, antiquary, and rabid Tory partisan. Dr Slop waddles through the pages of *Tristram Shandy*, dealing out advice to the Widow Wadman about Uncle Toby's groin, destruction to the nose of Tristram, and plastic surgery to either end of that diminutive character. His importance to the novel, however, is more profound than his ludicrous appearance suggests: Dr John Burton and his obstetrical writings underprop the first four volumes of the novel. The key ideas represent his actual theories, the key events are tragicomical extensions of his practices, and the key objects are the instruments of Dr Burton's own proud invention.

Dr Burton was excellently trained in his art. He completed the M.B. degree at St John's College, Cambridge, studied with the great Boerhaave at Leyden, and at Paris with Grégoire and Dusée, both eminent obstetricians. He received his M.D. degree from the university at Rheims and settled in York about 1736, where he quickly established a large practice among the poor influencing them to vote with his Tory party.

It is not likely that the mature Sterne satirised Dr Burton because of the political antagonism of their youth.[2] Sterne's treatment of Burton as Slop is not at all political. It has, however, a very personal tone, strongly suggesting that Sterne had been perennially amused by the irascible temper, papist sympathies, and portly, short figure of the doctor.

What really inspired Sterne, however, was Burton the 'scientifick operator', who

> had expressly wrote a five shillings book upon the subject of midwifery, in which he had exposed, not only the blunders of the sisterhood itself,—but had likewise superadded many curious improvements for the quicker extraction of the foetus in cross births, and some other cases of danger which belay us in getting into the world. [p. 44]

The reference is to Burton's *Essay towards a Complete New System of Midwifry*, 1751, the first of his indiscretions in the literature of science. It was followed two years later by a second and even greater blunder, *A Letter to William Smellie, M.D.*

To appreciate the foolishness which Sterne found in Dr Burton, we must visualise the doctor as a promising and prominent man in a burgeoning science. It was a great age for obstetrics. In 1733 Edmund Chapman had published the first full account of the obstetrical forceps, which offered a new and inspiring hope for the science.[3] The forceps had been invented a century before by the Chamberlen family, who unscrupulously guarded them as a secret for three generations. At length Hugh Chamberlen defrauded the faculty of the University of Amsterdam by selling them what he said was his 'nostrum'—one blade only of the forceps. However, the full secret was soon out, and the surge of experimentation which followed made of obstetrics the most advanced branch of medicine of the time. It was the age of Hendrik van Deventer, Richard Manningham, Fielding Ould, André Levret, William Gifford, Benjamin Pugh—the pioneers of the science. The greatest of all, by common consent, was that friend and countryman of Tobias Smollett, Dr William Smellie, who modified the forceps to the various sizes and shapes still used, devised the lock still standard, and taught the world how to use the instrument.

At the beginning of 1751, John Burton had in hand a half-finished manuscript of the *Essay towards a Complete New System of Midwifry* when he heard of a number of distressing developments. Brudenell Exton, William Clark, George Counsell and Benjamin Pugh were all publishing or preparing works on midwifery. André Levret, the very great French tocologist, was soon to bring out a description of some long, curved forceps. Most worrisome of all, William Smellie, whose reputation was then immense, was preparing to release the first volume of his monumental *Treatise on the Theory and Practice of Midwifery*. Burton, the historians are agreed, could no longer stand the anxiety: he took his unfinished manuscript to the printer.

The *Essay* is certainly not devoid of merit, but it is deficient in the standards and spirit of the new science. Burton is unreasonably hostile to the discoveries of his contemporaries and smug about his own. He writes well about matters in which he has had much experience, but insists upon erroneous anatomy and untested techniques. He is not quite able to separate his antiquarian self from the scientific, parading his learning ostentatiously and seriously vending the teachings of seventy writers on midwifery from the most ancient times, which he lists in a Preface. The Appendix alone would have secured for Burton an unenviable niche in the history of medicine even if Sterne had never written *Tristram Shandy*. In the Appendix he recommends a new forceps of his own devising, 'better than any yet contrived'. The historians, who treasure this instrument as the most odd, impractical, whimsical device ever suggested for insinuation into womankind, usually quote the words of Sir Alexander Simpson: 'an ingenious but very unserviceable forceps, working like a lobster's claws'. The laity are apt never to forget this curious forceps as the machine which crushed the infant Tristram Shandy's nose.

The inevitable happened: Burton was all but ignored, while Smellie won universal acclaim. Imagine the chagrin of the fiery little doctor when he read in the *Monthly Review* of September that his was 'a performance, which we cannot think will greatly illuminate or entertain any adepts in midwifery; some cautionary parts of which, however, and some of the cases, may be worth the perusal of beginners'.

Tristram Shandy might never have been born had Burton let the matter rest there. But the hot-tempered, egoistic little doctor could only rage. He must have raged for a full two years: he did not take comfort until he published, in 1753, *A Letter to William Smellie, M.D. Containing Critical and Practical Remarks Upon his Treatise* . . . This unprovoked attack, sometimes supercilious, sometimes vitriolic, could have been motivated by nothing but Burton's consuming envy. To be sure, he makes two or three good points,[4] but they are lost in the mass of sarcastic and picayunish sallies. He quibbles over minutiae—the ambiguous use of *sometimes* and *often*. He unjustly teases Smellie about his 'favorite instrument', his 'beloved forceps'. Ignoring the fact that Smellie had already caught a silly error (probably by some careless assistant) and corrected it in the second edition, Burton haughtily reprimands him for taking the words *Lithopaedii Senonesis Icon* to be the name of a writer when they had actually appeared under an illustration to which the words referred: 'a picture of a petrified child'. Sterne burlesqued the correction to make the most amusing footnote in *Tristram Shandy* (p. 150).[5] On the whole, Burton failed to detract from the great *Treatise*, and Smellie never deigned to reply, though his student, Giles Watts, calmly devastated Burton in a book called *Reflections upon Slow and Painful Labours*.

Just when or how Burton came to recognise his own errors I do not know. He never again published a medical treatise. Henceforth he channelled his creative energies into the antiquarian studies for which he was better suited, publishing his *Monasticon Eboracense* before Sterne had created Dr Slop, and winning thereby some measure of renown.[6]

Sterne found in Dr Burton and his books a new and inspiring vision of foolishness, one which impinged upon the most fundamental human experiences—generation, nativity, infanticide and hopeless surrender. Sterne read Burton pronouncing upon copulation and conception, and the vitality of the animal spirits. He considered Burton's ovular theory of generation against the animalcular theory of Smellie. He read Burton's warnings about possible damage to the nose or the genitals of a child during parturition (*Essay*, pp. 190–3; *Letter*, p. 108), and his defence of the Caesarean operation. He was fascinated to discover the danger of the cerebrum's pressing against the cerebellum in a strait delivery, but the harmlessness of the cerebellum's pressing against the cerebrum. He read a defensive argument that man-midwives preserve the heirs of gentry families (*Essay*, pp. 254–5). He was horrified with the vision of a woman dying, the severed head of her offspring lost in her womb. He learned of the dread operation whereby the too-large head of an unborn infant is opened so that it will pass and free the mother of her deadly burden. That such questions of life, and such actual decisions of how and when to take or save life should be left to John Burton! Ordinary fools, driven by passions and lusts, blundered across the surfaces of life. Dr Burton's foolishness was profound. It was the inspiration of Sterne's great comedy.

The extensive digressions of the first four volumes of *Tristram Shandy* are held together by the central episode, the birth of Tristram. Tristram must turn back to explain the history which preceded his birth—his conception (of course), his father's theories, his parents' marriage contract, and the stories of the players in his drama—Uncle Toby, Parson Yorick, the midwife. He must also move ahead to the events brought on by the manner of his birth—his misbaptism and his father's plea to the divines at the visitation dinner.

No child was ever more carefully planned. Tristram was as much the product of his father's intellect as of his loins. No father was ever less successful. From the very moment when Tristram, born and baptised, set out upon his life (p. 336), the family of which he was the intended bulwark was doomed. His uncle had refused to marry, his brother was at the brink of death,[7] and he himself had been condemned already by his begetting and birth to a life of impotence and an early death.[8]

Dr John Burton provided Sterne with the materials, not only for the central birth episode, but also for the genetic[9] and obstetrical theories of Walter Shandy which determined the circumstances of the birth.

Even the locus of Tristram's birth, a Yorkshire country house, was fixed obstetrically. The contract which Walter Shandy had been forced to sign when he married Elizabeth Mollineux gave to her the privilege of bearing her children in London, where she sought the care of Dr Richard Manningham (p. 44), the physician who founded the first lying-in ward in England.[10] However, if Mrs Shandy were ever taken to London at her own desire but on false tokens, she would forfeit her privilege for the next pregnancy. It happened that Mrs Shandy had been carried to London the year before only to discover that it was all wind and water.[11] Consequently, as Walter announced to his wife minutes after Tristram's conception, she must bear her child in Yorkshire (p. 43). There are many reasons for Walter's decision, including an elaborate theory about the pernicious effects of migrations towards the capital. They are all chimerical but one: 'Of all men in the world, Dr *Slop* was fittest for my father's purposes' (p. 153).

The exact reasons why Walter Shandy and Dr Slop had become 'two such allies in science' (p. 153) depended ultimately upon the squire's very liberal moral doctrine—liberal no less in our day than in his—the equality of man.

Now, as it was plain to my father, that all souls were by nature equal,—and that the great difference between the most acute and the most obtuse understanding,—was from no original sharpness or bluntness of one thinking substance above or below another—but arose merely from the lucky or unlucky organization of the body, in that part where the soul principally took up her residence. ... [p. 147][12]

The moral philosophy demanded a physiological prop. Walter read Coglionissimo Borri; he read the great Metheglingius; and he read Descartes (from whom Sterne surely took his idea, giving it an appropriate twist). The *sensorium* of the soul, he concluded, was 'in, or near, the cerebellum,—or rather somewhere about the *medulla oblongata*'. *Ergo*, Walter's first duty as a father was to preserve in his child 'this delicate and fine-spun web, from the havock which was generally made in it by the violent compression and crush which the head was made to undergo, by the nonsensical method of bringing us into the world by that part foremost' (p. 149). He was greatly distressed to discover that the force of the mother's efforts created a 'weight of 470 pounds averdupoise acting perpendicularly'.[13]

But how great was his apprehension, when he further understood, that this force, acting upon the very vertex of the head, not only injured the brain itself or cerebrum,—but that it necessarily squeez'd and propell'd the cerebrum towards the cerebellum, which was the immediate seat of the understanding.—Angels and Ministers of grace defend us! [pp. 150–1]

Walter's ideas about the jeopardy of the cerebellum during labour Sterne took directly from John Burton, who was at pains to explain how 'the Danger to the Child increases, as the Cerebellum is the more compressed'. True, he wrote about the danger, as Sterne says of Slop, 'not with a view to the soul's good ... as was my father's system,—but for reasons merely obstetrical' (pp. 153–4). Obstetrically speaking, prolonged pressures on the cerebellum could bring on convulsions in the new-born infant which were often fatal.

When, therefore, the Child's Head is ... large ... let the Force of the Mother's Effort, that propells the Child, be ever so strong or weak, the Cerebellum will, in such Proportion, become pressed; because Action and Re-action are, in this Case, equal; whence it follows, that the more the Head is squeezed ... the more the Brain [cerebrum] is forced towards the Cerebellum, and consequently, the Mischiefs abovementioned will ensue. [*Letter*, p. 123]

Walter's first solution to this terrible problem had the simplicity of genius—he could maintain the cerebellum intact if the child were delivered by Caesarean section. He casually mentioned this one day to Mrs Shandy, no doubt remarking upon what he had been thinking, that certain towering geniuses—notably Julius Caesar, Hermes

Trismegistus, Scipio Africanus, Manlius Torquatus and Edward the Sixth—all came sideways into the world: 'but seeing her turn as pale as ashes at the very mention of it, as much as the operation flattered his hopes, he thought it as well to say no more of it' (p. 153).

Well might Mrs Shandy pale, for the operation in the eighteenth century was always fatal. An Irish woman had survived it, though performed by an ignorant midwife, only to die a few weeks later. Fielding Ould, the first British obstetrician to mention the Caesarean in writing, called it an 'unparalleled Piece of Barbarity'. John Burton, interestingly, is the first Englishman to say a word in its favour. He did not believe a woman would be apt to survive it, but he cogently argued that it must be performed anyway if it were her last chance. In this he was vindicated by Smellie in the *Treatise*, who took a similar stand. It is apparent where Sterne got his idea for Walter's admiration of the operation, though Sterne gave it a unique turn. British obstetricians of this period always valued the life of the mother over that of the child. Burton and Smellie sanctioned the Caesarean only to save the mother's life. Walter has the honour of being the first Englishman to advocate it as a benefit to the child.[14]

Unable to convince his wife that she should deliver sideways, Walter put his hopes in a technique which today is called the 'podalic version': '... when a child was turn'd topsy-turvey, which was easy for an operator to do, and was extracted by the feet ... instead of the cerebrum being propell'd towards the cerebellum, the cerebellum, on the contrary, was propell'd simply towards the cerebrum where it could do no manner of hurt' (p. 151). It seems that Dr Slop 'had scattered a word or two in his book, in favour of the very thing which ran in my father's fancy' (p. 153)—as indeed he had. The very dangerous podalic version, widely practised in the early years, had been falling rapidly into disuse because of the forceps.[15] Dr Burton, however, out of his hatred for Smellie's clever forceps, vastly overstated the virtues of version in his *Letter*. In the course of his protest, he made Walter Shandy's argument: 'the more Liberty there is for the Brain to be squeezed from (instead of towards) the Cerebellum, the less ... Danger'. He supported his contention with the following theory:

> ... by turning and extracting the Child by the Feet ... the Child's Head is only compressed by the Bones of the Pelvis, and that too in such a Manner, as to do the least Injury to the Cerebellum, for the Pressure then is from the

lower Part of the Head, next to the Neck, towards the Os Bregmatis and Os Frontis, both which will yield and give Way; so that when the Head is squeezed on the Sides, the Cerebrum is pressed towards these Parts, and consequently does less Injury to the Cerebellum than when the Apex comes first. [*Letter*, p. 124]

The theory is sound enough in what it indicates about the structure of the brain and cranium, but it shows poor understanding of the mechanisms of parturition. In fact, there is very grave danger to the cerebellum of any child born with the head coming last. Walter's ultimate hope that this child might enter the world feet first was founded upon a very bad argument.

Because of this hope, little Tristram suffered a rural birth sponsored by a 'coalition' between the philosophic squire and the foolish doctor.

Walter, as well as the doctor, is a fool: he too expressed the mistaken ideas of Dr Burton. Yet Sterne created them as vastly different fools. Slop was Sterne's obstetric clown; Walter his confused philosopher. Walter remained the consummate father image—determined to beget, bring forth and rear his child judiciously. His hypotheses, though mistaken, reflect the more respectable ideas of Burton's books. The neurological theory of the various functions of cerebrum and cerebellum did not originate with Burton, but was learned by him from the admirable Boerhaave.[16] Consequently, as late as 1912 Dr W. H. Allport, in an appreciative essay called 'Tristram Shandy and Obstetrics',[17] announced that 'Shandy *père* . . . had views which would have done full credit to many of our present day obstetricians'. He thought that Walter's fears for the cerebellum were in accord with the most modern theories, and he especially admired Walter's intuition that delivery by Caesarean was less prejudicial to the child than natural delivery. One might add that Walter adumbrated a point of Freudian theory in suggesting that the foetal experience affected the psyche of the child. As a consultant obstetrician, Walter was foolish. As a philosopher of the life sciences, he was advanced.

Alas, neither his sound philosophy nor his questionable programme was to be realised. Dr John Burton had advocated podalic version only so long as he was quarrelling with Dr William Smellie and Dr Smellie's forceps. His attitude was rather different when he spoke of his own invention. Likewise, Dr Slop had 'scattered a word or two in his book' in favour of version, yet 'his new-invented forceps was the armour he had proved, and what he maintained, to be the safest instrument of deliverance' (p. 153). Poor Walter, who could better manipulate ideas than people, was destined to be disappointed.

Walter Shandy, caught up as he was in sapience about the cerebellum and theories of the preponderate influence of Christian names and noble noses, was insulated from the raw truths of human birth. He could not understand his wife's dread of Dr Slop. Yet birth in the eighteenth century was a fearful thing, and the sight of a man-midwife struck terror in the hearts of most women. Dr Slop entered the house as an Angel of Death among the hobby-horsical muses of the Shandy brothers—a suggestion Sterne planted at Slop's rap upon the door: 'ANALOGY, replied my father, is the certain relation and agreement, which different—Here a devil of a rap at the door snapp'd my father's definition (like his tobacco-pipe) in two,—and, at the same time, crushed the head of as notable and curious a dissertation as ever was engendered in the womb of speculation' (pp. 102–3).

Throughout its history, man-midwifery had been looked upon as an art of the abnormal. Men were seldom called in until the mother was in mortal danger and the foetus doomed. Such a grisly business drove away the more sensitive physicians and attracted such crude men as that described by Deventer:

> ... a Man in Liquor, almost void of the use of his Senses, both void of Pity and Compassion, furnished with a Knife, a Hook, an Iron Forecepts, and other Instruments horrible to Sight ... come to the Assistance of one in Agony ... commonly first begins, with rash Oaths to hurt the Mother, then kill the living Infant, then with a great deal of Pain to draw it out in Pieces, and at last to think no Reward satisfactory for such an extraordinary Piece of Work.[18]

Elsewhere Deventer gave an even more horrifying description of a man-midwife drawing out an infant with hooks while it was still alive and moving. Professional standards were certainly climbing rapidly by the middle of the century when obstetricians began to be accepted by the upper classes as a fashion. Still, the books on the subject by the most reputable practitioners, which circulated among the gentry, were hardly able to quiet the old fears since they were written without the merciful disguise of scientific language. Even the dispassionate Smellie knew not how to hide the drama when he told about doctors who, having turned the infant to bring it by the feet, 'pull at random with all their strength; so that the neck is stretched and separated, and the head left behind' (vol. I, p. 362). As a consequence of the fears so aroused, the men of the profession resorted to deceptions. Smellie advised doctors to hide their instruments in their pockets and to tie two corners of the bed-sheet about the waist or neck so that the instruments could be manipulated without being seen. When the child is delivered and handed to the nurse, 'the next care is to wipe the blades of the forceps, singly, under the cloaths, slide them warily into your pockets, and deliver the *Placenta*' (vol. I, p. 271).

The fears of expectant mothers, so naturally aroused, were reinforced by a constant, bitter antagonism of midwives toward the man-midwives. As early as 1668 Mauriceau reprimanded the sisterhood for maliciously putting '... Terror and Apprehension of the Chirurgeons in the poor Woman, comparing them to Butchers and Hangmen, that they chuse rather to die in Travail with the Child in their Womb, than to put themselves into their hands'.[19] The slander was still going on in 1751 when Smellie spoke of 'a general outcry ... raised against gentlemen of the profession, as if they delight in using instruments and violent methods' (vol. I, p. 242).

The women who raised this fuss were dismally trained in their work. They were licensed, if at all, by the bishop of the diocese without any regard for their medical knowledge. A letter of 1705 survives at the York Minster Library written by eleven women of Preston to the Archbishop of York recommending for a licence one Mrs Hannah Savage because she is 'a Woman of good fame and credit & due Frequenter of the Church. And one that hath been helpful to severall poore Women & their Labour in case of necessity.'[20] No more. Although Sterne sympathised with the taciturn, motherly midwife of *Tristram Shandy*, with whom he sided against Dr Slop, he did not hide the fact that she had no medical training (p. 11).[21]

The prolonged attack of this ignorant group of women upon the practitioners of the new science was reprehensible, but effective. The woman who made the most noise of all was Mrs Elizabeth Nihell, the Haymarket midwife, who published in 1760 *A Treatise on the Art of Midwifery*, in which she lambasted all 'he-practicers', whose ranks are filled, she said, with 'broken barbers, tailors, or even pork butchers, for I know one myself of this last trade, who, after passing half his life in stuffing sausages, is turned an intrepid physician and man-midwife'.[22]

As if the women were incapable of carrying on their own campaign of fright, two unscrupulous men joined their ranks. Frank Nicholls, a well-known man-midwife, turned traitor to his profession, had accepted from a midwife, Mrs Kennon, £500 for writing and publishing in 1751 *The Petition of the Unborn Babes to the Censors of the Royal College of Physicians*. Of all physicians, he wrote,

> the men midwives alone (as such) give no test of their learning, dexterity, or integrity, and yet these men are permitted on their single opinions avowedly and professedly to kill our children, and to treat our wives in such a manner, as frequently ends in their destruction, and to have such intercourse with our women, as easily shifts itself into indecency, from indecency into obscenity, and from obscenity into debauchery. [p. 6]

The most scurrilous attack of all, however, was that of Philip Thicknesse in *Man-Midwifery Analysed*, 1764, which must be read to be believed. Typical of its quality is Thicknesse's explanation of examination by 'touching', which is done, he said, 'to see if any emotions arise in the *touched* lady's breast, that the Doctor may take advantage of' (p. 8).

The attempts to frighten the women by painting the doctors as lechers reveals a puritanical attitude about the human body which we do not usually associate with the eighteenth century. We can only admire Sterne's taste in refusing to capitalise upon this irrational and embarrassing fear. His one reference to it comes through Uncle Toby, who was trying to help his brother understand why Mrs Shandy would not see Dr Slop: '—Then it can be out of nothing in the whole world, quoth my uncle *Toby*, in the simplicity of his heart,—but MODESTY:—My sister, I dare say, added he, does not care to let a man come so near her ****' (p. 100)[23]

The most insidious and knavish altercation of the midwives and their allies was on the danger of obstetrical instruments.

> That multitude of disciples of Dr. Smellie, trained up at the feet of his artificial doll [wrote Mrs Nihell], see the whole pack open in full cry: to arms! to arms! is the word; and what are those arms by which they maintain themselves, but those instruments, those weapons of death!
>
> ... crotchets, knives, scissors, spoons, pinchers, fillets, speculum matrices, all of which, and especially their forceps whether Flemish, Dutch, Irish, French or English, bare or covered, long or short, straight or crooked, windowed or not windowed, are totally useless or rather worse than good for nothing, being never but dangerous and often destructive.[24]

We should not be deaf to the funereal overtones when Dr Slop lays his hands upon his green baize bag.

When Dr Slop was dumped into the mud from his diminutive pony by the roaring past of Obadiah on the great coach-horse, he had only intended a casual call at Shandy Hall, not knowing that Mrs Shandy's labour had begun. '... what canst thou do?—Thou has come forth unarm'd;—thou has left thy *tire tête*,—thy new-invented *forceps*,—thy *crotchet*,—thy *squirt*, and all thy instruments of salvation and deliverance behind thee.—By heaven! at this moment they are hanging up, in a green bays bag, betwixt thy two pistols, at thy bed's head!' (pp. 109–10).

Sterne's irony is unmistakable: only one of the instruments in this 'tokological armamentarium', as Dr Allport called it, had anything to do with 'salvation'. The others were instruments of death.

The crotchet was a very ancient and very dangerous weapon, a hook used to destroy and extract a foetus which would not pass. No doubt Slop carried several forms of it, as did Burton. The most widely used types are seen in Plate Ia, taken from François Mauriceau, *The Diseases of Woman with Child*, 1668. The more merciful instrument on the left was often called the 'blunt hook'. That on the right, more properly spoken of as the 'crotchet', was merely a hooked knife. Dr Burton, however, was a great inventor. The green baize bag would have contained also the crotchet of his own design seen in Plate Ib. If it lacked the pretty silver handle of Mauriceau's, it sported an ingenious detachable handle complete with cross-member, a device Burton called his 'crutch'. Dr Burton used the crutch, he said, to push a foetus back into the womb, in the manner illustrated, when an arm presented first.[25] That particular presentation was one of the most feared, for the child could progress no further. The old procedure had been to amputate the arm.

The most common preternatural case was that of a child presenting the head naturally, which could not pass because the head was too large. Consequently, a great deal of ingenuity was expended upon devices which would destroy the child by opening the head, and extract by attaching the head from within the cranial vault. For this dread operation, the most commonly used instrument was the *tire tête* of Mauriceau. Sterne, by speaking of the *tire tête* in the bag, was teasing Dr Burton, who had elaborately criticised that instrument. What was

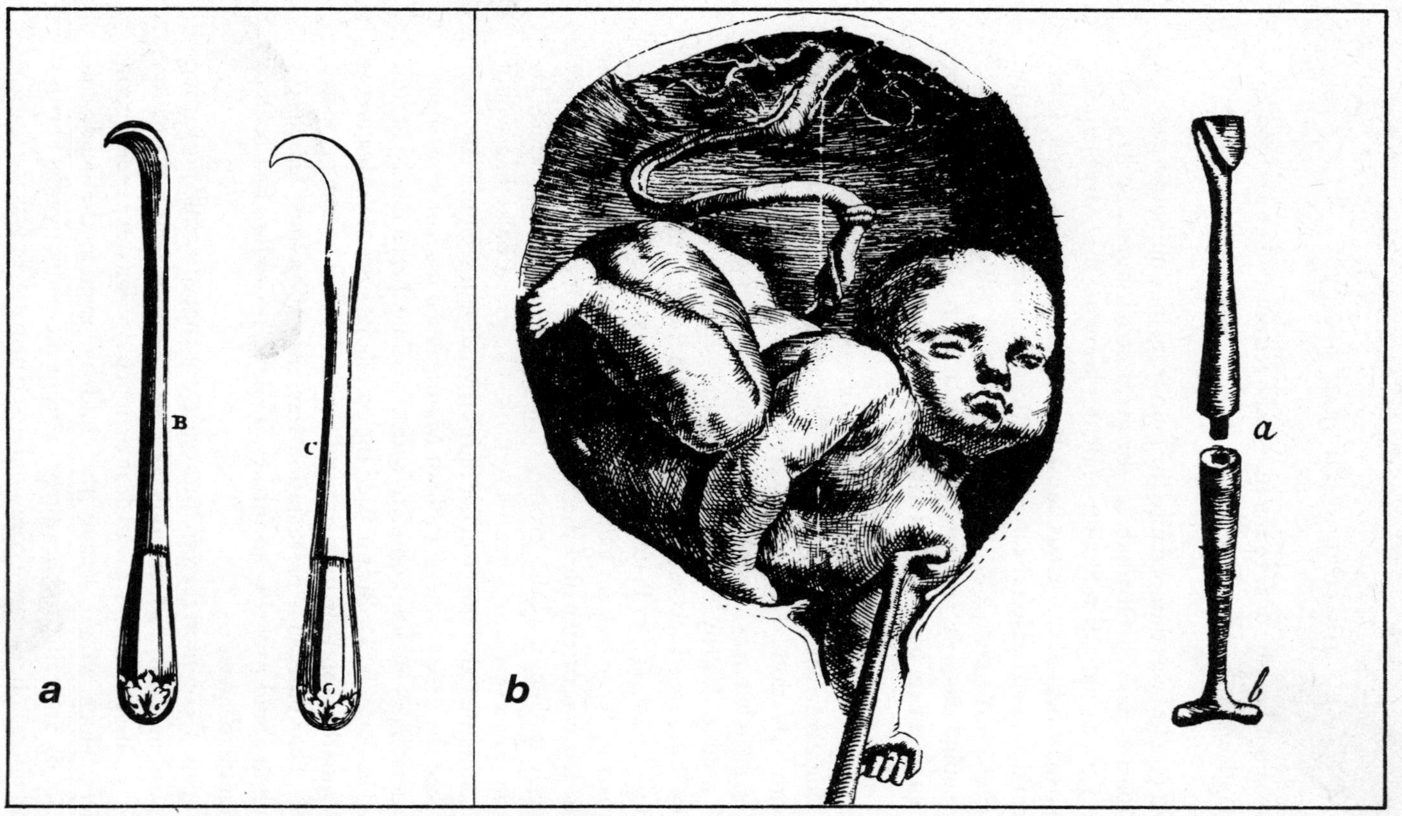

Plate 1a Blunt hook and crotchet from *The Diseases of Women with Child*, 1668, by François Mauriceau.

Plate 1b Dr Burton's crotchet with detachable crutch used to push a foetus back into the womb, from the *Essay Towards a Complete New System of Midwifry*, 1751.

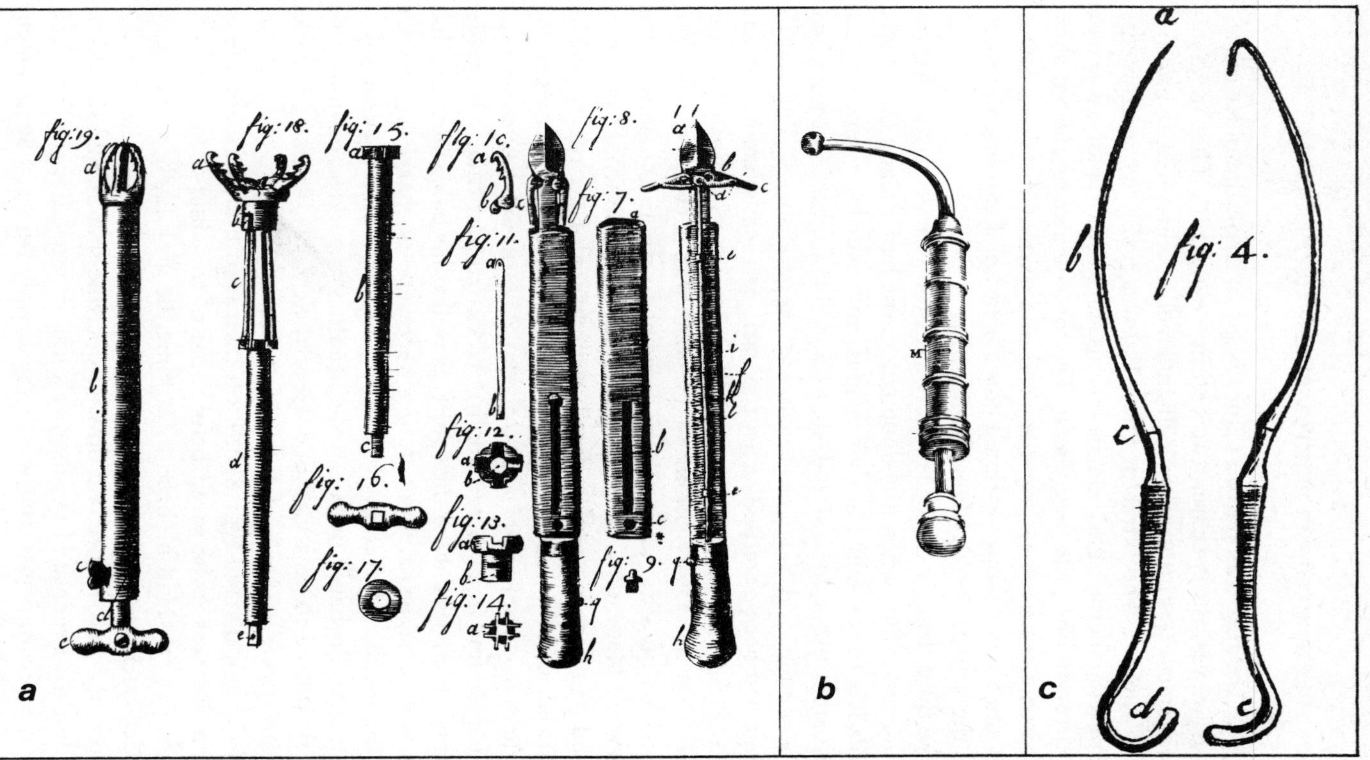

Plate IIa Dr Burton's extractor, from the *Essay Towards a Complete New System of Midwifry*, 1751.
Plate IIb Mauriceau's squirt, from *The Diseases of Women with Child*, 1668.
Plate IIc Forceps of the Chamberlen type, from the *Essay Towards a Complete New System of Midwifry*, 1751.

really in the bag was Burton's improvement upon the older device, which he was always careful to call his 'extractor'. That it was an improvement was attested by William Smellie, who spoke in praise of it (vol. I, p. Iv). The extractor (Plate IIa) was really two instruments. The portion on the right, seen in various stages of assembly, was used by Burton to open the foetal head. The three figures on the left show the instrument used to grip the head and extract the dead foetus. Tristram Shandy comes within a hair's breadth of entering the world with the help of this terrifying implement.

The third deathly device is the 'squirt', the syringe used to baptise the unborn infant when it is doomed. Sterne had already introduced his readers to the squirt in that magnificent joke about baptising 'all the HOMUNCULI at once, slap-dash, by *injection . . . par le moyen d'une* petite canulle, and *sans faire aucun tort au père*' (p. 62). Baptism by syringe had been practised at least as early as 1668, when Mauriceau spoke of it,[26] Sterne, however, got his information about this expedient from the *Observations* of Hendrik van Deventer, who had quoted his question about the sacrament to the theologians of the Sorbonne. Had Sterne read their original reply, he would not have missed one very interesting detail: the efficacy of the rite would be enhanced, said the good doctors of the Sorbonne, if the opening in the nozzle were in the form of a cross.[27] Alas, Mauriceau's squirt, the only one I could find in a plate (Plate IIb), lacks that particular advantage.

Sterne's remarks about the squirt, as well as his bald statement that Slop was a papist, amounted to a very serious charge against Dr Burton, for the infiltration of the Roman Church into Yorkshire was still feared. Probably Burton had Catholic sympathies; obviously he was rumoured to be a Catholic. Nevertheless, his obstetrical works contain strong evidence of the Protestantism he always claimed. He took the moral stand typical of Protestant man-midwives: the life of the mother was to be saved before that of the child (*Essay*, p. 208; *Letter*, p. 117). Had he been a Catholic, he very likely would have avoided such statements, as did most continental writers: for the Church had long before laid down a doctrine that a child should be saved at the expense of the mother's life, if necessary, so that it can have the benefit of baptism which she already enjoys.[28] Burton mentions no squirt in his books.

The one instrument which offered some hope for the life of Tristram was the forceps.

In the course of his career, Dr Burton used three forceps. His earliest instrument, for which he gave instructions in the body of the *Essay*, was a crude forceps of a type invented by the Chamberlens. The curved blades had no lock. They were placed at the sides of the foetal head and articulated, if at all, by holding the shanks together with the fingers of one hand. In Plate IIc we see Burton's plate, but a side view only of unmatching blades. The left one, when paired with an identical blade, made up the forceps. That on the right, a hooked blade, is one of a pair called the 'double crotchet', which could deliver only a dead foetus.

In his third and last period, Dr Burton used a more modern forceps of the sort designed by his old master, Dusée. This instrument, new at the York Medical Society, has long, straight, unfenestrated blades articulated with a removable pin—a passable instrument, though decidedly inferior to the several forceps designed by William Smellie. This instrument was found among his things at Burton's death. Apparently he had learned the truth about the forceps he designed, but had refused to the very last to admit the worth of the forceps invented by Dr Smellie.

If either of these devices is in the green bag, neither is withdrawn from it. The instrument which delivered Tristram Shandy was Slop's 'new invented forceps'. The three references to their newness (pp. 110, 153, 186) make it abundantly clear that Sterne meant the instrument of Burton's own invention described and illustrated (Plate III is Burton's plate) in the Appendix hastily tacked to the *Essay* of 1751—so hastily added, in fact, that the implement is not mentioned in the text itself. The arguments Burton advanced in its favour were brief in the original Appendix, but long in the *Letter to Dr William Smellie* appearing two years later (pp. 141–3). It could be placed in one operation, said Burton; and the blades could be fixed in a rigid position once the set screw at the bottom was tightened. 'This Instrument is less prejudicial to the Child's Head, because the wings can be fixed, at any determinate Degree of Expansion, as not to compress the Head more than necessary; whereas, with other Forceps, the more you pull, the more you squeeze . . .' (*Essay*, pp. 389–90). For all that, the machine is not well designed, as we can see in the photograph of the actual forceps, now at the obstetrical museum of the University of Edinburgh (Plate IV).[29] The blades are too narrow and the curve poorly designed for a child's head. The major objection is to its bulk. 'A very whimsical

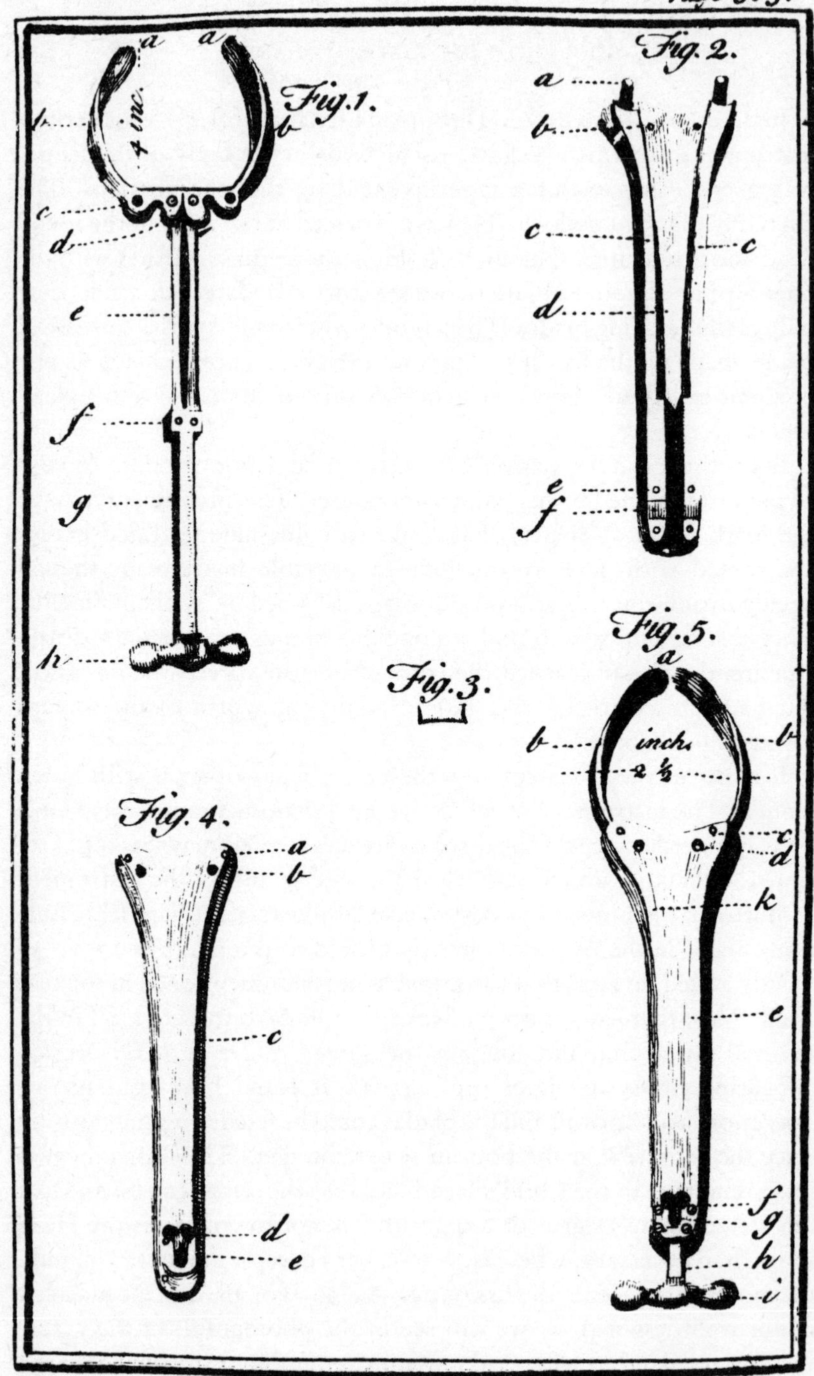

Plate III Dr Burton's forceps, from the *Essay Towards a Complete New System of Midwifry*. 1751.

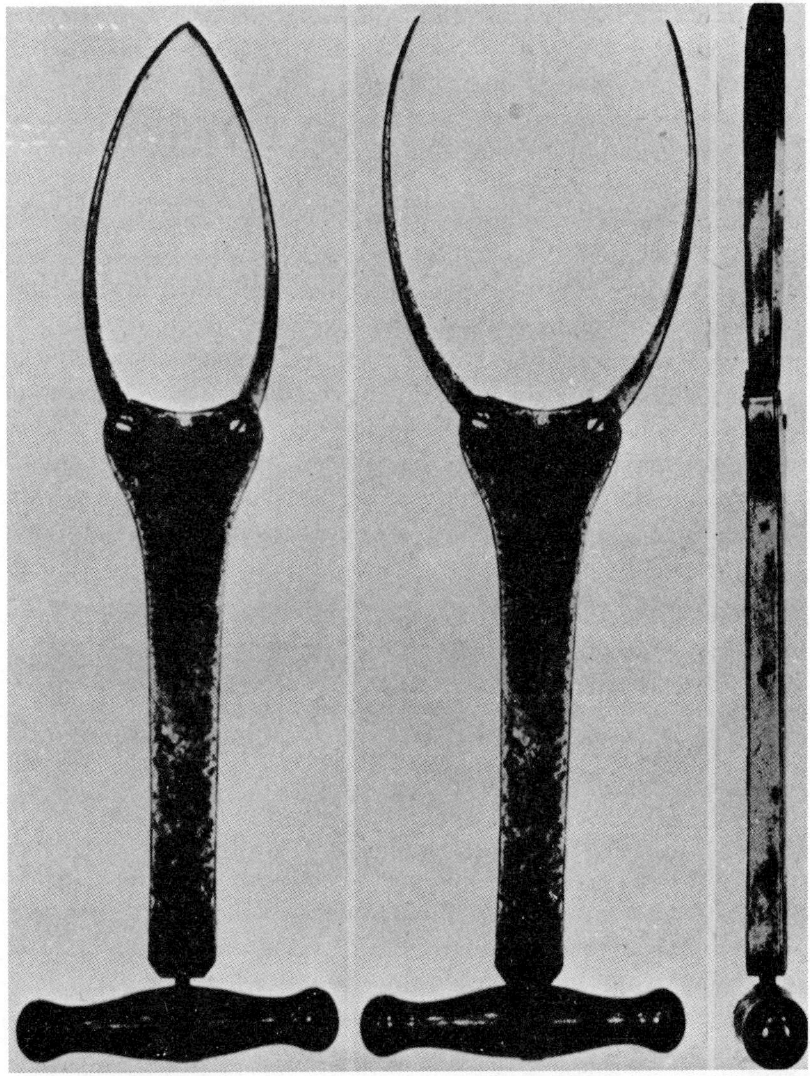

Plate IV Dr Burton's forceps. Now in the obstetrical museum, University of Edinburgh.

contrivance', commented Dr Lowder in 1782, which requires 'more room than we expect to have when we use forceps'.[30] To these criticisms I would add a point discovered by Dr Margaret Rowbottom and myself when she recently demonstrated for me the facsimile forceps at the Wellcome Medical Museum in London. So great is the magnification of force between the screw handle and the claw-like blades, that the operator has no sense of the pressure being exerted by the blades. The discovery was made, to my sorrow, upon the bones of my hands, which, like those of Uncle Toby's, were nearly broken as Dr Rowbottom casually turned the handle.

Imagine to yourself now the scene in the back parlour. Dr Slop has been washed up, after his fall into the mud, and rubbed down and fitted out, or into, a pair of Obadiah's pumps. Obadiah has returned from his second trip upon the great coach-horse, this time to get the green baize bag, which he has placed before Dr Slop and Uncle Toby and his master. But Obadiah, so that he could hear himself whistle as he trotted home, had quieted the 'terrible jingle' in the bag by taking cord and tying and cross-tying the bag with many roundabouts and hard knots. 'A sudden trampling in the room above' and a groan from Mrs Shandy startles Dr Slop into action. He cannot undo the knots. Now the 'most virtuous way' would be to take fingers and teeth to them.

> Dr. *Slop* had lost his teeth—his favourite instrument, by extracting in a wrong direction, or by some misapplication of it, unfortunately slipping, he had formerly in a hard labour, knock'd out three of the best of them, with the handle of it:—he tried his fingers—alas! the nails of his fingers and thumbs [in accordance with Burton's instructions in the *Essay*] were cut close. [p. 168]

Dr Slop borrows a penknife and cuts his thumb to the very bone. 'Curse the fellow ... I am undone for this bout.' Thereupon Walter Shandy lifts down his copy of Bishop Ernulf, and Dr Slop stands anathematising Obadiah as above the innocent unborn moves closer to the point which will determine his life or death.

Susannah runs downstairs. 'Bless my soul!—my poor mistress is ready to faint,—and her pains are gone,—and the drops are done,—and the bottle of julap is broke,—and the nurse has cut her arm,—(and I, my thumb, cried Dr *Slop*) and the child is where it was' (p. 184). But more: 'the midwife has fallen backwards upon the edge of the fender, and bruised her hip as black as your hat'. Perhaps she was tugging hard at a fillet when it slipped off. (A fillet is a slit linen sling placed over the head.) '... the midwife would gladly first give you an account how things are, so desires you would go up stairs and speak to her this moment ... No, replied Dr *Slop*, 'twould be full as proper, if the midwife came down to me.—I like subordination, quoth my uncle *Toby*' (p. 184).

The midwife has come down subordinately to make her report. Dr Slop does not feel rushed. He first must demonstrate his forceps to the gentlemen.

> Upon my honour, Sir, you have tore every bit of the skin quite off the back of both my hands with your forceps, cried my uncle *Toby*,—and you have crush'd all my knuckles into the bargain with them, to a jelly.
>
> ... the points of my forceps have not been sufficiently arm'd, or the rivet wants closing—or else the cut on my thumb has made me a little aukward,—or possibly—'Tis well, quoth my father ... that the experiment was not first made upon my child's head piece. [p. 187]

Slop discounts the suggestions, explaining that the head of a foetus is 'naturally as soft as the pap of an apple;—the sutures give way'—a point Burton had frequently made in his books.

'And besides,' continues the doctor, 'I could have extracted by the feet after', to which the old midwife standing by comments eloquently, 'Not you.' Walter, of course, pricks up his ears: 'I rather wish you would begin that way.'

The doctor, beginning to enjoy his power, turns to the midwife. 'Will you take upon you to say, it may not be the child's hip, as well as the child's head? 'Tis most certainly the head, replied the midwife', in the second and final speech of that delightful character.

> Because, continued Dr. *Slop*, (turning to my father) as positive as these old ladies generally are,—'tis a point very difficult to know,—and yet of the greatest consequence to be known;—because, Sir, if the hip is mistaken for the head,—there is a possibility (if it is a boy) that the forceps
>
> * * * * * * * * * * * * * *

Thereupon Dr Slop picks up the green baize bag and trips 'pretty nimbly, for a man of his size', across the room and up the stairs.

From these few hints we can know exactly Mrs Shandy's condition. Her labour has been short, stopping two hours and ten minutes after it began.[31] It was a critical labour from the first, as evidenced by Susannah's sudden, fearful flight for the old midwife. The short, violent labour indicates that Mrs Shandy's waters had suddenly broken. Consequently, the baby has moved well down towards the pelvis. The head presents, as the midwife well knows, for she has been attempting some sort of manual extraction and has had a grip, which did not hold, upon the head. The difficulty is clear: Tristram's head is too large for the opening. The case is a common one, to be found described in every eighteenth-century obstetrical treatise, including Burton's *Essay* (pp. 191, 215) and *Letter* (pp. 118–19). As the midwife knows, in such an advanced stage there is no chance at all for the podalic version Walter wants so badly, Dr Slop's bragging notwithstanding. The possibilities have been narrowed to two: Tristram *must* be delivered by the forceps or by the *tire tête*.

A calm falls upon the Shandy household. At least a quiet falls, for the two gentlemen in the parlour fall asleep. When they awake Dr Slop is in the kitchen preparing for a brave attempt at plastic surgery. ''Tis a bridge for master's nose,' reports Trim. 'In bringing him into the world with his vile instruments, he has crush'd his nose, *Susannah* says, as flat as a pancake to his face, and he is making a false bridge with a piece of cotton and a thin piece of whalebone out of *Susannah's* stays, to raise it up' (pp. 214–15). Thus, too, is crushed another hope of the father, for in Walter Shandy's opinion a good, generous nose (next to a proper begetting, a birth feet first, and an inspiring Christian name such as Trismegistus) is the most important asset a man can have.

The forceps, as Dr Burton's *Essay* (p. 217) or any obstetrical work of the time will explain, are to be placed over the foetal head at or close to the temples, the exact position being determined by the operator's first feeling the ears. The instrument could slip. But slipping from the narrow dimension, side to side, to the longer dimension, front to back, is out of the question—especially for Dr Burton's forceps, the blades of which will not move once the set screw has been fixed. As bungling as Slop appears, it is hard to believe he could misplace the forceps out of sheer stupidity. His error was caused by the cut on his thumb. The gash having robbed his hands of their sensitivity, he misjudged the location of the ears.[32] When he tightened down the blades, the device being made as it was, he could not feel any resistance.

Worse still, the delivery was too slow. The head had remained under pressure in the narrow pelvic passage. While Dr Slop haughtily called down the midwife and foolishly questioned her, while he demonstrated his forceps on Uncle Toby's fists, the cerebellum, or soul, of the infant (depending on the point of view) was being slowly pressed above. Hence the evening of Tristram's birth: 'There is not a moment's time to dress you, Sir, cried *Susannah*—the child is as black in the face as my—As your, what? said my father, for like all orators, he was a dear searcher into comparisons—Bless me, Sir, said *Susannah*, the child's in a fit' (p. 287). *Fit* was a good medical term in those days, one used to describe the convulsions in the new-born, often fatal, brought on by too great and too prolonged pressures upon the cerebellum. The baby, black in the face and presumed dying, is rushed to the silly curate, while Walter is trying to climb into his breeches, and misbaptised with the name Tristram—of all Christian names, the very one his father thought the worst. All of Walter's fears, without exception, have been realised in the birth of his son.

It might have been worse, replied my uncle *Toby*—I don't comprehend, said my father—Suppose the hip had been presented, replied my uncle *Toby*, as Dr. Slop foreboded.

My father reflected half a minute—looked down—touched the middle of his forehead slightly with his finger—

—True, said he. [pp. 280–1]

Tristram's birth was utterly circumstantial and accidental—the exact opposite of his father's inspired ideal of planned, rational creation. Dr Slop did save the life of the Shandy heir, but not because his ideas were sound or his inventions clever. Tristram survived, the 'sport of small accidents' (p. 166), of an odd marriage contract, a too-large head, a clumsy machine, and a cut thumb. Not reason, but Fate, gave to Tristram Shandy his life and his inadequate configuration.

Slop reappears from time to time to play the medical clown, farcically in the cataplasm-throwing fight with Susannah over the prone Tristram after the falling window sash had circumcised the small hero (p. 413); more subtly in his prediction that the wound 'will end in a *phimosis*' (p. 401), although a phimosis is cured by circumcision, not caused by it.[33]

Dr Slop's real role in the story, however, was finished once Tristram was born. In the birth episode, he and Walter Shandy had represented truthfully the theories and practices of Dr John Burton. In these Sterne had discovered his profound comic vision of man's utter foolishness before the mysteries of life and death.

The melancholy literature of midwifery gave to Sterne a paratactical life–death image, his informing symbol, his own myth. The image remained with him to the last. Speaking of the *Sentimental Journey*, he wrote to George Macartney three months before his death, 'I am going to ly-in; being at Christmas at my full reckoning—and unless what I shall bring forth is not *press'd* to death by these devils of printers, I shall have the honour of presenting to you a *couple of as clean brats* as ever chaste brain conceiv'd—They are frolicksome too, *mais cela n'empeche pas*.' That life should begin with a threat of death. For an age which assumed a reasonable world, this was the most nonsensical of mysteries. It was the germ of Sterne's great frolic.

NOTES

1 Quotations from *Tristram Shandy* are taken from the James Aiken Work edition (New York, 1940).

2 They opposed each other in the York by-election of 1741/2, when the young Sterne edited a newspaper and wrote pamphlets for the Whigs. Sterne, however, had sold his services for a prebend stall at York Minster, and his heart was not in politics. When Walpole resigned in 1742, Sterne publicly apologised for his part in the recent campaign and quit politics for good. Thereafter Burton and Sterne found themselves sharing an unenviable position as the two men most hated by that maniacal Whig, the powerful Archdeacon of Cleveland and Precentor of York, Dr Jaques Sterne, the uncle of the novelist. One would think that the persecutions each suffered at the hands of this terrible man would have created a bond of sympathy between them.

In *The Politicks of Laurence Sterne* (London, 1929), p. 18, L. P. Curtis suggested that Sterne had a hand in Burton's imprisonment during the revolution of the Pretender of 1745/6. Burton was arrested by Dr Jaques Sterne, who was also a Justice of the Peace and second in command of the defences of York, after he was captured and released by the rebels (as he maintained), or met with them by assignation (as Dr Sterne said). In Burton's published defence (*British Liberty Endanger'd*, London, 1749), he spoke of a letter written by a 'relation' of Jaques Sterne which had accused him of inviting the rebels to York. Curtis surmised that Laurence Sterne was the author, but I cannot agree. A more likely person is Thomas Pulleyn, Clerk of the Peace for the West Riding, a nephew of Jaques Sterne by marriage, who is frequently mentioned in Burton's book. There is something suspicious in Burton's inadequate account of his capture. Nevertheless, no formal charge was ever brought against him, though he was incarcerated for more than a year and forced into bankruptcy. Jaques Sterne, on the other hand, was guilty of inciting false witness against Dr Burton while the man was in prison (Leeds City Library, Temple-Newsam Papers PO/3C: ff. 143, 162). On the whole Burton seems more sinned against than sinning, a candidate for the compassion of Sterne, who was waiting out the revolution, so far as I know, at his rural parish.

3 For my facts about the history of obstetrics here and throughout the article I am indebted to a number of medical historians: J. S. Fairbairn, 'The Development of Obstetrics from the Embryonic State', *St. Thomas's Hospital Gazette*, XIX (1909), pp. 163–81; John Byers, 'The Evolution of Obstetric Medicine', *British Medical Journal* (1912), I, 1345–50; H. R. Spencer, *The History of British Midwifery from 1650 to 1800* (London, 1927); I. H. Flack (pseud. Harvey Graham), *Eternal Eve; the History of Gynaecology and Obstetrics* (Garden City, N.Y., 1951); D. T. Atkinson, *Magic, Myth, and Medicine* (Cleveland, Ohio, 1956); L. S. King, *The Medical World of the Eighteenth Century* (Chicago, Ill., 1958); B. L. Gordon, *Medieval and Renaissance Medicine* (New York, 1959).

I especially appreciate several studies of Dr Burton by medical men: J. Glaister, *Dr William Smellie and his Contemporaries* (Glasgow, 1894), ch. 16; A. Doran, 'Burton ("Dr Slop"): His Forceps and His Foes', *Journal of Obstetrics and Gynaecology of the British Empire*, XXIII (1913), 3–24, 65–86; R. W. Johnstone, *William Smellie, the Master of British Midwifery* (Edinburgh and London, 1952), ch. 13; W. Radcliffe, 'Dr John Burton and his Whimsical Contrivance', *Medical Bookman and Historian*, II (1948), 349–55.

4 Glaister, Doran and Radcliffe (see note 3) evaluate Burton's criticism in detail. His most telling points seem to have been (1) that the uterus includes a muscle structure, and (2) that the blades of the forceps should not be wrapped in leather, as Smellie believed.

5 Sterne's name for Smellie in this joke was 'Adrianus Smelvgot', a corruption of a name Sterne found in Burton's *Letter*: listed among the 'moderns' of midwifery whom Smellie should have studied is one 'Joh. Adriani Slevogt'.

6 Vol. I of the *Monasticon Eboracense, or The Ecclesiastical and Monastic History of Yorkshire* appeared in 1758. Soon afterwards Burton was made a Fellow of the Society of Antiquaries of London. He had not completed the second volume when he died in 1771.

7 T. Baird. 'The Time-scheme of *Tristram Shandy* and a Source', *Publications of the Modern Language Association of America*, LI (1936), 803–20. Brother Bobby died in 1719, a short while after Tristram's birth on 5 November 1718. Uncle Toby's courtship of the Widow Wadman had taken place earlier, in 1713, albeit the narrative of that frustrated love concludes the novel. As Baird showed, the events of the novel are exactly arranged within the military and political history of England. Within medical history, however, the birth of Tristram makes no chronological sense. In 1718, the year of Tristram's birth, forceps were unknown in England and Dr John Burton was only eight years old.

8 My general idea about the structure of the novel is taken from W. B. Piper, *Laurence Sterne* (New York, 1966). Piper convincingly argues that all the digressions are related to a core plot having to do with the frustrated attempts of the Shandy family to prolong their line.

9 Sterne went far beyond Burton's few comments on genetic theory. See L. A. Landa, 'The Shandean Homunculus: the Background of Sterne's "Little Gentleman"', in Carrol Camden (ed.), *Restoration and Eighteenth-Century Literature: Essays in Honor of Alan Dugald McKillop* (Chicago, Ill., 1963), pp. 49–68. Sterne's interest in generation theory, however, may have been sparked by the remarks of Burton and Smellie. Especially curious is an amusing exchange between Burton and one Kirkpatric, the reviewer of Burton's *Essay* for the *Monthly Review*, V (Sept. 1751), 286–92. Kirkpatric, deriding Burton's speculations about how the semen stimulated the ovum, made a joking implication about Burton's masculinity which left the doctor fairly sputtering in print: 'For where is the Conclusion that mine is a defective Birth, because I leave the Use of the Semen Masculinum (which is here a Thing merely speculative) to be discussed by some abler Hand?' (*Letter*, p. 242). How Sterne must have laughed at that! Is it possible that this banter about a congenital impotence, occurring as it does within a dialogue about conception, could have suggested to Sterne Walter Shandy's idea about 'due care' in propagation? Tristram, who lost the benefit of such care because of his mother's unhappy association of ideas, was later plagued with impotence (see pp. 517–18).

10 Established in Jermyn Street, 1739, the ward became eventually Queen Charlotte's Hospital. A second ward was opened at Middlesex Hospital in 1747, and 1749 saw the establishment of the British Lying-In Hospital (later called the British Hospital for Mothers and Babies). Although the greatest contribution of Sir Richard Manningham was the founding of his ward, he is more often remembered as the man who exposed in 1721 the 'rabbit breeder', Mary Tofts, who had convinced much of the world that she gave birth to rabbits. Manningham was a conservative operator—too conservative, one suspects, for Walter Shandy's purposes.

11 'There are natural great Bellies, containing a living Child, and these we call true; and others against Nature, in which instead of a Child, is engendered nothing but strange Matter, as Wind mixed with Waters ... they are called false Great-Bellies'—François Mauriceau, *The Diseases of Women with Child* (first published Paris, 1668), trans. Hugh Chamberlen, edition of 1752.

12 Comically, but consistently, Walter is assuming an ideal equality among embryos as he (or Tristram speaking for him) had already assumed among *homunculi* (pp. 5–6). In the earlier instance, Tristram referred to Cicero's *De Legibus* and Pufendorf's *De Jure Naturae et Gentium*, thus aligning Walter's spermatozoic ethic with the great latitudinarian legal tradition which culminated with Jefferson and the Declaration of Independence.

13 I have not found the source of this interesting statistic, though I suspect it was taken from André Levret, *L'Art des accouchemens démontré par des principes de physique et de mécanique* (Paris, 1753), a copy of which I have been unable to obtain.

14 So far as I know, continental writers did not openly approve the Caesarean, but they reveal that another attitude sometimes prevailed. Mauriceau, in *The Diseases of Women with Child*, has this to say of it: 'I know very well they palliate it with a pretence of baptizing the Infant, which else would be depriv'd of it. . . . But I do not know that there ever was any Law, Christian or Civil, which doth ordain the martyring and killing the Mother, to save the Child: 'Tis rather to satisfy the Avarice of some People, who care not much whether their Wives die, provided they have a Child to survive them' (p. 236).

15 During the sixteenth century, when it was taught by Ambrose Paré, it had been the only hope for the child's life in preternatural cases. Burton, though he recognised its dangers, was wrong to advocate it over delivery by forceps. Walter Shandy stands alone in recommending it for births which might be normal.

16 See King, *The Medical World of the Eighteenth Century*, pp. 103–4.

17 *American Journal of Obstetrics*, LXV, 612–17.

18 H. van Deventer, *The Art of Midwifery Improv'd*, English edition of 1746, p. 14. See also p. 325.

19 Mauriceau, *The Diseases of Women with Child*, pp. 155–6.

20 York Minster Library MSS., Ad. A 4 (3) b.

21 She had been licensed by Didius, a Commissary of the Archbishop. Didius was Sterne's satiric portrait of Dr Francis Topham, who indeed held among his many offices the Commissaryship of the Exchequer and Prerogative Courts of the Archbishop of York.

22 Quoted by Flack, *Eternal Eve*, p. 292.

23 Radcliffe, in 'Dr John Burton and his Whimsical Contrivance', suggests that Sterne's asterisks become more meaningful when we know that Burton placed his patients in an unusual position, thereby risking a heightening of their feelings of shame. 'In France the left lateral position in delivery is still known as Burton's position, for he was an ardent advocate of its use on all occasions. . . . It will be remembered that the custom was to deliver in the supine position, or a modified lithotomy position.'

24 Quoted by Flack, *Eternal Eve*, p. 292.

25 This illustration, as the others from Burton's *Essay* (Plates IIa, IIc, III), was made for the doctor by George Stubbs (1724–1806), later famous as a painter of horses and lions.

26 First noted by Dr John Ferriar in 'Comments on Sterne', *Manchester Philosophical and Literary Transactions* (1793), republished in the *Annual Register* (1793), pp. 379–98. Dr Ferriar used the 1681 edition of *Maladies des Femmes Grosses*, from which he quotes: 'il n'y a pas d'occasions ou on ne puisse bien donner le baptême á l'enfant, durant

qu'il est encore au ventre de la mere, estant facile de porter de l'eau nette par le moyen du canon d'une seringue jusque sur quelque partie de son corps . . . et il seroit inutile d'alleguer que l'eau n'y peut pas etre conduite, á cause que l'enfant est envelopé de ses membranes, qui en empéchent; car ne sçait-on pas qu'on les péut rompre tres aisement, en cas qu'elles ne le fussent pas, apres quoi on peut toucher effectivement son corps' (p. 394).

27 This information is from Flack, *Eternal Eve*, p. 328. Flack dated the original document 30 March 1733. Sterne, in his note to *Shandy*, pp. 57–8, dated the document he quoted from Deventer 10 April 1733. I cannot explain the discrepancy. Philip Peu also discussed baptism by squirt in 1694; see Radcliffe, 'Dr John Burton and his Whimsical Contrivance', p. 354.

28 Glaister, *Dr William Smellie and his Contemporaries*, p. 263. Also see the quotation from Mauriceau in note 14.

29 The photograph is reproduced from R. W. Johnstone, *William Smellie, the Master of British Midwifery* (Edinburgh and London, 1952). I wish to thank the publishers for permission to use the photograph.

30 From a manuscript lecture quoted by Doran in 'Burton ("Dr Slop")', p. 20.

31 Two hours and ten minutes lapsed between Slop's entrance and his tripping upstairs (p. 188). Labour had begun when Susannah went for the midwife and Obadiah for Dr Slop (p. 99). If we allow about ten minutes for Obadiah's fetching of the horse, his accident with Slop at the corner of the garden wall, and Slop's dragging himself to the house, then the labour began two hours and twenty minutes before Slop goes upstairs. But by then the labour had been stopped for about ten minutes—from the time Susannah first ran downstairs (p. 184).

32 Tristram tells us (p. 166) that had Nature set up a race with Dr Slop to see if she could deliver before Slop untied all the knots made by Obadiah, Tristram's nose would not have been depressed. The passage might be taken to mean that Nature could have decided to deliver the boy normally, but that reading would not fit with the facts of Mrs Shandy's condition. The passage means, rather, that had Dr Slop untied the knots instead of cutting them (thus cutting his thumb), he would have delivered Tristram whole.

33 A phimosis is a narrowing of the preputial orifice. Robert James, in *A Medicinal Dictionary*, vol. III (London, 1743–5), explained its causes as either a too long foreskin, or 'impure coition'. Its cure, he said, if medication failed, was circumcision. There remains, however, some argument in favour of Dr Slop's prognosis. If only a small part of the prepuce were amputated and mangled by the sash, irregular scar tissue might form, resulting in a phimosis.

This paper first appeared in R. F. Brissenden (ed.), Studies in the Eighteenth Century: Papers presented at the *David Nicholl Smith Seminar 1966* (Canberra, Australian National University Press, 1968), pp. 133–54.

ROBERT ADAMS DAY

Sex, scatology, Smollett

> That I might, however, mortify his vanity, which had triumphed without bounds over my misfortune, I thrust his sword up to the hilt in something (it was not a tansy) that lay smoaking on the plain, and joined the rest of the soldiers with *an air of* tranquility and indifference.[1]

Thus Roderick Random after the battle of Dettingen, having chastised the insolence of a Gascon soldier (and begun the physical part of the quarrel by administering 'a kick on the breech').

Everyone knows that Smollett is bawdy, earthy, robustious, and other clichéd adjectives that come to a mind surfeited with the 'hype'-advertising version of the eighteenth century. But to survey both the fictional *œuvre* of Smollett and his factual works to discover just how bawdy and earthy he is, and *how* he is bawdy and earthy, is to uncover something quite different: an underlying myth, Smollett's personal, self-manufactured picture of the sexual universe. Everyone unconsciously builds such a myth as he progresses from the polymorphous sexuality of infancy to the more focused and specialised sexual behaviour of adulthood, but most of us are scarcely aware that we have made so idiosyncratic a myth unless we have sought the assistance of an analyst. The artist is psychologically different in that he continually talks about his myth in public, using the language of art—symbol, sequence, frequency, grouping, transformation, condensation. These may be decoded (at least, as they reveal themselves within the work of art) by the intelligent reader, even if he is innocent of psychoanalytic technique. They give, as it were, the 'thumb-print' of their maker, repeated in work after work, as Charles Mauron has brilliantly shown.[2] The sexual myth of Smollett was a highly unconventional one for his day; but, curiously, it is shared by a remarkable quartet of writers in our own—Hemingway, Mailer, the Lawrences (D. H. and T. E.). I shall try to demonstrate that, just as the Sword in the Stone (or the great tree) energizes the myths of King Arthur and the Volsungs, so Smollett's idiosyncratic story of sex constructs its revelatory paradigm around the Sword in the Turd.

So far as we know (and the evidence is very meagre), Smollett's own sex life was tepid, blameless, conventional and happy. Shortly after attaining his majority, in 1742 or 1743, he married Miss Ann (Nancy) Lassells of Jamaica. For twenty-eight years of 'perfect harmony' they appear to have spent but little time apart; and in any case Smollett's heavy literary drudgery throughout his married life, and his wretched health, would have made sexual adventures highly unlikely.[3]

But—as Richardson, Fielding and Sterne amply demonstrate—there is no necessary relation between connubial bliss (or at least tepidity) and novels of high and violent sexual tension. And there is no denying that Smollett's heroes are not anchorites. Besides their sporadic pursuit of the ladies with whom they are to be rewarded at the dénouement, Roderick and Peregrine not only blithely enjoy the favours of complaisant widows, matrons, peasant girls and assorted wenches, but Roderick pays the usual penalty of venereal disease (p. 114). (Fathom, of course, and Greaves are exceptions: Greaves is a sexually refrigerated Quixote figure throughout most of the narrative, and Fathom is an anomaly in the picaresque tradition—a cold-hearted seducer and thoroughgoing villain, and also the only picaro who comes to mind as being rendered by the narrator in the unsympathetic and distancing third person.) Smollett's subheroes or squires—Strap, Pipes and so on—take their sex *en passant*, when and as they can get it. Sex, then, is abundantly provided by Smollett; and at this point the reader may be tempted to accept the clichés, lump the major eighteenth-century novelists together as robustly sexy, and let it go at that.

But also at this point a major difference can be seen. Smollett, so to speak, turns the sex on and off. *Pamela* and *Clarissa* are pervaded from start to finish by the sexual question around which they revolve—a woman's chastity and its perils. So are *Joseph Andrews*, *Amelia* and (after its first six books). *Tom Jones*. *Tristram Shandy* scarcely allows the sexual innuendo to falter for more than a page or so. But with Smollett the situation is different. To be sure, Emilia, Narcissa, Aurelia and Monimia (limply melodious all) are from time to time in danger of ravishment; but not perpetually, and for much of the narrative they are simply shelved in favour of the male world of combat and trickery. Seldom allowed to speak for themselves, they are seen only by the heroes, in a few stilted love-scenes, where both narration and dialogue ape the stereotyped vocabulary of the melodramatic stage ('Heavens! Do I see my charmer?' etc.). Moreover, as characters they are pale indeed compared to the girls of Richardson or Fielding; such feeble life as they have, and such individuation among the clichés, is provided by the never-failing exuberance of Smollett's style. Thus in Smollett the female side of the sexual equation is not well sustained by the heroine, either by her perpetual presence or by her vitality as a character.

There remains the element of casual sex, common to all the novelists in question. Joseph Andrews's chastity is sorely and often tried, Tom Jones and Billy Booth have their brief loves, Mr B and Lovelace have had theirs, and most of the male characters in Sterne are bathed, so to speak, in sex—even if it seldom or never achieves itself. The difference between Smollett's characters and these is simple and clear: the casual amour as practised by Smollett's males has been characterised as 'a successful evacuation'.[4] A desirable and desiring female presents herself, arousal is briskly but chastely described, the bedroom door closes—and that is that. Or, perhaps, 'I made bold to slip into bed to this charmer, who gave me as favourable a reception as I could desire. Our conversation was very sparing on my part' (*RR*, p. 102). Or, more elaborately:

> I must own, to my shame, that I suffered myself to be overcome by my passion, and with great eagerness seized the occasion, when I understood that the amiable Nanette was to be my bedfellow.—In vain did my reason suggest the respect I owed to my dear mistress Narcissa; the idea of that lovely charmer, rather increased than allayed the ferment of my spirits; and the young Paisanne had no reason to complain of my remembrance. Early in the morning, the kind creatures left us to our repose. [*RR*, p. 240][5]

The reader need only think of Mr B's attempts on Pamela or the rape of Clarissa, Joseph with Lady Booby or Mrs Slipslop, Tom Jones with Mrs Waters, or Uncle Toby and the Widow Wadman, to perceive the difference. In every case, whether the author's intention is to be comic, prurient, terrifying or merely sensual, he 'works up' the scene—leads into it, lingers over it, fills it with vivid detail. 'Perfunctory' is the only word for casual sexual encounters in Smollett; or perhaps 'stereotyped'. Few of them last for more than a page; and if they do, as with the amorous Mrs Hornbeck in *Peregrine Pickle* (pp. 200–4, 218–20, 222), most of the wordage is taken up with the comic details of pursuit, concealment and discovery, not with dalliance. (We cannot, of course, expect to find overtly salacious or even frank writing in eighteenth-century novelists' descriptions of sexual encounters. Drugstore pornography is unique to our own time, and in Smollett's the careers of Fanny Hill and her sisters were confined to the clandestine purchaser and reader; they did not surface for general consumption or discussion. Yet even Richardson, however pure his language, had reason to regret his 'warm scenes', and *Pamela* underwent a gradual purgation throughout the rest of his life, as 'sweat' became 'effluvia' and 'shirt' 'garment'.[6] Pornography in the mid eighteenth century seems almost to have been superfluous.)

But, one might ask, what happens in Smollett when the ardent hero's long trial is over, the perfect heroine is wedded and bedded, guilt is banished, and unrestrained sensuality is illuminated by Hymen's encouraging torch? The answer is, not much. One commentator has observed:

> Smollett's nuptial narratives conform to a curious stereotype. Roderick relates how after Narcissa has gone to bed on their wedding night 'I broke from the company, burst into her chamber, pushed out her confidant, locked the door ...' but then reminds himself not to 'profane the mysteries of Hymen'. ... Emilia is 'elegantly dished out' on the same occasion in *Peregrine Pickle* for a husband who is described as 'maddening with desire'. ... and here Renaldo is incongruously described as 'a lion rushing on his prey'. It is perhaps just as well that Smollett draws 'the decent veil' on these events.[7]

In short, sex is abundant in Smollett—in a sense; but it is not integrated into his fictional fabric, not pervasive, not rich, certainly not 'bawdy, earthy', etc. One might compare the effect to being told that one is to see a remarkable tropical garden and then discovering that what is meant is an acre of sand planted with several hundred curious cactuses.

There is, however, another side to Smollett's expression of sexuality. It was perceived by a reviewer in the *Gentleman's Magazine*, who characterised one of his works as being narrated with 'great spirit and humour; but there is a mixture of indelicacy and indecency which though it cannot gratify the loosest imagination, can scarce fail to disgust the coarsest'.[8] The reviewer was referring to *The History and*

Adventures of an Atom (1769), a political satire in which no sexual act takes place. And he alluded to the fact that, if we extend sexuality to coprophilia/phobia and the podex, the *Atom*, which contains no unchaste word, may be the sexiest work in English.

How so? A detailed enumeration would require many pages, and a selection must suffice. The Emperor of Japan (George II of England) turns his rump on people as a snub (I, 21) and constantly kicks his ministers in the breech. His prime minister (the Duke of Newcastle) soothes himself after these encounters by having his arse kissed by bishops, whose beards produce exquisite (in fact, orgasmic) pleasure (I, 35–43). He constantly befouls himself, as terrifying news bulletins arrive one after another. The elder Pitt, on resigning from the Cabinet, claps his hand to a part that shall be nameless; there are learned digressions on haemorrhoids, kicking, breeches (II, 100; I, 90–2; II, 77–82). It is safe to say that at no point in the *Atom* are we spared for more than three of its duodecimo pages in large type a more or less extensive reference to the podex and what comes out of it (or goes into it, as with enemas), given with the greatest possible stylistic gusto. The characterisation 'obsessive' is hardly too strong, one concludes.

But it may be that the *Atom* is an aberration. Little known, and perhaps (it used to be thought) not even certainly by Smollett,[9] is it not unfair evidence in a discussion of his universe of imagery? Let us then examine his acknowledged masterpiece, *Humphry Clinker*. In this work of mellow maturity we find that one of the main plot lines concerns the state of Matthew Bramble's bowels—obstinately constipated for months, easy and relaxed as emotional growth and the salubrious ambience of Scotland produce the desired effects. (Too many critics forget that Bramble's 'healing journey' is chiefly a quest for intestinal tonus.) The puns on 'shit' in the uncouth letters of Tabby and Win are numerous; at Bath Dr Linden discourses on its aromas as an admirable replacement for hartshorn (pp. 17–18), and it is, alas, as eighteenth-century writers never tired of pointing out, a notable feature of the streets of Edinburgh, where the costive find release (p. 220). Lismahago's sword, like that of Roderick's challenger after Dettingen, is passed through a privy in token of dishonour (p. 283). One of the earliest tokens of Humphry's gentle descent is the accidentally revealed but exquisite whiteness of his buttocks (p. 81); those of Lismahago, seen by firelight as he crawls down a ladder, make a callous spectator think of 'a fine Descent from the Cross' (p.

300), and those of the fair Win, discovered by the breezes on a similar occasion, kindle Cupid's flame in the bosom of Clinker (p. 175). Micklewhimmen tricks a clothier from Leeds into profuse discharges (mind over matter, pp. 174–5), and the intestinal troubles of both Tabby and her dog Chowder make much mischief.

In short, if we eliminate from our considerations the difference in tone between savage satire and relaxed comedy, a tabulation of the scatological units of narration (scatemes?) in the two works would make them seem to be close rivals.

Both, however, are productions of Smollett's last years, and it may be that his own distresses (the Italian doctor who attended his last illness found chronic diarrhoea)[10] unduly coloured the fabric of his fictions at this time. It is true that Roderick Random (1748) escapes Cloacina; it is Strap who receives the contents of a chamber pot (p. 68). But the elaborate chamberpot trick that Peregrine Pickle (1751) plays on his stepmother (too much, apparently, even for early readers, since it was suppressed after the first edition; pp. 65–7), the various evacuations of Pallet and the guests at the Dinner in the Manner of the Ancients (pp. 236–9), the asafoetida contest in *Fathom* (p. 195), and dozens of other incidents, either tricks or the result of embarrassing accidents, amply demonstrate that, like the machine of government that he characterised in the *Atom*, in terms borrowed from the introduction to the *Continuation* of his *Complete History of England*, Smollett's fictional machine could not move unless its wheels were amply greased 'with the ordure of corruption' (II, 78; I, iv).

Nevertheless, this is to say nothing new. If they have been reluctant to paddle in it, few critics of Smollett have failed (albeit with a pursing of the lips and a quick changing of the subject) to remember that ordure and to note that Smollett is scatological. So are Swift and Pope. And, with the exception of Victorian Thackeray or Bright Young Person Aldous Huxley and his followers, few have gone into spasms of disgust at their scatology.[11] After all, it is sensibly argued, Swift may have been one of the few genuinely fastidious persons in that dirty age; moreover, a recent level-headed treatment of his scatological satire has made the simple point, hard to refute, that from the point of view of mere effectiveness, what more satisfactory device for the satirist who wishes to mount an all-out, devastating attack than to equate his victims with excrement?[12] Again, mere scatology is one thing and scatological sex is another (coprophilia is not a subject extensively treated, even in discussions of *psychopathia sexualis*). It remains to be shown, then, that Smollett's scatology is different from Swift's and Pope's and, more important, that rather than being merely a part of the satirist's armamentarium it is connected with the sexual element of his fantasy world.

Pope's scatology (in his published works) is largely limited to parts of the *Dunciad* and of the late, savage satires. Swift's is more prevalent; but if we eliminate a handful of poems, one or two short passages from each book of *Gulliver's Travels*, and a few bits from *A Tale of a Tub*, nothing remains beyond the ordinary coarseness of realism. But Smollett's type of fiction, though intimately connected with satire, is arguably not satire *per se* and in primary intention, as *Gulliver* certainly is. It would be very difficult to maintain in the face of the evidence that Smollett's scatology is not gratuitous, or is chiefly used for satirical attack, or does not pervade his whole *œuvre*. Therein lies the difference, though to demonstrate it conclusively and in detail would require a treatment by instances at a length impossible here. The more important point is to show the connection, if any, between the buttocks and excrement of Smollett and sex as he fantasised it.

Smollett's treatment of conventional sex, licit and illicit, in comparison with the performance of his great contemporaries in the novel, does not appear to have his heart in it. What of his treatment of unconventional sex? One critic, perhaps rashly, notes in *Random* 'the first account of homosexuality in European fiction since that of Petronius himself'[13]—Roderick's encounter with the depraved Earl-Strutwell, who recommends 'the exquisite pleasure attending the success of ... this inclination' (p. 310). Roderick of course is properly horrified and immediately breaks the connection, though not before having been cajoled out of his watch. It is true that, with the possible exception of Old Coupler in Vanbrugh's *Relapse* (1697), Strutwell seems unique in English literature up to Smollett's day. Yet he certainly is not leniently treated by Smollett or his spokesman Roderick, who quotes Smollett's own satire *Advice*,

> Eternal infamy the wretch confound
> Who planted first, this vice on British ground!

and one swallow does not make a summer. But Strutwell has been preceded by Captain Whiffle, described in great and pictorial detail as outrageously effeminate, and as furnished with a companion, Simper, with whom he is suspected of 'maintaining a correspondence ... not fit to be named' (p. 199), and a valet named Vergette; a name, as *Random*'s most recent editor has ingeniously noticed, meaning 'clothes-brush', but also 'little penis' (p. 460). And Strutwell is followed by the Italian count, three years later in *Peregrine Pickle*, who vanquishes the chastity of a German baron, after the Dinner of the Ancients, by singing a languishing love-lyric of Guarini about burning desire, snatching a kiss, and tickling the baron's ribs. Not content with this prelude, Smollett and Peregrine urge the landlady to investigate; she finds the pair lewdly engaged and drives them ignominiously from the house (pp. 242–3). Pallet's adventures in Paris when disguised as a woman include relieving himself in the men's retiring-room and thereby attracting the amorous advances of a French fop, together with a threat of castration manufactured by the ingenious Peregrine, complete with animadversions on the life of eunuchs (pp. 244–5, 252–3).

It is true that these pranks are never condoned, and they may be seen as merely extravagant variations on slapstick comedy by an author intent on pushing *semper alter et idem* as far as it will go. But they are by no means Smollett's only excursions into the image-cluster of buttocks–their products–ambiguous sex–phallic symbols–sodomy. For example, toward the end of the *Atom* the Duke of Newcastle, who bears the name (not very difficult to decode) of Fika-kaka,[14] and who is already an old woman in the sense of being timorous and fussy, turns into a woman by losing his genitals, as one of the arse-kissing bishops discovers, and begins to incubate eggs, while Smollett throws in a reference to the legend that after a papal election the youngest cardinal-deacon inspects the new Pope through a *chaise percée* and announces: 'Mas est; Deo gratias' (II, 114–17). In a review in the *Critical* of a work on cockfighting and the rearing of fighting cocks, the writer (not, of course, provably Smollett) condemns the sport as barbarous and remarks of the author, 'His cares extend to the earliest period of incubation; and so explicit are his rules, that we cannot help thinking he has devoted some part of his time to the very act of hatching' (XIV, 155 [August 1762]). A curious fancy, but it is not without parallel. In Smollett's first substantial published work, the Popean satire *Advice* (1746), a mysterious reference to 'C——'s prolific bum' (l. 29) is annotated as follows:

This alludes to a phenomenon, not more strange than true. The person here meant, having actually laid upwards of forty eggs, as several physicians and Fellows of the Royal Society can attest; one of whom, we hear, has undertaken the incubation, and will no doubt, favour the world with an account of his success. Some virtuosi affirm, that such productions must be the effect of a certain intercourse of organs not to be named.

The identity of 'C——' has not transpired, and one may wonder at Smollett's eagerness to introduce this obscure occurrence, whether or not it was apocryphal (one may also suspect that the Royal Society could have been duped by one of those skilful persons, not unknown at private entertainments, who have acquired sufficient control over their anal sphincters to admit and extrude eggs without breaking them).

These seem to be Smollett's only discussions of oviparous men, but not 'of a certain intercourse of organs not to be named'. We may speculate that the young Smollett, making his début on the London literary scene as a Popean satirist, gave *Advice* careful thought, and that he was out to shock. He must have succeeded, for *Advice* is as homosexually iconoclastic as *Roderick Random* would be. Its epigraph, from Juvenal's second satire, would hardly have been selected thoughtlessly, and it runs thus (in Nahum Tate's 1696 rendition):

> To see't [the podex] so sleek and trimm'd the Surgeon smiles
> And scarcely can for laughing launce the Piles.
> O Peers of Rome! need these stupendious Times
> A Censor or Aruspex for such crimes?

The laughing surgeon who wrote *Advice*, after a survey of cowardly generals and foolish or knavish statesmen, focuses on how one may rise in the world 'with honours bright, / His master's pathic, pimp, and parasite' (l. 80), like Lord Strutwell's jealous valet or like 'Brush' Warren, who owes his present affluence to 'the most infamous qualifications ... from having been a shoeblack ... was kept by both sexes at one time' (l. 90n.). (Warren has likewise never been identified.) We pass on to 'Pollio', who is 'the pride of science, and its shame' and has apparently trafficked with a 'prostituted groom' (ll. 95–7); to Sir John Chardin of Kempton Park, who 'kept two rosy boys for the entertainment of his guests' (l. 106n.); to the tastes of Virgil, Anacreon and Horace; and to 'unnatural orgies' at Oxford, denounced with passion (ll. 109–10n.).

It may be that the youthful Smollett was merely moved by Roderick's 'generous indignation' at the 'sordid and vicious disposition of the world' (p. xlv) to lash at malefactors whose misdoings were obscure enough to have escaped even the rage to identify of modern editors; but there is surely something gratuitous about the editorial behaviour of the mature Smollett when in annotating the prose writings of Voltaire in English translation he pauses to speculate unnecessarily on sodomy among the Jesuits (XVIII, 54), interrupts a discussion of Semitic customs to wonder whether circumcision causes homosexuality (I, 43) or, in giving the character of William of Orange, remarks that while 'some' have accused Bishop Burnet of remarking that William 'was fond only of back doors', he said no such thing (VII, 99). In the *Atom* farts and haemorrhoids are too numerous to cite. The White Horse from the arms of Hanover 'eats pearls by the bushel and voids corruption by the ton' (I, 85). In one of the *Atom's* digressions, on witchcraft, Smollett fathers on King James I, in his *Daemonologie*, a remark which is to be found nowhere in its pages; that at witches' sabbaths the Devil gambols about with a lighted candle stuck in his breech (I, 197). The omniscient particle that tells the story discourses learnedly on the itching sensations in the anal region of the Duke of Newcastle and how, before he had discovered the virtues of bishops' beards, these *pruriti* were imperfectly assuaged by a series of curious *torche-culs* borrowed from Rabelais: 'a poke, a slipper, a pannier, a hen, a cock', etc. (I, 33). Later the elder Pitt wipes himself voluptuously with the poetical works of Frederick the Great, printed on 'a very fine, soft, smooth Chinese paper made of silk' (II, 56). Newcastle, on his way to becoming an old woman, wipes babies 'if they were foul . . . with every appearance of pleasure' (II, 114). And Smollett wrote (or approved) a review in the *Critical* of a satire on Lord George Sackville's conduct at Minden (Sackville was responsible for the one flaw in the English triumph; he refused to bring up his troops when ordered to do so, and was cashiered for this). The pamphlet says that Sackville must have been at stool when the attack occurred; the reviewer recommends that its pages be used by him as 'a much more soft, commodious, and comfortable *detersorium* than the hard stiff paper used for cartridges' (VIII, 257 [September 1759]). The *Critical* also began a review of a work on madness, whose author quarrelled with others' theories, by producing a general paragraph of comment on the folly of medical controversies; the reviewer remarks that in a 'recent' quarrel of this kind the 'great prosyndic of Padua' had befouled himself after having taken his own laxatives too profusely. The 'recent' controversy had taken place twelve years before; Smollett had been involved in it; but it is very doubtful whether more than a handful of readers would have remembered the controversy, who the 'prosyndic' was, or that one of the issues (and far from the most important one) had been the use of purges.[15]

This very miscellaneous list of references to the anus and its uses conventional and bizarre is most probably not exhaustive. But the fact that a not very assiduous investigation has sufficed to produce it should convince the reader that 'scatological' is not idly applied to Smollett. The nature and variety of the items, though, should equally demonstrate that, however repellent or trivial we may consider scatology to be, it is not a trivial item in the furniture of Smollett's mind—at least that part of his mind that governed his authorial tics and obsessions. The very gratuitousness of most of these references, their clearly sexual connections, the richness of fantasising that characterises them, are all significant; also, they reach their fullest flowering in a work that is wholly satirical, personally motivated beyond any other production of Smollett's, and very possibly not originally intended for publication in his lifetime—the *Atom*.[16] Nevertheless, their earlier and later occurrences, in contexts where they are only marginally satirical or not so at all, suggest that Smollett could not help, or resist, putting them in.

Before going on to consider the meaning of sexual scatology in Smollett's world of fantasy we should take note of one of its sources (a source that Smollett seems to have been unique among the authors of his time in using)—the scurrilous political cartoons that issued in a flood from the print-shops. These are little known today, and they are scatological to an extent that modern cartoons do not and cannot parallel. Eminent persons expose their buttocks in derision, enemas are freely given and taken, arses are kissed, and personages high and low spray one another with ordure. Smollett's specific indebtedness to the details of many of these in the *Atom* is very clear, though lack of space prevents its discussion here. But the prints he used relate to political and military events of 1756–66, and most of these are *not* scatological, though in one some women expose their buttocks, in another Dr Smollett gives Britannia an enema, and in a third the Earl of Bute incubates; Smollett *reverses* these, with Bute's enemy Newcastle incubating, a man (Newcastle) exposing buttocks, and Pitt giving enemas.[17] The political prints must not be left out of our calculations; but Smollett's scatology both postdates and antedates them by some years, and his uniqueness in using them is another respect in which he notably differs from his contemporaries.

One case of pictorial influence, however, must be noted, because among other reasons it involves the eminent Hogarth. In *Greaves* the wicked Justice Gobble (p. 95) and in the *Atom* the detestable Newcastle (I, 94) are described in almost identical words as resembling Felix on his tribunal, 'humorously delineated by the inimitable Hogarth . . . in the *Dutch* style'. The reader is expected to know (or more probably Smollett obsessively forgets that he may very well not know) the details of Hogarth's print parodying his own serious painting *Paul before Felix*. The Roman governor, terrified by the Apostle's fervour and righteousness, has befouled himself, and his attendants grimace or stop their noses.[18] Smollett must have treasured this not very famous representation; and we are entitled to suspect that he found it paradigmatic.

Paradigmatic of what? The evidence is now in: does it offer clues to the structure and relationships that govern Smollett's scatological-sexual world?

Heterosexual relationships, casual and frivolous or serious and involving courtship and marriage, are certainly not absent; paradoxically, they are *conventional*. If we are willing to classify Smollett's novels, with Ronald Paulson, as following the line of more-or-less picaresque/satirical, where narrative development is subordinated to pictorial satire and constant variety,[19] we may say that Smollett was content to follow the model for the distribution, treatment and importance of such material laid down by his mentor Lesage in *Gil Blas*. We may also say that Smollett was more interested in following the 'tamed-picaresque' recipe than in energising his notions of love by any idiosyncratic fantasising. But the coldly perfunctory nature of his treatment of love is masked by the exuberance of his style in general, and indeed becomes visible only by high-contrast methods (to borrow a term from photography); we see it only if we are seeking the warm vitality that Richardson, Fielding and Sterne bring to their handling of the sexual dimension of life, and that Smollett totally lacks.

Homosexuality in Smollett is also best seen by high contrast. No dramatist writing in English, no novelist, no poets except Charles Churchill, Marlowe and Walt Whitman, between antiquity and World War II, has so much to say on the subject. (We should omit the scene of sodomy in Cleland's *Woman of Pleasure*, and other overtly pornographic works such as the *Teleny* sometimes attributed to Oscar Wilde, or the pseudo-Rochesterian play *Sodom*; these are of questionable literary merit, had at most an 'underground' existence, and were certainly never intended for general consumption.) Churchill deals with homosexuality only once, in lines occupying about one-fourth of his savage satire *The Times* (1764), and Marlowe's and Whitman's homoerotic poetry is couched in a language so evasive and ambiguous that it permitted them, and has, permitted the bulk of their critics until recently, to deny or ignore any such inclination or intention. The same may be said of the mass of inferior Victorian poetry and fiction that is sentimentally homoerotic, and of the novels of Horace Walpole, Beckford, 'Monk' Lewis and Oscar Wilde, who avoided the explicit by many stratagems. But there is no question of what Smollett is talking about. It may be said, then, that of major writers in English before our own day, Smollett is the only one to deal with homosexuality in plain, explicit language and with some length and frequency. But in every case he is equally explicit, indeed vehement, in his condemnation of it. As for scatology, the occasional chamber pot is a standard prop in the repertory of robust comedy, and even the peerless Sophia Western once has her posterior charms briefly revealed in *Tom Jones* as the result of a tumble from a horse (Bk. XI, ch. 2).

True, a somewhat chilly treatment of heterosexual love, homosexual episodes, *outré* but few, and some overemphasis on the coarser side of slapstick do not amount to very much. These, however, represent only the conscious side of Smollett the novelist. The unconscious dimension, manifested in gratuitous references, repetition, imagery, odd turns of thought, symbolic pictures, puns, transformations—the material of poetic imagery and of Freud's dream-work—must be speculatively (and controversially) reconstructed. The resulting figures may displease the reader, and surely would have displeased Smollett had they been perceived by him *tous nus*. But we have already seen them enumerated, and it now remains, by generalising and categorising, to make sense of them—or rather, myth.

Excrement is always evil. Only a fool, like Dr Linden, would praise it, only fools (Tabby, Win) inadvertently name it, only fools or knaves are tricked into involuntary contact with it (Peregrine's stepmother, the Leeds clothier), only the base, if innocent (Strap) are befouled with it by others. Only the very evil (Gobble, Felix, Fika-kaka) cannot control it and discharge it at the wrong time, but this they do often. On the other hand, it is a means of torment if retained; the potentially good (Bramble) or the neutral or mildly bad (Tabby, Chowder) may suffer from constipation and be constrained to resort to (often treacherous) purgatives. Only a fool-and-knave of the worst kind (Fika-kaka, as he wipes foul infants) could actually take pleasure in it. Thus one's relations with excrement are an index of one's moral worth, but so, it would seem, is the state of one's bowels. Nothing too much; Aristotle's good man, in Smollett's world of scatology, rests in the golden mean between costiveness and diarrhoea. But courage is also a mode of virtue, and the imputation that Lord George Sackville (Smollett was one of his few persistent defenders in print)[20] could have been at stool during the battle of Minden is abhorrent.

Buttocks and the anus (though excrement is there produced) are quite other things. Those of Humphry reveal him as a person of quality; those of Win are Venus's snares; Lismahago's are merely comical. Showing the buttocks may be a sign of derision, as in the cartoons, but this mode of expression is used by the king himself, not only in fiction but in fact.[21] Arse-kissing may be a universal metaphor for sycophancy, but the descriptions of its effects in the *Atom*, though they are enjoyed by the loathsome Fika-kaka, are also relished at considerable length and in great and elaborate detail by his creator. (The modern reader should not need reminding that anilinctus is a branch of erotic activity). Arse-wiping for Smollett, at least in the *Atom* and at Minden, can be positively voluptuous, and the connoisseur may well devote time and effort (as, to be sure, in Rabelais) to the search for the most exquisite 'detersorium'. As noted earlier, in the *Atom* Smollett is letting himself go, and we should therefore not be surprised at its luxuriance of detersorial imagery; but if in its pages arses are often erotically wiped, they are erotically kicked equally often (by 'Got-hama-baba' or George II of England, Smollett's imagination being assisted by historical fact and by an imitation of Voltaire).[22]

In this clustering of imagery we can see Smollett making the transition from the merely anal to the anal-erotic, to violence, and, following his linked images one step further, to homosexuality. And here we find the most grotesque and bizarre, but perhaps most basic myth-collocation of all—the one which links together all of Smollett's scatological-sexual figurations and ties them in with a myth not only personal to him but basic in many cultures; unsavoury and fantastic, but surfacing in folklore and linking Smollett with certain twentieth-century writers—the Lawrences, Mailer, Hemingway—by way of a grim joke of the locker-room variety. We have a useful key to this deeply buried fantasy in two decodable puns, one visual, one verbal: the name Fika-kaka and Roderick Random's performance after Dettingen.

Roderick has vanquished a thoroughly despicable opponent, the boastful Gascon, in a fair fight. But the Gascon had previously bested him with the sword, and only after some hasty schooling in swordplay can Roderick match him. Resting after a display of masculinity (the battle) the Gascon denigrates the English; Roderick rather unnecessarily takes umbrage, rebukes him, kicks him in the breech, disarms him, and, when he refuses to plead for his life, humiliates him (or so he intends) by thrusting his sword into a 'smoaking' (therefore fresh) turd and 'with an air' of (therefore pretended) 'tranquility and indifference' rejoins his comrades. That is to say, if we decode or abstract the myth from its symbolic wrappings: a male, humiliated by a male from another group by means of a symbolic phallus, acquires a powerful phallus himself, defeats his rival, figuratively sodomises him without contaminating his own virility symbol, and departs, concealing his relief and triumph.

Smollett detested the timid, silly, vacillating Duke of Newcastle more than any other figure satirised in the *Atom*, and gave him the most loathsome name of all. 'Caca' in many Indo-European languages is baby talk or adult talk for defecation; 'fica', Italian for fig, is also, from the appearance of a ripe fig, a euphemism for the vulva. But 'Cunt-Shit', whatever else it may mean, clearly equates two orifices that are never equated in man or the mammals, but are one and the same in birds and reptiles. We remember that Fika-kaka receives pleasure anally from kissing and kicking, that he turns into an old woman, enjoys wiping infants, and incubates eggs. We also remember 'C———'s prolific bum' from *Advice*, with its grimly jocular suggestion that sodomy might make a man lay eggs. It would appear that Smollett's unconscious mind manufactured a curious myth very early in life and retained it tenaciously until the end of his career: the anus is a sort of vulva; bad, equated with effeminate, men may or ought to be 'punished' by sodomy; they will then turn into females (inferior beings) and do what birds do, but in any case they will thus be effectively destroyed or eliminated from consideration. In some way excrement is a magic agent in effecting this horrid transformation and is therefore loathsome, but is doubly loathsome if juxtaposed with the phallus that represents honour, virility, courage. Thus in the *Atom* Smollett has the Picts and Scots being 'unbreached' or conquered by the Romans and so adopting their skirted mode of dress (I, 92). Fika-kaka, or Prime Minister Newcastle, the target of Smollett's most concentrated venom, is the most powerful man in England, fulfilling the prophecy of the earliest work, *Advice*. He flourishes in his fictional guise by being 'his master's pathic, pimp, and parasite', for a pathic is a passive sodomite, a catamite or kept boy.

Space does not permit a detailed recapitulation of the anthropological parallels to such a myth in customs and taboos, but it is not unique to Smollett. One may suggest that the reader should consider the ancient Greek and medieval Japanese taboos regarding who is to practise active and passive sodomy, the grounds of the Judeo-Christian horror at *emissio in ano*, the Yiddish slang word, *fagele*, or bird, for a homosexual, active sodomy as a rite of triumph among South American Indians, and various jokes and expressions of loathing in the more robust of all-male conversations.[23] If we are willing to entertain the contention that Smollett's fantasies were energised by some such myth as has been outlined, unseen but deeply felt, the pluses and minuses of his sexual world are readily accounted for. The tepidities of conventional love clearly run a poor second to the obsessive and fascinated horror and desire that attend sexual excrement-magic.

As remarked earlier, this aspect of Smollett's fantasy has affinities among imaginative prose writers in our own day. These may be quickly sketched. T. E. Lawrence, the *preux chevalier*, superhumanly courageous and fanatically cleanly, who, he would have us believe, underwent collapse and metamorphosis as a result of being beaten and buggered at Deraa by soldiers after repulsing the amorous advances of the Turkish bey, is one such fantasist. Another is Norman Mailer, ostentatiously virile. A *TLS* reviewer once characterised *The Naked and the Dead* as having more bowel movements than any other novel in English; he had not read the *Atom*.[24] Mailer recommends buggery, has annoyed feminists by his 'male chauvinism', celebrates male–male bedding in *Why Are We in Vietnam?*, and has his hero Rojack bugger the maid in a triumph-rite after having negotiated a perilous circuit of his apartment building on a narrow ledge. Hemingway, a byword for flaunted masculinity, tends to harp on the loathsomeness of effeminates in *Death in the Afternoon* and several of his stories. Critics have lamented the implausibility of his love scenes and of his female characters; he tells us in *A Moveable Feast* how as a boy on the lake-boats that plied Lake Michigan he learned that one must always carry a knife as a precaution against the ever-present danger of being forcibly sodomised by the brutal boatmen.[25] D. H. Lawrence is a more complex case, but one may mention his remarkable ability to portray feminine reactions to the act of love, his frequent praise of men's buttocks or 'suave loins', the wrestling-initiation scenes in *Women in Love*, *Kangaroo*, *The Plumed Serpent* and *Sons and Lovers*, the *Blutbrüderschaft*, and lastly the scenes of (heterosexual) sodomy, ecstatically described from the woman's point of view, in *Women in Love* and *Lady Chatterley's Lover*.

These examples are given not so much with the intention of tracing a particular line of sexual fantasy in modern writers (which can and should be done at much greater length) as of persuading the reader that, if it exists in four writers close to us in time, something like it may equally have existed in Tobias Smollett two hundred years ago. Smollett remarkably resembles D. H. Lawrence in his frail physique, his fastidiousness, his tubercular affliction, his sensitivity, his indignation and bellicosity, the tremendous range and vivacity of his style; to my mind he strikingly resembles Lawrence as well in this strand of his depiction of sex and love.

Lastly, the squeamish reader who may be partly persuaded but who is inclined to reject the whole argument on the grounds that its matter is too repulsive to be considered objectively, may reflect that if indeed a deeply buried homosexual-excremental myth furnishes the motive power for Smollett's fictions, its repellent nature and existence are justified by the vivid and arresting results. Such a reader is well advised to take Swift's counsel in 'The Lady's Dressing-Room', suppress his natural revulsion, hold his nose, elevate his eyes, and honestly admire

> Such Order from Confusion sprung;
> Such gaudy Tulips rais'd from Dung.

NOTES

1 Tobias Smollett, *Roderick Random*, ed. Paul-Gabriel Boucé (Oxford; 1979), p. 250; italics mine. Subsequent references to Smollett's works are given parenthetically in the text and refer to the following editions. For the novels the Oxford English Novels Series is used: *Humphry Clinker*, ed. Lewis M. Knapp, 1966; *Sir Launcelot Greaves*, ed. David Evans, 1973; *Ferdinand Count Fathom*, ed. Damian Grant, 1971; *Peregrine Pickle*, ed. James L. Clifford, 1964. Other works: *The History and Adventures of an Atom* (2 vols., London, 1769); *The Continuation of the Complete History of England* (5 vols., London, 1760–5); *The Works of Mr de Voltaire* (English translation of the prose writings; 25 vols., London, 1761–5).

2 In *Des Métaphores obsédantes au mythe personnel: introduction à la psychocritique* (Paris, 1968).

3 See Lewis M. Knapp, *Tobias Smollett: Doctor of Men and Manners* (Princeton, N, J., 1949), pp. 42, 298, 257, 73, 298–9; *The Letters of Tobias Smollett*, ed. Lewis M. Knapp (Oxford, 1970), pp. 18–20, 113–14.

4 Donald Bruce, *Radical Doctor Smollett* (Boston, Mass., 1965), p. 68.

5 For the purposes of this discussion it is worth noting that 'us' means Roderick and a Capuchin friar, with whom he is enjoying an eighteenth-century version of the American custom of 'double-dating' in a barn. The next night they sleep together on a flea-ridden mattress; nevertheless during the night the Capuchin is able to rifle Roderick's pockets, or in Smollett's words, 'had made free with my cash' (p. 242).

6 See T. C. Duncan Eaves and Ben D. Kimpel, *Samuel Richardson: a Biography* (Oxford, 1971), pp. 426–7, on this never-ended project of refinement.

7 Damian Grant, notes to *Fathom*, pp. 383–4. *Greaves* conforms to the stereotype: 'Mrs Kawdle conducted the amiable Aurelia, trembling, to the marriage-bed; our hero, glowing with a bridegroom's ardour, claimed the husband's privilege. Hymen lighted up his brightest torch at Virtue's lamp. . . .' (p. 207).

8 XXXIX (April 1769), 205.

9 Although the *Atom* was issued anonymously and we have no documentary evidence from Smollett for his authorship (Knapp hesitates for these reasons to ascribe it unequivocally to Smollett, pp. 281–3), the external and internal evidence is abundant and conclusive. The latter will be given and discussed in the introduction and notes to my edition of the *Atom* (forthcoming from the University of Delaware Press), the former in my article, 'The Authorship of the *Atom*', *Philological Quarterly*, 59 (1980), 187–93.

10 Knapp, p. 298.

11 For an enlightened recapitulation of various opinions, see Donald

Greene, 'On Swift's "Scatological" Poems', *Sewanee Review*, 75 (1967), 672–89.

12 Jae Num Lee, *Swift and Scatological Satire* (Albuquerque, N.M. 1971). Significantly, the sociobiologist Edward O. Wilson notes in *On Human Nature* (Cambridge, Mass., 1978), p. 26, that one of the famous 'talking' chimpanzees ordered its trainer out of the room in a paroxysm of rage by signing 'You green shit'.

13 Bruce, p. 77.

14 Not difficult, at least, if one is acquainted with Italian; see the discussion below.

15 See my article, 'When Doctors Disagree: Smollett and Thomas Thompson', *Etudes Anglaises*, 32 (1979), 312–24.

16 I discuss this point in the article mentioned in note 9, above.

17 These are described in my article, '*Ut Pictura Poesis*? Smollett and the Graphic Arts', *Studies in Eighteenth-Century Culture*, 10, ed. Harry Paine (Madison, Wis., 1981), pp. 297–312.

18 See Ronald Paulson, *Hogarth's Graphic Works* (2 vols. New Haven, Conn. and London, 1965), I, pp. 215–16; II, pp. 205–6.

19 Though Smollett's fictions certainly have affinities with the picaresque mode, to call them merely 'picaresque' is highly erroneous. See the excellent discussion in Paul-Gabriel Boucé, *The Novels of Tobias Smollett* (London and New York, 1976), pp. 71–99; and on the structural force of the satiric mode in his works, Ronald Paulson, *Satire and the Novel in Eighteenth-Century England* (New Haven, Conn., 1967), pp. 165–216.

20 Robert D. Spector, *English Literary Periodicals and the Climate of Opinion During the Seven Years' War* (The Hague, 1966), pp. 56–61. (It is worth noting that Sackville was generally thought, justly or not, to be homosexual.)

21 On George II's rude habit of 'rumping' see Maynard Mack, *The Garden and the City* (New Haven, Conn., 1969), pp. 130ff.

22 The king was notoriously rude and undignified toward ministers in the Closet, once kicked an attending physician, and kicked his hat or wig about in fits of rage. Smollett's immediate source, however, is the spurious Part II of *Candide* (Voltaire, XVIII, 157), where a king honours his courtiers by kicking them thus, and arouses their envy by bestowing an unprecedented number of kicks on Candide. See also Mack, pp. 130ff.

23 See in particular K. J. Dover, *Greek Homosexuality* (London and Cambridge, Mass., 1978), and Tobias Schneebaum, *Keep the River on Your Right* (New York, 1969).

24 Michael Mason, 'Beginning in the Asylum', *TLS*, 5 May 1978, p. 493, col. 2 (including an interesting discussion of Mailer's obsessive imagery).

25 New York, 1964, pp. 18–19.

PAT ROGERS

The breeches part

I

In 1852, at the age of thirty-eight, Charles Reade completed his first novel. His career up to that date had been unremarkable. At Oxford he had taken a third in *literae humaniores*, but in the manner of the times had subsequently become a fellow, Vinerian scholar, bursar and vice-master of his college, Magdalen. According to *DNB*, 'his suite of five rooms in the college ... was beautifully situated, looking southwards on the cloisters and tower'. But, though he retained this set until his death thirty years later, Reade spent less and less time in Oxford. He had been called to the bar in 1843 and at one time had projected a serious career as an advocate: but, to quote the same source, 'his interest in law was evanescent, and he sought more congenial occupation in the study of music and literature'. He began to make a collection of cuttings and extracts with a view to compiling some great work on a subject not yet properly defined. In fact, his first literary productions were stage works, that is adaptations and amputations performed on existing works, by Scribe, Victor Hugo, George Sand and others. His fortune turned with the success of a comedy entitled *Masks and Faces* (on which the miscellaneous writer Tom Taylor collaborated). Staged in November 1852, it was followed within a matter of weeks by another version in the form of a novel—speed which present-day compilers of the book of the TV series might envy. The novel marked the beginning of Reade's true vocation as a writer. Reade was to achieve fame as the writer of two modes of fiction: contemporary realism and medieval quasi-epic. His first book lies between these categories: it is eighteenth-century costume drama, and its subject is the actress Peg Woffington.

To tell the truth, *Peg Woffington* is not a very good book, and still less is it a work in touch with modern taste. The heroine, presented through the majority of the text as a vivacious and mercurial extrovert, turns penitent in the last few pages, and offers a case-history in holy living and dying. Like other authorities, Reade is vague about the 'internal complaint' which killed Mrs Woffington in her mid-forties, although the symptoms may mean cancer. Unlike the biographers, Reade has Peg retire from the stage prior to the onset of her illness—converted in a moment by a sermon of John Wesley, a giant in times of 'sapless theology'. The noble calm with which the actress confronts death (her fate having been clumsily revealed to her by the unfortunately named Dr Bowdler) stirs Reade into a grand peroration. Public taste eagerly responded to the novel, and J. Fitzgerald Molloy, 'author of *Court Life below Stairs*', was probably not exaggerating when he prefaced his *Life and Adventures of Peg Woffington, with Pictures of the Period in which She Lived* (1884) with these remarks:

> No biography of Peg Woffington, the most brilliant actress of her century, has up to this time been written. Her very name might have been forgotten had not a great novelist rescued her memory from oblivion and directed interest to her career. Yet this has been achieved by the aid of fiction, as he acknowledged to me a little while before laying down his pen for ever.[1]

J. Fitzgerald Molloy does not altogether disdain fiction, when it comes to it; but he has no imaginary characters equivalent to Reade's gallery—the feeble *jeune premier* Ernest and his beloved Mabel (not, one might think, the most authentic period names), the stock Sir Jasper figure here named Sir Charles Pomander, and the starving poet Triplet, a hack with a heart of gold.

One of the aspects of Peg's career which clearly fascinated Reade, and figures in all the Victorian fan-gossip which his book provoked, is her adoption of male attire in some of her best-known roles. The topic occurs in the very first chapter:

> She played Sir Harry Wildair like a man, which is how he ought to be played (or, which is better still, not at all), so that Garrick acknowledged her as a male rival, and abandoned the part he no longer monopolized.
>
> ... It has been my misfortune to see ——, and ——, and ——, and ——, et ceteras, play the man; nature forgive them, if you can, for art never will; they never reached any idea more manly than a steady resolve to exhibit the points of a woman with greater ferocity than they could in a gown. But consider, ladies, a man is not the meanest of the brute creation, so how can he be an unwomanly female?

After this smug reasoning, Reade apostrophises 'mesdames les Charlatanes' and repeats himself: 'In Sir Harry Wildair she parted with a woman's mincing foot and tongue, and played the man in a style large, spirited, and *élancé.*' Later on, Peg herself claims that in this role she had been 'taken for a man'. In Chapter II, Kitty Clive quarrels with Peg 'because [John] Rich breeched her, whereas Kitty . . . wanted to put delicacy off and small clothes on in Peg's stead'. The heroine relates the story of an errant lover, whom she paid back by disguising herself as a man, 'with a little coal-black moustache, regimentals, and what not'. In this dress she made love to the man's new inamorata, and managed to get him jilted on the wedding-eve.[2]

Finally in Chapter III, Sir Harry Wildair appears in all his brilliant finery:

> Her bright skin, contrasted with her powdered periwig, became dazzling. She used little rouge, but that little made her eyes two balls of black lightning. From her high instep to her polished forehead, all was symmetry. Her leg would have been a sculptor's glory; and the curve from her waist to her knee, was Hogarth's line itself.
>
> She stood like Mercury new lighted on a heaven-kissing hill. She placed her foot upon the ground, as she might put a hand upon her lover's shoulder. We indent it with our eleven undisguised stone.
>
> Such was Sir Harry Wildair, who stood by Mr Vane, glittering with diamond buckles, gorgeous with rich satin breeches, velvet coat, ruffles, *pictai* [sic] *vestis et auri*; and as she bent her long eye-fringes down on him, (he was seated) all her fiery charms gradually softened and quivered down to womanhood.

The profound sexual ambiguity in this description corresponds to other aspects of the text, where Peg is both admired as a woman and allowed to 'quiver' into nineteenth-century femininity.[3]

At the end the various personages are dispatched according to a well-tried formula. The rakish Sir Charles 'lived a man of pleasure until sixty. He then became a man of pain . . . and died miserably.' Triplet 'made his final exit in the year 1799'. Less latitude is possible with characters such as Colley Cibber and James Quin, whose role in the proceedings has been to provide local colour, with a host of exclamations and Latin phrases: both had been easily deceived by Peg's act as Mrs Bracegirdle early in the book. The ending has a cheerful nostalgia about it—'My reader knows that all this befel long ago. That Woffington is gay, and Triplet sad no more. That Mabel's, and all the bright eyes of that day have long been dim . . .' Only the heroine's timely repentance invades the sweet inanity of the bogus eighteenth-century world of oaths, green-room bitchery, competitive epigrams and, above all, dressing up.[4]

It is an essential part of Reade's unconscious strategy that the quaintness and distance of the preceding age (Triplet's failure to survive *quite* into the nineteenth century is symbolic) should go with all this emphasis on borrowed finery. For Reade, the protean quality of his heroine is attractive but dangerous; in her last years of pious retirement, 'far from dust, and din and vice' (by which he possibly means Teddington), she would not have been allowed any glamorous transformation. It will have been apparent that Reade disapproves of the play in which Wildair appears, that is Farquhar's *The Constant Couple* (1700). The play had been successful since its first staging: its author had failed in the leading role at Dublin, but Wilks had made it tremendously popular in the early decades of the century. Even the less impressive sequel entitled simply *Sir Harry Wildair* enjoyed revivals from time to time. Reade passes over what some might have expected the Victorians to find tasteless, that is the male disguise used on the stage and, as we have seen, transferred to off-stage situations in the novel.

But the contradictions are deeper than that. Did Peg really play Sir Harry 'like a man'? If so, is there not something odd about her get-up, as Reade describes it? The passage quoted indicates a considerable duplicity of attitude. Peg is Mercury, yet her lightness of foot connotes not just speed but a lack of masculine bulk. Her 'periwig' is part of the eighteenth-century male's normal appurtenances, but historically it seems an epicene if not a feminine piece of apparatus. One can test this point by imagining how Reade could have coped with Peg in Victorian male attire. Beards, mutton-chop whiskers, stove-pipe hats, subfusc uniform, trousers, all connote male power, sexuality and authority. No woman could put on such contemporary drag without raising awkward questions about unsexing herself to claim the privileges of the dominant segment of society. But the buckles and breeches are almost genderless: they permit the wearer (from a Victorian standpoint) to create a simulacrum of masculinity, without any disturbing threats of a subversive maleness.

Of course, things cannot have felt quite like that to an eighteenth-century theatre audience, since ruffles did not express effeminacy in the context of the age, especially in a stage setting. But when Reade goes on to emphasise such features as Peg's rouge and long eyelashes, he points to a genuine ambiguity present all along. It was attractive actresses who were given the chance to play breeches parts—that is, women who had been found attractive to men. Their costume did not preclude the use of stage make-up to enhance their best features, and that would produce results quite different from any 'painting' by the beaux of the age (whatever cosmetic effects Lord Hervey's unguents may have had, nobody called his eyes 'two balls of black lightning'). Again, the display of leg enhances the sexual display of womanhood even as it pretends to mimic manhood. When Reade says that the curve from Peg's waist to her knee resembled Hogarth's curve of beauty, he gives the game away. For sinuosity in the hip and thigh region is not just a secondary female characteristic, but one of the most obvious features of female attractiveness to the male. Having said earlier that Peg did not mince her way through the male roles she played, Reade now assigns her a grace and softness quite at odds (as the age would see it) with masculine deportment. He does not seem quite sure whether Peg is to be admired for resembling a man in the role, or admired for not doing so.

II

Some of these ambiguities date back to the first popularity of breeches roles on the Restoration stage. The usual explanation given follows the lines of this sensible account by Marion Jones:

> More than one excuse served to get actresses into breeches for the delectation of a predominantly male audience. First, of course, came revivals of old plays with parts written for boys playing women, where the plot demanded assumption of male disguises at times during the action: with the advent of actresses, titillating dénouements with bared bosoms and flowing tresses became popular, and new plays were written to exploit this 'disguise penetrated' motif. Next, increasingly popular after Nell Gwyn played the madcap Florimel in Dryden's *Secret Love* (1667), came the 'roaring-girl' type of part, where the heroine adopted men's clothes as a free expression of her vivacious nature: prologues and epilogues were sometimes given by favourite actresses in men's clothes with no other apparent reason than to provide the same arbitrary thrill. Something akin to this was the practice by which an actress took the part of a male character just to amuse the audience: Peg Woffington made a great hit of Farquhar's 'Sir Harry Wildair', though the role—very far from epicene—had been made to measure for its creator, the dashing Wilks. Occasionally a whole play would be performed by women—Pepys relished

Killigrew's 'bawdy loose play' *The Parson's Wedding* done like this in 1664, and there are several instances of the novelty in the early eighteenth century.[5]

In its broad analysis, this résumé corresponds to J. H. Wilson's section in *All the King's Ladies* (1958). Wilson calculates that of more than three hundred plays first performed in London between 1660 and 1700, eighty-nine contained roles in which actresses donned male clothes.[6] Some of these may have been slightly exotic, for instance a girl 'disguised as a eunuch', and many resemble the comparatively—but not totally—sexless page disguises of an Imogen. Nevertheless, the fad was well marked and lasted out the century with ease, long after the boy players had been forgotten and when most of their roles had gone out of the repertory.

Many stars of the Restoration stage made a considerable impact in one or other of these travestied roles—not just Nell Gwyn, but also Mrs Elizabeth Barry, Mrs Mountfort, Mrs Bracegirdle. No particular set of qualities seems to have been required for such casting. One might have supposed that the roaring girl, at least, would need something in the way of stature, presence or contralto voice: but there is no real evidence to this effect. In all the categories listed by Marion Jones, it appears that sheer acting skill and (female) attractiveness were the main attributes. With each role, in varying degrees, the thin pretence could be concealed or emphasised: since there was no attempt to portray anything other than a notional or stylised masculinity, the actress did not risk losing any glamour or sex-appeal—usually, quite the opposite.

The practice went on in the new century, but it was only with the second generation of actresses that it attained full prominence. In Dublin during the 1730s Mrs Bellamy (mother of the celebrated George Anne) scored a hit in the role of Silvia in *The Recruiting Officer*, which involves disguise as a soldier. Peg Woffington made her breeches début in *The Female Officer*, before her great triumph as Wildair at Aungier Street in April 1740. We may take it as dramatic licence when critics claim that overnight the hitherto 'standard' performance by Wilks was eclipsed: but the impact was undoubtedly very great, justifying the management's unusual expense in buying a bespoke suit of clothes to deck out the star in appropriate style. Later in the year Peg played the role at Covent Garden, and she gave it 'by desire' at Drury Lane several times in the following years. A royal command performance before the Prince and Princess of Wales in January 1742 marked the peak of her renown as Wildair. No other breeches role produced quite the same popular reaction, with verses in the press implausibly describing Peg as 'the chief of the belles and the beaux':

> That excellent Peg
> Who showed such a leg
> When lately she dressed in men's clothes—
> A creature uncommon
> Who's both man and woman
> And chief of the belles and the beaux![7]

However, Woffington did essay other male roles, notably Lothario in Rowe's *Fair Penitent*, another part of theatrical rakishness which had been pioneered by previous actresses. When Peg returned to Dublin in the early 1750s, at the then astronomic rate of £400 a season, it was as Lothario that she enjoyed one of her greatest triumphs. No longer in her greenest youth, she could still carry off the dash and energy which, apparently, were what the audience desired to see.

Both the roles mentioned, along with others more remote from the usual 'breeches' repertoire, were played in the same period by Charlotte Charke, of whom more presently. But no considerable actress seems to have attempted Wildair in the major London theatres until Mrs Ann Barry, wife of the tragedian Spranger, took the role at Drury Lane in 1771. Of course, other brands of travestied playing went on. Silvia in regimentals remained a popular feature in the enduringly successful *Recruiting Officer*, and there are other cases of this type. But nothing quite rivalled the splendid apparition of Wildair as impersonated by Woffington. In 1777, with one eye cocked towards the social reformers such as Sir John Fielding, Covent Garden put on a 'much-discussed production' of *The Beggar's Opera*, in which Mrs Farrel took the role of Macheath. She is described as a 'counter-tenor', which must mean contralto, and though the vocal effect must have been odd, dramatically the rather supine hero does not seem outside the range of a good actress. It was for this production that Thomas Arne wrote the famous song 'A-Hunting we will go', sung by his pupil Mrs Farrel. To later taste, it would seem incongruous that the vicious elements in *The Beggar's Opera* might be mitigated by the substitution of a woman in the hero's role: but this perhaps connects with the sexless nature of the transformation, as usually practised. All this was orthodox, beside the Covent Garden production of 1781 in which all the sexual roles were reversed: mostly slapstick, but with Charles Bannister as Polly Peachum taking the songs straight, without any attempt at falsetto. Tate Wilkinson took such productions to the provinces, but it was a short-lived fashion.[8]

One could point to other isolated manifestations of the practice in eighteenth-century Britain. In the opera house there was Signora Galli, who occupied the role of 'second man' in the 1770s. According to C. S. Terry, 'Her voice being contralto, and her figure rather large and masculine, she was frequently invited to sing male parts', and many examples survive from the playbills of the time.[9] We know from the Dublin newspaper advertisements in the mid-century that publicity often featured references to actresses 'in Boy's Cloaths' or 'in Breeches', a fairly sure sign that the audience appeal of the device was high.[10] In fiction, Garrick's Hamlet was witnessed by a certain Mademoiselle de Richelieu, ogled at in her masculine disguise as she sat in a box by women who sat in the pit.[11] Private theatricals sometimes included *travesti* playing, especially in the more abstract and allegorical items of dramaturgy: though I do not know of quite such an elevated example in England as that of Madame de Pompadour, disporting herself as Prince Charming—in a demure riding habit—at her playhouse in the north wing at Versailles. Otherwise we are reduced to the female soldier Hannah Snell, appearing in full regimentals at Sadler's Wells around 1750. Freaks and oddities apart, the practice never quite died out on the legitimate stage, and Mrs Jordan, a notable Miss Hoyden, undertook breeches parts late in the century—as well as a part called Priscilla Tomboy in a play unknown to me, *The Romp*.

This rapid summary leaves out one significant figure, who stands in many ways quite apart. This is the sad daughter of Colley Cibber, best known as Charlotte Charke, who published some rather unreliable memoirs as *A Narrative of the Life of Mrs Charlotte Charke* in 1755.[12] The very title-page of this engrossing work listed 'Her Adventures in Mens Cloaths' as a leading inducement to prospective buyers, and it would be safe to say that Mrs Charke was the only specialist in breeches parts who publicly extended her cross-dressing to life outside the theatre. The *Narrative* tells of various escapades in which Charke became involved whilst in the guise of a man, including the virtually inevitable affair with a deluded woman. This is a human document on quite a different level from the materials so far discussed in this essay. However, it is worth stressing at the outset that Charke did make a considerable career out of breeches parts, with appearances recorded in such different roles as Plume and Archer in Farquhar, Pistol, George Barnwell, Macheath and Lothario. She even took off her father in his great part as Sir Fopling Flutter: a considerable task for her, because there can be few more difficult feats for a woman than that of portraying male effeminacy. In the light of Mrs Charke's longtime connection with the theatre, and especially her repertoire of breeches roles, her own social and psychological alienation acquire even greater interest.

She was in all probability homosexual, and the use which Maureen Duffy makes of her story in *The Microcosm* (1966) is surely altogether legitimate. It is a lesbianism which might be described as part-cultural, in that Charke seeks a more active and dynamic role outside bed as well as in it. In Maureen Duffy's rendition, the character 'Charles' defines his transformation in explicitly theatrical terms: 'You are pleased to compliment me, Madam, answered our adventurer, playing her new role as the Man Charles with as much assiduity as ever she had applied herself to the part of Young Bevil or Captain Plume.' And again: 'The next day the child was duly presented to Mrs Dorr, after being well versed in her part in which she proved as convincing as her mother.' Charles finds work as an actor difficult to get and at one time sets up as proprietor of an inn: he maintains good relations with his old profession, being 'unable to refuse anyone styling himself a comedian'. Returning to the stage, Charles finds himself on one occasion doubling the parts of Plume and Silvia in *The Recruiting Officer*. As far as staging the drama goes, this makes for a totally impossible situation, since the pair are lovers and not by any directorial ingenuity doublable roles. I do not know if Maureen Duffy recognised this in the *Narrative*, but the circumstance makes an obvious metaphor for Charles's divided condition. Subsequently the strolling company gives a disordered rendition of the other great Farquhar favourite, *The Beaux' Stratagem*: the scene is drawn from Charke's *Narrative*, but achieves more point in the third-person relation of 'Charles'.[13] Mrs Charke was obliged to spend a good deal of her theatrical life presenting burlesques of the classics, in fairgrounds and in country barns, and one could reasonably see in her theatrical adventures an image of the 'inauthentic' way of life which her sexual tastes dictated to her.

To take male roles is here a form of protest, not so much against the inferior quality and range of the repertoire of women's roles in the theatre, as against the limitations of propriety at large, which so constricted the available modes of being, personal and existential, for women everywhere.

Here, just for a moment, the adoption of a male role can be associated with wider sexual attitudes. Female protest was a very muted voice in Charke's day, and it is not surprising that no contemporaries express the seemingly obvious attitudes which Erica Jong gives to her eighteenth-century heroine, Fanny Jones, taking the road in the 1720s:

> To dress as a Boy gave one Privileges no Woman could e'er possess: first, the Privilege of being left in Peace (except by Robbers, who prey'd almost equally upon both Sexes); second, the very substantial Privilege of Dining where'er one wisht without being presum'd a Trollop; third, the Privilege of moving freely thro' the World, without the Restraints of Stays, Petticoats, Hoops, and the like. For I had form'd the Theory that Women should ne'er be entirely free to possess their own Souls until they could ride about the World as unencumber'd as possible. The Hoop Skirt, I reason'd, was an Instrument of Imprisonment. I might shudder with Horror at the Idea of the legendary Amazons cutting off one Breast, but sure I could not but understand their Motives.

Similarly, later on in the novel: 'For my part, I am content to be in his Attire; for wearing a Man's Disguise always fills me with a Sense of Freedom, e'en Wantonness. I chase him round the Bed again, delighting in the Novelty of this Change in Status.'[14] Perhaps the 'theory' smacks too much of the liberated 1960s, and one can hear the accents of Isadora Wing behind those of Fanny. But Erica Jong projects on to the eighteenth century what is surely a widely shared sense among women, and it would be rash to assume that no female theatregoer felt a sense of release by identification with the rakish actress in breeches.

As it was, such occasions as masquerades gave women a limited opportunity to try out the costume and with it some of the social freedom of a man—one of the many things opponents of masquerades had against this class-denying mode of pleasure. The flaunting unrealism of carnival disguise permits the acting out of forbidden fantasies: but of course it also limits the meaning of these gestures, by its very theatricality. This lack of real human import is well caught by Mandeville, in Remark P to *The Fable of the Bees:*

If a Woman at a Merry-making dresses in Man's Cloaths, it is reckoned a Frolick among Friends, and he that finds too much Fault with it is counted censorious: Upon the Stage it is done without Reproach, and the most Vertuous Ladies will dispense with it in an Actress, tho' every Body has a full view of her Legs and Thighs; but if the same Woman, as soon as she has Petticoats on again, should show her Leg to a Man as high as her Knee, it would be a very immodest Action, and every Body will call her impudent for it.[15]

This looks like a stock Mandevillian paradox: but in essence it remains fairly applicable, and from this circumstance derives the appeal of the actress in breeches (or tights), which in an age of full frontal nudity still represents a special unveiling. To have no clothes on at all is one thing. To be dressed, but in such a way as to disclose more of the anatomy than clothes usually allow—this is quite different. And if to many the latter is more sexually exciting, that makes good enough sense and scarcely constitutes a paradox.

What is missing in eighteenth-century accounts (and so may or may not have existed, we cannot be sure) is a sense of the discovery of a new self through disguise. This is marvellously conveyed in a very fine passage of *War and Peace*, Book II, in which the young people, after discussing metempsychosis, receive a visit from a party of mummers. They immediately rush away to transform themselves.

Half an hour later there appeared in the ballroom among the mummers an old lady in a farthingale—this was Nikolai. A Turkish girl was Petya. Dimmler was a clown. A hussar was Natasha, and a Circassian youth Sonya with burnt-cork moustaches and eyebrows.

After being received with well-feigned surprise, non-recognition or praise from those who were not mumming, the young people decided that their costumes were so good they ought to be displayed somewhere else.

They decide to pay a visit to their neighbours the Melyukovs. Sonya, 'generally so timid and reserved', takes the lead in these plans. Her costume was best of all: 'Her moustaches and eyebrows were extraordinarily becoming to her. Everyone said how pretty she looked, and she was keyed up to an unusual pitch of energy and excitement. Some inner voice told her that now or never her fate would be decided, and in her masculine attire she seemed quite another person.' The party make off in sledges, unnaturally hilarious, and shouting to each other through the frosty air. At one point Nikolai glances at Sonya, and sees in her 'quite a new, sweet face with black eyebrows and moustaches that peeped up at him from her sable furs—so close yet distant—in the moonlight'. He reflects: 'That used to be Sonya.' Later on, still bemused by the moonlit scene and unfamiliar atmosphere, Nikolai hears a remark by 'one of the strange, pretty, unfamiliar figures sitting by him—the one with fine eyebrows and moustaches'. Again he muses: 'I believe that was Natasha.' Then he adds, 'And that's Madame Schloss [the chaperon], but perhaps I'm wrong, and I don't know that Circassian with the moustache, but I love her.' That he cannot properly distinguish either his sister or the girl with whom he is inconveniently falling in love is beautifully apt to the novel's purposes: but it is also convincing as a lyrical interlude. Before the party returns, Nikolai finds himself outside the Melyukovs' house and meets Sonya in the dark. 'She's quite different and yet exactly the same', he thinks as he embraces her, kissing her 'on the lips which wore a moustache and smelt of burnt cork'. In his masterly control of the episode, Tolstoy shows how play-acting can light up what was mysterious.[16]

III

The later history of *travesti* performance would require a separate treatment. The story would touch on Cherubino; Madame Vestris, with her early success as *Giovanni in London*; the pantomime principal boy; and of course Sarah Bernhardt, whose notable performances included Reichstadt in Edmond Rostand's verse drama *L'Aiglon* (1900)—that is, the central role of Napoleon's son François-Charles-Joseph. Other actresses have followed Bernhardt in offering a straight portrayal of Hamlet—most recently in London Frances de la Tour—and the twentieth century has produced at least one great operatic role in *Der Rosenkavalier* (1911). In both cases the element of masquerade has become less important, and the sexual frisson has more or less disappeared. Even as I write, the well-known actress Felicity Kendal is to be seen at the Edinburgh Festival in the part of an adolescent male, in Tom Stoppard's adaptation of a play by Johann Nestroy. Press reviews comment on her excellent portrayal of the youth without registering any particular surprise.

The sexual dynamics of the original breeches role were obviously very different. It was central to the effect that the actress's femininity showed through: indeed, the aim seems to have been to draw special attention to her charms, either physically or through some dramatic nudge (e.g., the girl-as-page witnessing a love affair of her inamorato, but unable to reveal herself). Most actresses given the opportunity to take a prominent breeches role were young, instantly identifiable by the audience, and familiar in the stock female repertoire. No matter which category of part they took (as set out by Marion Jones), they were judged by canons altogether different from those applied to a man or a boy in similar roles.

It might seem that Peg Woffington marks an exception, since her Wildair is commonly praised as having replaced that of Wilks as the standard interpretation. Now it is true that contemporaries do sometimes speak of her performance as superior to that of any male actor, as for example the author of a life of James Quin in 1766:

> ... There was no woman that ever yet had appeared on the stage, who could represent with such ease and elegance the character of a man. Every one who remembers her must recollect that she performed Sir Harry Wildair, in the *Trip to the Jubilee* [the sub-title], far superior to any actor of her time. She was so happily made, and there was such symmetry and proportion in her frame, that she would have borne the most critical examination of the nicest sculptor. She had besides dispossessed herself of that awkward stiffness and effeminacy which so commonly attend the fair sex in breeches.[17]

This patronising account, with its emphasis on Peg's anatomy, treats the performance as a feat, and whilst I do not for a moment rule out the possibility that a woman *might* indeed be the best stage rake of her day, the underlying sense here is of a *tour de force* rather than of an authentic portrayal from within. Similarly Tom Davies in his life of Garrick (1780):

> Sir Harry Wildair, acted by a woman, was a novelty; this gay, dissipated, good-humoured rake, she represented with so much ease, elegance, and propriety of deportment, that no male actor has since equalled her in that part: she acquitted herself so much to the general satisfaction, that it became fashionable to see Mrs Woffington personate Sir Harry Wildair....
>
> In Dublin she tried her powers of acting a tragedy rake, for Lothario is certainly of that cast; but whether she was as greatly accomplished in the manly tread of the buskin'd libertine, as she was in the genteel walk of the gay gentleman in comedy, I know not; but it is certain that she did not meet with the same approbation in the part of Lothario, as in that of Wildair.[18]

Despite the references to 'ease' and 'elegance', one cannot escape the impression that the novelty and *outré* quality are what matter. Davies mentions that 'her choice of character excited the curiosity of the public', and the exploitation of this curiosity value depended on a recognition of the underlying paradox. Even when Garrick abandoned the role of Wildair (having played it opposite the Lady Lurewell of Mrs Woffington and Mrs Clive in March 1743), the reaction suggested a timely surrender to commercial considerations.

That an accomplished, if not great, actress such as Peg Woffington might have been able to unlock secrets of male characterisation not available to a man would have been too advanced a notion. Mrs Charke never attained much recognition, and gave her convincing breeches performances in the fringe theatre. Perhaps she managed to make herself too like a man for comfort—at least to the extent that the audience forgot about the impersonation during the play, and then what had become of the breeches role? Its *raison d'être* lay in the *imperfect* masculinity of the performer: when this gap narrowed, the easy acceptance of a rakish Woffington moved insensibly towards a feeling of embarrassment or rejection.

In the end it is Reade's depiction of Peg Woffington, with all its bogus 'Georgian' furniture, which probably renders the nature of the phenomenon as well as any. The smooth-thighed Mercury, 'fiery' in charms but poised ready to soften and quiver into the received pattern of femininity, exactly defines the limits of sexual tolerance. In bending, momentarily, the conventions of a society in which both men and women knew their sexual place, the actress in breeches serves to confirm rather than discredit these conventions.

NOTES

1 J. Fitzgerald Molloy, *The Life and Adventures of Peg Woffington* (London, 3rd edn., 1887), p. vii. Other sources include Augustin Daly, *Woffington* (Philadelphia, Pa., 1888); Janet Dunbar, *Peg Woffington and her World* (London, 1968); and various shorter treatments.

2 Charles Reade, *Peg Woffington: a Novel* (London, n.d.), pp. 12–13, 28, 32, 51–3.

3 Reade, *Woffington*, pp. 70–1. The ambiguity of Peg's appeal is suggested by a story, though probably an apocryphal one: namely, that she once ran off the stage, flushed with applause, and remarking, 'I have played the part [of Wildair] so often, that half the house believes me to be a real man.' The sharp-tongued Quin retorted, 'By God, madam, if they do, the other half knows you to be a woman.' (Quoted by Carola Oman, *David Garrick* (London, 1958), p. 51.) For many reasons the first claim was obviously one that could not be substantiated: nor, for that matter, is there much hard evidence to support Quin's riposte.

4 Reade, *Woffington*, pp. 238–55.

5 Marion Jones, 'Actors and Repertory', in *The Revels History of Drama in English*, Volume V, 1660–1750 (London, 1976), pp. 148–9. Other aspects of the breeches part are discussed by Peter Ackroyd, *Dressing Up* (London, 1979), pp. 96ff.

6 J. H. Wilson, *All the King's Ladies* (Chicago, Ill., 1958), pp. 67–86.

7 Quoted by Dunbar, *Woffington*, p. 39. Information on theatrical events is mostly taken from standard sources, that is *The London Stage*; the *Biographical Dictionary of Actors*; *DNB*; and similar works.

8 See Roger Fiske, *English Theatre Music in the Eighteenth Century* (London, 1973), pp. 402–6.

9 C. S. Terry, *John Christian Bach* (London, 1967), p. 146. In *opera seria* women continued to be assigned male roles long after the demise of the castrato.

10 Esther K. Sheldon, *Thomas Sheridan of Smock Alley* (Princeton, N.J., 1967), p. 187.

11 R. G. Noyes, *The Thespian Mirror* (Providence, R.I., 1953), p. 128.

12 The *Narrative* was reprinted in facsimile, ed. L. R. N. Ashley (Gainesville, Fla., 1969): this is the edition cited.

13 Maureen Duffy, *The Microcosm* (London, 1967), pp. 68–94.

14 Erica Jong, *Fanny* (London, 1980), pp. 61, 228. Fanny actually mentions as the spur to her disguise her knowledge of 'certain famous Actresses in London ... dressing up in Men's Clothes to play "Breeches Parts" ' (p. 55)—though I do not know of any such imitative behaviour in real life.

15 Bernard Mandeville, *The Fable of the Bees*, ed. Phillip Harth (Harmondsworth, 1970), p. 191.

16 L. N. Tolstoy, *War and Peace*, tr. Rosemary Edmonds (Harmondsworth, 1957), I, pp. 614–26 (Book II, part 4, chapters 10–11).

17 *The Life of Mr James Quin, Comedian* (London, 1887), p. 40. This anonymous life was first published by S. Bladon in 1776.

18 Thomas Davies, *Memoirs of the Life of David Garrick, Esq.* (London, 1780), I, pp. 306–7.

Selective Index